SHARON

Why Humans Like Junk Food

Enjoy the Book !

Dr. Steve

1/2012

WHY HUMANS LIKE JUNK FOOD

The Inside Story on Why You Like Your Favorite Foods, the Cuisine Secrets of Top Chefs, and How to Improve Your Own Cooking Without a Recipe!

Steven A. Witherly, PhD

iUniverse, Inc.
New York Lincoln Shanghai

Why Humans Like Junk Food
The Inside Story on Why You Like Your Favorite Foods, the Cuisine Secrets of Top Chefs, and How to Improve Your Own Cooking Without a Recipe!

Copyright © 2007 by Steven A. Witherly, PhD

iUniverse books may be ordered through booksellers or by contacting:

iUniverse
2021 Pine Lake Road, Suite 100
Lincoln, NE 68512
www.iuniverse.com
1-800-Authors (1-800-288-4677)

ISBN: 978-0-595-41429-1 (pbk)
ISBN: 978-0-595-85780-7 (ebk)

Printed in the United States of America

CONTENTS

Acknowledgments

First, I dedicate this book to my wife, Caroline, and our dear little daughter, Clarissa (sweet pea). Caroline convinced me that I must finish this work and assisted in proofing and designing the look and contents. Clarissa managed to keep busy—with her many friends and playthings—to allow me time to write. And I hope my two sons, Eric and Ryan, both of whom like to cook, will find this work at least a little interesting. (Hey guys, I *finished* it!)

Second, I must remember and thank my mentor and sensory sciences professor, Rose Marie Pangborn, for encouraging me to think outside the physiological box on food palatability and pleasure. Without her support and helpful guidance I would never have come this far in explaining the surprisingly complex world of food perception. Cancer ended the life of this great researcher, and I keep her in my prayers.

Third, I must thank my good friend Dr. Bob Hyde (professor at San Jose State University), whose natural genius in solving scientific riddles formed the basis of many of the theories herein. And to think it all started with a casual chat in my kitchen back in 1986, while we both sipped merlot (yes, that's right, merlot—way before the popular movie *Sideways*).

I'd also like to thank Mike Dauria, Nestlé Foods, for his helpful editorial comments; Bruce Horovitz (*USA Today* staff writer) for his inspirational idea of the food diagrams; the Restaurant Guys (restaurantguysradio.com), Francis Schott and Mark Pascal, for their kind comments on the rough draft of this book; and *Uberchefs* Thomas Keller and Anthony Bourdain, whose cookbooks and keen insights into culinology were a personal inspiration. Mr. Bourdain's entertaining quotes are reprinted by permission of Bloomsbury USA. And the culinary wisdom of Keller is quoted by permission of Artisan, A Division of Workman Publishing Company, Inc., New York. Finally, scripture quotes are taken from the New American Standard Bible, Copyright 1995 by the Lockman Foundation.

This work is also a reflection and, in a sense, a culmination of the genius of many researchers in food perception and sensory science. In the past, I have recognized their contributions by naming some food perception phenomena after these researchers' last names. While this is unconventional in science, it is a simple way to remember some of the more important food principles. I have tried to the best of my ability, using the wisdom and insight from the scientific literature, to explain and simplify the many food phenomena and behaviors.

I would like to mention just a few of the names of those great scientists whose work is both illuminating and inspirational.

Gary Beauchamp	David Booth	David Wingate
Thomas Scott	Barbara Rolls	Dana Small
Edmund Rolls	L. L. Birch	Morley Kare
Anthony Sclafani	Harry Kissileff	Patricia Pliner
Elizabeth Capaldi	Jacques Le Magnen	Ilene Bernstein
Rose Marie Pangborn	Leann Birch	Ann. C. Noble
Linda Bartoshuk	Paul Rozin	Eric Block
Michel Cabanac	Adam Drewnowski	Patricia Pliner
John Blundell	Kent Berridge	L. Wisniewski
Mark Fantino	Marion Hetherington	Robert Hyde
Susan Schiffman	Harold McGee	Louis J. Minor
Thomas Scott	Rachel Schemmel	Gilbert Leveille
Julia Child	Emeril Lagasse	David Mela
Ernie Strapazon	Dale Romsos	Morten Kringelbach

Ted Williams   A. W. Logue   Michael O'Mahony

Alton Brown   Martin Yan   C. Broberger

And there are many others …

The reader can learn much by Google-ing these names and reading their many interesting papers. To this day, I am amazed that their works have not received the general recognition they deserve—after all, food scientists, chefs, and the home cook would greatly benefit by an understanding of food perception and the pleasures of the palate!

Preface

To the Reader:

In this book, I have tried to simplify and outline the various food pleasure principles as much as possible in general observations, aphorisms, and theories; I've often used bullet points in a teaching manner.

To the **Dietitian**: I would hope these principles may be used to make healthy food taste good. It is certainly possible! Pleasure is the major driver of food ingestion and behavior, but without an understanding of the nature of food pleasure and perception itself, no useful modifications to food can be made. Salt, fat, and sugar, classically considered a nutritional enemy, can still be used for good.

To the **Food Scientist**: Sadly, the principles of good food construction are not part of any food-science curriculum that I am aware of—probably because of the sheer complexity of the subject and the lack of physiological training in the food sciences. This book, then, may be your first exposure to the interrelated world of food physiology, psychology, and neuroscience. In your profession, you create foods that millions eat; use these principles to elevate your own understanding of good food construction.

To the **Professional Chef**: Many excellent chefs use the principles described in this book without actually knowing it; they use tradition, training, and talent in their food design. Hopefully, I will demystify what you may already know. The time-honored principles of French cooking were actually the impetus behind my scientific investigation of the "why" of classic cuisine, which was presented at the 1985 Geneva Nutritional Conference and published in the 1986 book: *Food*

Acceptance and Nutrition titled: "Physiological and nutritional influences on cuisine and product development." Twenty years later, food intake and neuroimaging research coupled with advances in taste and smell perception have completely transformed the fields of food science and sensory perception.

"Nothing would be more tiresome than eating and drinking if God had not made them a pleasure as well as a necessity."
Voltaire (1755–1826)

Final Note: Any errors in punctuation, syntax, or grammatical correctness are mine alone—blame them on Sentence Specific Satiety.

CHAPTER 1

▼

FOOD PLEASURE THEORIES AND PRINCIPLES

The brain's pleasure centers prefer salt, sugar, and fat mixtures.[1,2,3]

All of our favorite foods have unknown physiological and neurobiological explanations as to why we prefer them and why they have endured as best sellers over the years. In fact, I started studying the psychobiology of the popular snack food Doritos in an effort to understand why this billion-dollar brand is a huge success year after year in the United States—and many foreign countries as well. I studied the food intake and chemical senses literature—over five hundred research reports and four thousand abstracts—in order to discern the popularity of Doritos. In the process I developed the Food Pleasure Equation (Capaldi-inspired) and, in collaboration with Dr. Robert Hyde (San Jose State University), the important theory of *Dynamic Contrast* in foods.

There are hundreds of food palatability theories and influences (and seemingly endless neurotransmitters, neuropeptides, and hormone effectors). The list we will discuss includes what I think are the most important and useful food perception theories. In my evaluation process I used the philosophy of the renowned physicist Albert Einstein, who once said (I paraphrase) that a good theory must have three properties: it should *explain* the phenomenon, it must *predict* future behavior of the phenomenon, and it must be *simple*, the simpler the better—but not any more than that. It is the hope of this author that the principles enumerated below will help explain why you eat what you eat (food enlightenment), elevate your own cooking prowess (it's fun to prepare meals for your friends), and perhaps even make good-for-you food tasty and delicious. Please note that not all researchers will agree with my list, and some may not even want to be associated with the phenomenon—but after twenty years of giving lectures and talks, I think it is both honorable and heuristic to put names behind the science.

In 1825, a French lawyer, Jean Anthelme Brillat-Savarin, wrote a brilliant treatise on food and philosophy called the *Physiologie du Goût*. Quite ahead of its time, and still quoted today, *The Physiology of Taste* contains insights and musings on the sense of taste, food pleasure, gastronomy, coffee, chocolate, and even the first description of the "umami" taste of MSG (called the osmazome). I found his work inspiring (see my chapter on chefs), and I have tried to update his treatise with this current work using the very latest research in food science and neurophysiology—just as he predicted in the first chapter of his book. For a complete copy of his work on the Web, see http://etext.library.adelaide.edu.au/b/Brillat-Savarin/savarin/b85p/.

The following is a list of the most important food palatability theories of particular interest to food scientists, chefs, dietitians, and those who just like to cook. This is not in order of importance, but merely a listing. I selected these sixteen theories from over a hundred published food-perception phenomena in the scientific literature. I believe they explain most of the food behavior we see in our daily life.

Major Food Perception Theories

1. Food Pleasure Equation (Hyde/Witherly)

   a. Sensation Plus Calories

   b. Taste Hedonics

   c. Emulsion Theory

   d. Salivation Response

2. Dynamic Contrast (Hyde/Witherly)

   a. Ping-Pong Pleasure Contrast (Hyde)

    b.   Tostada Effect (Witherly)

    c.   Meatloaf Effect (Witherly)

3.   Sensory Specific Satiety (Rolls) or "Variety Effect"

4.   Supernormal Stimulus (E. O. Wilson)

5.   Evoked Qualities (Hyde) a/k/a Emeril "BAM!" Effect

6.   Flavor-Flavor Learning (Pliner)

7.   Mere Exposure Effect (Pliner)

8.   Taste-Aversion Learning (Bernstein/Rozin)

9.   P. Rozin's Principles of Food Likes and Dislikes

    a.   Disgust Theory

    b.   E. Rozin's Flavor Principles

10. Energy Density Theory (Drewnowski)

11. Vanishing Caloric Density (Hyde)

12. Post-Ingestional Conditioning (Booth, Capaldi)

13. Human "Cookivore" Theory (Wrangham)

14. Aroma and Essential-Nutrient Encoding (Goff and Klee)

15. "Liking" Versus "Wanting" Theory

16. The Stomach: the Second "Taste" System

Six Most Important Food Theories:

1.   Taste Hedonics (salt, sugar, and umami)

2.   Dynamic Contrast (food arousal and surprise)

3.   Evoked Qualities (when food sensory properties evoke past memories)

4.   Food Pleasure Equation (Food Pleasure = sensation + macronutrients)

5.   Caloric Density (humans like food with a CD of about 5.0)

6.   Emulsion Theory (taste buds love foods in emulsified forms)

Food Perception Theories

The reality is that scientists know very little about food choice or preference.[4] Food pleasure appears to involve both the opioid and cannabinoids reward circuitry that interact in complex ways.[5] Moreover, if we wish to understand the nature of overeating and obesity we must explore the science behind what makes food taste good.[6]

1. The Food Pleasure Equation

"O taste and see that the Lord is good."
Psalms 34:8 (NASB)

"You are the salt of the earth; but if the salt has become tasteless, how will it be made salty again?"
Matthew 5:13 (NASB)

A. Food Pleasure = Sensation (Taste, Aroma, Orosensation) + Calories (Macronutrients)

Sensation	plus	Caloric Stimulation
❖ Gustation (taste)		❖ Protein
▪ Salt, MSG, 5'Nuc.		▪ Casomorphins
▪ Sweet		▪ Gluteomorphins
▪ Fat Taste		▪ Amino acid stimulation
▪ Vanilloid activation		❖ Carbohydrates
▪ Water Taste		▪ Sucrose
❖ Olfaction (Smell)		▪ Glucose
▪ Aroma (pure)		▪ Fructose
▪ Trigeminal		▪ Starch
❖ Dynamic Contrast (Feel)		❖ Fat
▪ Temperature change		▪ Linoleic Acid
▪ Snap, Crackle & Pop		▪ Linolenic Acid
▪ Texture Contrast		▪ Omega-3's?
▪ Rapid Meltdown		❖ Caloric Density
❖ Supernormal Stimulus		▪ Vanishing Caloric Density (Hyde)
▪ Wansink Effect		
❖ Variety Effect (SSS)		

Food pleasure is a combination of sensory factors (sensation) and caloric stimulation by the macronutrients (protein, carbohydrate, and fat). Sensory factors that most contribute to pleasure are salty taste, sweet taste, umami taste, and orosensation from the oral cavity (feeling). Aroma is important in food discrimination but not a primary hedonic driver like taste. Dynamic contrast in the food plays a major role in food pleasure (texture and taste contrasts, food meltdown, and temperature changes).

The body regulates all three macronutrients with intricate feedback mechanisms—but uses the total amount of calories as the general sensor. And as we will learn, high caloric density foods are preferred over lower—brain scans show a reduced hedonic response when subjects view a plate of vegetables versus a higher calorie alternative. Depressing, isn't it?

The Food Pleasure Equation postulates that the brain has the ability to quantify the pleasure contained in an eating experience as performed by certain dopamine neurons in the brain and the sensing of calories by the gut. When you have a food choice, the brain actually calculates how much pleasure will be generated during the eating and digestion of a particular food. The goal of the brain, gut, and fat cell is to maximize the pleasure extracted from the environment, both in food sensation and macronutrient content. If a food is lowered in calories for health reasons, the gut has the ability to sense this, and the food will become less palatable over time (think frozen yogurt or light potato chips). To keep the food pleasure elevated, one must add additional sensation, e.g., more taste, greater dynamic contrast, or added orosensation. The biggest mistake I see in the commercial marketplace is creating a light food (that tastes and looks exactly like the original) without adding more pleasure sensation(s). Given the choice of two foods exactly alike in sensory terms, the brain, with instructions from the gut and fat cell, will always choose the higher-calorie original.

B. Taste Hedonics

As mentioned above, certain solutes (salt, sugar, MSG, and the 5'-nucleotides in solution) in foods contribute most to food pleasure. In numerous studies, we find that the taste of sugar, particularly sucrose, and salt drive taste hedonics and ingestion. Monosodium glutamate (MSG) taste, or "umami," is now firmly entrenched as the fifth hedonic taste. Umami means "deliciousness" in Japanese and is believed to signal the presence of protein in your mouth. Protein, by itself, does not have much taste (try chewing on a raw steak if you are a skeptic). MSG, interestingly, does not have that much taste on its own either; kind of brothy and a little salty, but add sodium chloride to it, and the hedonic flavors just explode!

C. <u>Emulsion Theory</u>

Taste buds (and higher-order brain structures) like the taste of emulsions, whether they are salt-fat or sugar-fat combinations. The most *agréable* foods are true emulsions, whether they are butter, chocolate, salad dressings, ice cream, hollandaise sauce, mayonnaise, or *crème*. One major reason for this is the concentration effect of the hedonic taste solutes when made into an emulsion. For example, butter is about 2.5 percent salt by weight, but this level of salt is concentrated into the 15 percent water phase of the butter emulsion. In effect, the true salt concentration is 10 percent—a true hedonic salt rush.

French chefs are masters of emulsion creation, and the humble mashed potato is no exception. In the *French Laundry Cookbook* (p. 86), Thomas Keller describes the exacting technique of using a *chinois* (cone strainer) to create the perfect emulsification of potatoes, butter, and cream—or *pomme purée*. Chef Rowley Leigh, food columnist for the *Financial Times USA*, writes about the extraordinary (unctuous) mashed potatoes of French chef Joel Robuchon—finest *ratte* waxy potatoes emulsified with equal parts of unsalted Normandy butter.[7]

D. <u>Salivation Response</u>

My salivation theory states that we prefer foods that are moist or evoke saliva during the mastication process. Saliva is critical for hedonic solute contact with taste buds; simply put, no taste, no pleasure. Saliva also fosters food lubrication and enhances the entire eating experience. Even dry foods like saltines have salt on top and a flaky texture that fosters salivation as it melts down in the mouth. Add fat to a dry food (potato chips are 50 percent fat calories), and you have *additional* oral lubrication—the perfect "salivation" food. Thin potato chips have a texture that melts down very quickly and stimulates salivary flow. The tastiest foods should evoke saliva or at least provide lubrication and moistness. Culinologists and great chefs know this secret. French chefs are masters of food saucing; Chinese (and Asian food in general) and Indian cuisines are almost entirely finished with a sauce or glaze.

We have all experienced "mouth watering" when presented with tasty food, especially when we are hungry. Salivation is tied into the whole experience of eating. And Temple et al. (2006) found that as we eat more of the *same* food, we secrete less saliva—we are actually habituating to the food in a manner similar to Sensory Specific Satiety.[8] This amazing response actually means the food becomes less pleasurable as you continue to eat it, and you salivate less! Taken to another level, this means that superior cuisine that keeps you stimulated with texture, colors, and taste will not allow this salivation habituation response to occur. In fact, salivation to a food may be an independent measurement of how much you like it. (Dr. Robert Hyde and I performed a number of salivation experiments under the direction of Professor Rose Marie Pangborn at UC Davis.)

2. Dynamic Contrast (DC)

"So because you are lukewarm, and neither hot nor cold, I will spit you out of
My mouth."
Revelation 3:16 (NASB)

The Witherly and Hyde theory of DC states that people prefer foods with sensory contrasts—light and dark, sweet and salty, rapid meltdown in the mouth, crunchy with silky, and so on. Temperature changes in the mouth are also highly arousing and pleasurable. "Ping-Pong Pleasure" refers to an ingestion pattern, in which people tend to alternate between foods that cleanse the palate, like drinking beer (which is low sodium) with salty snacks, or wine with food (wine is very low sodium and acidic). Studies indicate that the brain has a craving for novelty, which produces a "thrilling effect" via the release of brain opioids (endorphins).[9] In fact, we used to call our theory "dynamic novelty," wherein the mouth delights in texture, flavor, and orosensory novelty. In 2006, Biederman and Vessel proposed that humans are "infovores"; where pleasure systems (using mu-opioids) actually guide human behavior for learning (and preference for novelty) in a constantly changing or challenging environment—hence, the addictiveness of video and Internet gaming.[9] In the same way, gustation and orosensation excite mu-opioids in the medial and forebrain sections (our pleasure centers), guiding our pleasures of ingestion.

Many foods with high DC have the same feature, which I call the Tostada Effect—an edible shell that goes crunch followed by something soft or creamy and full of taste-active compounds. This rule applies to a variety of our favorite food structures—the caramelized top of a *crème brûlée*, a slice of pizza, or an Oreo cookie—the brain finds crunching through something like this very novel and thrilling. No doubt, higher-order brain mechanisms release opioids—and probably a separate population of neurons distinct from the activation of the classic taste centers. This phenomenon name is derived from the only dish that I cooked in college that was popular with my roommates—sometimes we would eat it once a week. (Cooking the tostada shells can be hazardous; one roommate, while trying to deep-fry the corn tortilla, ignited the paper-towel rack with the hot oil. A well-aimed dousing with beer saved the apartment.)

The exact opposite of adding contrasting flavors, textures, and tastes is what I call the "meatloaf effect", affectionately named after this most quintessential American dish that evokes sensory yawns and feelings of apathy—a taste bud dud. Top French chefs know this effect well and take great lengths to reduce or eliminate it entirely. Thomas Keller is one of the best at this—he crafted *The French Laundry* and *Bouchon Cookbook* recipes to eliminate the accidental blurring of sensation and diminution of pleasure. (See my chapter on secrets of the chefs). The meatloaf effect is very prominent in canned foods or in stews and soups that sit around for a long period. The intense heating called retort processing or, to a lesser extent, aseptic processing, transforms fresh and bright looking ingredients into muted colors and unidentifiable flavors. Not only does the meatloaf effect reduce food pleasure, but consuming such foods creates a bad-food memory complex. To this day, the taste and smell of a tinny, canned vegetable evokes the sensory shudders of my youth. Julia Child writes of this effect as well and provides culinary guidance on how to eliminate it.[10] She describes culinary techniques that transform ordinary canned beef bouillon into a tasty brown sauce. I often use Thomas Keller's favorite (fresh thyme and bay leaf) flavoring complex to revitalize sauces that use canned chicken or beef broths.

3. Sensory Specific Satiety (SSS)

SSS is a very important theory in food pleasure appreciation. It states that as we eat food, the pleasure response to the sensory properties of the food decreases within minutes. This involves parts of the brain (orbitofrontal cortex) that sense the taste, aroma, texture, and even visual aspects of foods.[11] A decrease in pleasure response is the body's way of encouraging the intake of a wide variety of foods—differing in flavors and textures. The opposite or reciprocal of SSS has been called the "variety effect" or the "smorgasbord effect," wherein we eat more when presented with food variety. The SSS effect is quite rapid (as little as ten minutes) and has culinary implications for creating the most interesting and pleasurable food. Thomas Keller (of *The French Laundry* fame), understands this effect, he calls it the law of diminishing returns, and specifically designs his tasting courses to counteract this negative effect on food pleasure.[12]

4. Super Normal Stimulus *or* Supersize Me

This is a long-held biology principle stating that rare and important stimuli in the environment (like energy-dense foods) become magnified and more desirable (or Super Normal) if made *larger* than expected—like a supersized order of French fries or the 1,400 kcal Monster Thickburger. Meat is a valuable and precious macronutrient in our evolutionary past, and half a heifer on a bun is visually exciting and stimulates the overall ingestive response. Several studies indicate that big portions excite the palate, and people just eat more. Although the supersize phenomenon is waning, big portions are still the norm in many restaurants. Many of our favorite foods are supernormal combinations of salt, fat, and sugar that exceed anything available to our wandering ancestors. We evolved to crave these valuable and rare nutrients. Hence, we respond with an exaggerated eating response (hyperphagia) to the super normal sundae.

Super normal stimuli exist in other avenues, such as the entertainment world. The cartoon drawing of Jessica Rabbit (from the movie *Who Framed Roger Rabbit*) and, to a more limited extent, Barbie, are popular examples of obvious accentuation of physical attributes beyond normal physiological probability, with the intent of enhancing female desirability. For a discussion on this phenomenon, see E. O. Wilson's book *Consilience: The Unity of Knowledge*.

Brian Wansink, marketing professor at Cornell and author of *Mindless Eating*, has studied this phenomenon and found that portion size can even supersede taste as a driver of ingestion.[13] Similar to the supersize phenomenon in fast food, he found moviegoers given popcorn in large buckets ate 34 percent more. I can't wait to read his book.

5. Evoked Qualities (EQ)

Dr. Robert Hyde's hypothesis states that the act of eating food creates memories, not only the sensory properties of that food, but the event of eating, and even the people you ate with. This food-environmental experience creates a permanent memory engram. Later on, this memory can be "evoked" or relived by exposure to the sensory properties of the food or one's mere presence in the same environment. Food cravings are often triggered by sight, smell, and caloric memories of restaurants past. One EQ example is Emeril's ubiquitous use of his excellent "Original Essence" seasoning—or "BAM!" spice blend. It contains a number of culinary spices (onion, garlic, Italian herbs) whose aromas evoke past memories of food ingestion and happy times. And, according to the theory, one does not need to be consciously aware of the underlying memories being recalled. Neuroscientist Sarah Leibowitz has also noted that every food experience creates a sensory memory response to the food, the caloric level, and the social surroundings.[14] Another example is Chef Thomas Keller, who reminisced that every time he prepares onion soup it brings back memories of every bowl of soup he has ever consumed.[12]

6. Flavor—Flavor Learning

This theory states that food preference to a neutral stimulus that is paired with a preferred flavor or taste, will increase liking for the previous neutral or even disliked food.[15] An example would be adding sugar to oatmeal to induce preference or the use of garlic in a vegetable to induce liking (works well with kids). This should not be confused with post-ingestional conditioning, which is caloric-induced liking to a food after digestion.

7. Mere Exposure Effect

In studies on food preference, the mere exposure to a sensory stimulus (so-called neutral stimuli) will increase familiarity and liking.[16] Familiarity actually increases liking *more* than contempt as we acquire tastes for things over time with repeat exposure. As an example, kids may not like broccoli, but if you keep exposing them to it, for instance, by just placing it on their plates, liking will occur even without ingestion. In time they will at least try it; and if it is made tasty (butter, garlic, and salt), kids will be enticed to consume it. Once consumed, the calories (butter or cheese sauce) will help *burn-in* permanent liking. We call this post-ingestional conditioning (see below).

8. Taste-Aversion Learning

This principle states that food ingestion with negative gastrointestinal side effect creates a permanent flavor or taste-aversion to that food.[17] It is likely that all of us have about half a dozen of these aversions buried in our brain stems. An easy way to acquire one (and I have not, of course, done this personally) is to drink too much, get sick, and throw up—alcohol is a gastric irritant, and all those interesting flavors and tastes on the way up become instant food aversions. Also known as the "Southern Comfort Effect" in the not-so-scientific food intake literature, certain sweet liquors, or drinks with umbrellas, can slow gastric emptying, allowing alcohol a longer and more damaging gastric contact time—

with sometimes unpleasant results (vomiting). Once during a lecture on food aversions, an executive came to the podium and confided that his company is aware of this sugar-gastric-irritation phenomenon and is developing a line of less sweet alternatives.

9. Rozin's Fundamental Principle

Food psychologist Paul Rozin suggests that it is easier to dislike a food than to learn to like it. His observation is an important protective feature of the human omnivore, where we eat anything and can be poisoned by everything! Children, with lower body weights and less developed detoxification systems, become very picky and prone to eat the same foods over and over. Pregnant women, with a developing fetus, must be very selective with foods—especially novel ones, where even *small* amounts of ingested food can have lasting biological effects.

a.   Disgust. This is a powerful motivation to reject food because the food tastes bad or is considered dangerous (a worm in an apple).[18] A basic, core emotion, disgust involves the sense of taste, perhaps gastric nausea, and stereotypical facial (disgust) expressions—*yuck*! This factor is probably largely overlooked in food likes and dislikes—most of which are based on texture and animal products. My favorite examples of disgust from Rozin's research include his attempt to get adults and kids to consume a cockroach-in-a-drink (after the cockroach has been removed) or his request for people to drink apple juice from a bed pan—now that's *disgusting*.

b.   Elisabeth Rozin's Flavor Principle. An outstanding cook and food anthropologist, Ms. Rozin observes that cuisines have core techniques and flavors that define their character (sensory signature). Cuisine-curious cooks may want to check out her cookbooks (*The Flavor Principle Cookbook,* now known as *Ethnic Cuisine;* and *Crossroads Cooking*) and try preparing the flavor signatures of various cuisines. The function of Flavor Principles is to allow people to experience novel foods in their diet without inducing *neophobia*, or rejection. In Asian cuisine, for example, adding soy sauce to a new dish brings back the familiar and encourages food exploration. Here is an example of a flavoring principle: Indonesian cuisine is characterized by a combination of soy sauce, brown sugar, peanut, and chile. So by recreating this *combination* of flavors and ingredients you have formed the flavor "signature" of that cuisine. (For college students and serious foodies, reading anything from Paul and Elisabeth Rozin will advance your culinary and sensory knowledge.)

10. Energy Density (ED) Theory

Adam Drewnowski (nutrition and sensory expert) has discovered in his research that high energy density food is associated with high food pleasure. In addition, energy-dense foods are tasty but not filling, whereas foods with low energy density are more filling but less tasty.[19] Although humans never evolved in an energy-rich food environment (with the exception of nuts), but we crave the calorically dense foods when we see or sense them—we call this modern fast food. Even French cuisine techniques increase the tastiness and density of foods with butter and cream—visit the mashed potatoes recipe of *Puree de Pomme de Terre* in the *Bouchon* cookbook (page 250) to get the idea. His preparation technique is worth noting; it creates an emulsified potato mixture with rapid meltdown on the palate.

Energy density is a number from 0–9, and it is calculated by dividing calories (kcals) by the gram weight of a food. Foods' ED ranges from water (0) to pure vegetable fat (9). Most vegetables are near 1, meats climb to 2–3, fast and junk foods hover around 4–5 and butter climbs to 7.2.

11. Vanishing Caloric Density

A hypothesis by Dr. Robert Hyde states that we tend to like foods with high oral impact, plenty of taste and dynamic contrast, but with low satiating ability or immediate gastric feedback. Now, few foods qualify (meringues, diet soda, cotton candy, and pretzels), but popcorn is perhaps the best example. Buttered, salted popcorn is very tasty, and you can eat a lot of it, repeat oral stimulation, since it isn't that filling. In fact, I've seen some people actually accelerate their eating rate due to the absence of gastric satiety. Eating a whole bowl of popcorn for dinner is not a rare occurrence. Foods that exhibit this rapid (oral) meltdown response may actually signal the brain that the food being ingested is lower in calories than it really is. The reduced satiety response to high dynamic contrast foods (ice cream, chocolate, and French fries) may partially explain Dr. Drewnowski's observation that energy-dense foods that meltdown rapidly in the mouth, often lack satiety. Hence, foods that quickly "vanish" in the mouth are more rewarding, reduce gastric satiety, and encourage over ingestion.

12. Post-Ingestional Conditioning

"The belly rules the mind."
Old Spanish proverb

Consuming the macronutrients (fat, protein, and carbohydrate) will quickly condition the human (and animals) to prefer the taste of *that* food. Sweet foods condition readily, sometimes after one pairing—sweet taste is a reliable and potent inducer of mu-opioid in the brain reward center. Foods high in fat calories also condition readily; studies reveal that feeding people yogurts with higher fat content will condition the food flavor faster and stronger. This is part of the problem with junk food—unusually rich in taste-active components like salt, fat, sugar, and umami, with high caloric density, they readily create potent food preferences. As food is digested, receptors in the stomach and intestines relay information on the food to the brain via direct contact with the vagus nerve, resulting in the release of many different peptide hormones. High-fat foods are particularly *bienvenue*; specific hormones relay fatty acid information (calories) to the brain and the fat cells. There are plenty of peptides in the brain that respond to the presence of fat. Such peptides include orexin, galanin, leptin, and insulin. In the appetite center, certain peptides are released that can stimulate the taste for fat (opioids, galanin) and carbohydrate (neuropeptide Y) and encourage hyperphagia (overeating).[20]

13. Human Cookivore Theory

Richard Wrangham, professor of anthropology at Harvard University, noticed the close evolutionary relationship between humans and fire over the past five hundred thousand years.[21] Cuisine may be in our genes. Cooking made modern man and influenced gastronomy, nutrient assimilation, and flavor preferences. There is much evolutionary support for this theory: human stomachs are smaller than primate herbivores, and we prefer nutrient-dense foods. Although our olfactory receptors have degenerated over the past hundreds of thousands of years, our higher-order aroma brain processing (secondary and tertiary areas) has actually increased. Aroma perception touches more parts of the brain than any other sense. The use of fire greatly expanded what we could digest and eat safely. This, in part, explains our seemingly built-in liking for the smell of smoke and BBQ— it's the smell of survival! To this day, hickory smoke can give me pleasure chills— similar to a favorite piece of music.

Scientists have discovered "meat-adaptive" genes in humans that were a very important nutritional adaptation to meat eating. Human ancestors ate meat as long as 2.5 millions years ago, and despite what we currently think about meat and bad health; these gene changes protected us against the adverse consequences of a higher protein diet (high cholesterol and iron). Chimps and other apes that are fed our type of fast food diet clog their arteries very quickly—while we are relatively resistant.[22] I've also expanded Wrangham's cookivore theory a bit to include fermentation aromas. Fermented foods and their aromas can also signal survival, whether it is in the form of cheese, beer, wine, miso, or *Kimchi*.

Further evidence for the cookivore theory comes from researcher Peter Lucas, author of *Dental Functional Morphology*, who suggested that cooking makes food softer and easier to chew, and the use of utensils makes cutting food much easier, thus reducing the need for a huge jaw.[23] Bernard Wood, a paleoanthropologist at George Washington University, believes we are evolving to eat mushy food.[24] Actually, we are evolving to eat cooked foods, prepared in ways to increase caloric density.

Zoologist Desmond Morris in the now-classic *Naked Ape*, says that humans are meat-eating carnivores, but have kept their plant-eating ways (like all other primates) for the pleasures of food variety and the hedonic taste of sugar.[25] Typical primates have a wide and diversified palate of tastes and flavors from plant foods, consuming roots, leaves, flowers, shoots, and fruits with deliberate and obvious relish. Desmond also suggested that we prefer warm or hot food, primarily to increase food flavor generation—a strict meat diet is simply too boring. Hence, humans are mostly meat-eating omnivores, who like to consume plant foods for variety, flavor, and sweet taste (energy). Most importantly, we like to cook these foods *together*. This is, in effect, the foundation of modern cuisine (it's in our genes).

14. Aroma and Essential Nutrient Encoding (Goff and Klee)

This novel theory states that human olfaction and the perception of essential nutrients in plants coevolved in a mutually beneficial way.[26] Many plants derive their volatiles from essential nutrients such as vitamins, minerals, and fatty acids. Their detection and perception may have helped guide human olfaction—fine-tuning the olfactory system to detect useful aromas. This fits in well with the cookivore theory. As we have seen, over hundreds and thousands of years of evolution our olfactory discrimination may have degenerated, but higher-order olfactory pathways were fine-tuned to pay attention to survival aromas in the environment: detecting food, foes, and sex. The authors suggest that volatiles that signal nutritional significance (Vitamin C, B-vitamins, and carotenoids) are epigenetically (preprogrammed) preferred—and this has *very important* food pleasure implications—especially in flavor manufacture and cuisine design.

15. "Liking" Versus "Wanting" Theory

Neurophysiologist Kent Berridge suggests (with strong scientific support) that our desire for food (and drugs) must be distinguished into two separate phenomena: *liking*, or pleasure induced during eating, and *wanting*, the (non-hedonic) desire to choose that food.[27] Berridge's work is tough reading and difficult to understand because it is not biologically intuitive. (But the good doctor is always quick to answer my e-mails when I need further clarification.) In an article on liking versus wanting, scientist David Mela (2006) explains that the key to understanding food behavior involves physiological cues, anticipated pleasure, and external cues (conscious and unconscious).[28] He says that oral *pleasure* is not the only food-purchase criteria; the other dimension is a desire for "wanting" that food based on a non-hedonic choice. He suggests that wanting may be related to the experience of food boredom—we simply want food with differing sensory properties. Low calorie foods, he hypothesizes, must be optimized for both *wanting* and *liking*. Why is this important? Well, it is fairly easy to measure and to manipulate how much you like something, but measuring how much you *want* something, especially when you are not aware of it, is quite another matter! Mela believes that this new dimension of wanting is a major factor in purchase intent and deserves much more serious study. In the future, manipulation of food "wanting" may be a major product development endeavor.

Berridge and his colleagues disclose that the intense liking of sweetness is due to mu-opioid stimulation localized in the rostrodorsal region of the nucleus accumbens shell (a pleasure circuit in the limbic brain) and the ventral pallidum.[29] Dopamine was widely believed to be the major pleasure neurotransmitter in the brain, but this may not be the case at all. Mice that are bred to have *no* brain dopamine still experience pleasant taste, however, they lack the *will* to work for it.[27] Shimura et al. (2006) also found that GABA, opioid, and D_1 receptors in the ventral pallidum (brain pleasure structure) are involved in the consumption of hedonically positive taste stimuli.[30] The authors suggest that many common motivated behaviors activate the ventral pallidum such as consuming food, mating behavior, sexual activity, and in the liking for number of drugs such as alcohol, heroin, and cocaine. The brain pleasure response, it appears, likes to share a final common pathway.

16. The Stomach: the Second "Taste" System

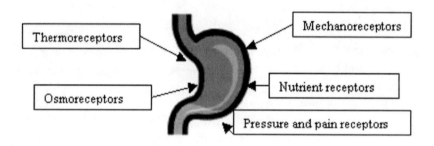

Many chefs and food scientists have focused on the oral cavity as the major dictator of what we eat. The tongue does contain many thousands of taste buds and chemoreceptors that constantly monitor the gustatory and orosensations of the food we eat, and they certainly guide food selection and pleasure. But this view of oral fixation changed when researchers found that the stomach and small intestine have the great ability to sense what we eat as well—in fact, these organs contain many more "sensing receptors" than our taste buds! The stomach, small (and even the large) intestines' major roles are to evaluate incoming food (called a bolus), facilitate digestion, and prevent you from ingesting potentially toxic compounds. I became aware of the importance of "stomach sensing" from a presentation in Geneva by the physiologist N. Mei in 1986. He was one of the first to note the amazing richness and complexity of the sensory information arising from the digestive territory.[31]

The stomach and small intestine have the following systems to evaluate what is consumed:

1. Mechanoreceptors. These receptors located in the mucosa and muscular layers sense the distention or contraction of the digestive wall.

2. Chemoreceptors. These receptors are sensitive to all three main types of nutrients: carbohydrate, amino acids, and lipids. In addition, they are pH responsive to acids or alkali substances.

3. Thermoreceptors. The stomach can sense the temperature (and the intensity) of the nutrients and the water of the food eaten.

4. Osmoreceptors. The stomach can sense "osmolality" or the number of dissolved particles in solution. If one consumes a very high sugar and fat food, the stomach secretes water in an effort to dilute the contents to lower the osmolality back to normal. This can stress the stomach lining, and cause a feeling of malaise (upset).

The wall of the gut has an impressive array of sensors that can relay information to the brain stem and ultimately to the sensory cortex of the brain (right next door to the taste areas). The gut has nutrient receptors for: sodium chloride, amino acids, fats, fatty acids, glucose (especially rich), and other simple sugars. In fact, the intestine may have more taste receptors than the oral cavity, and non-nutrient receptors abound as well. These receptors sense the volume of food, osmotic pressure, the temperature of food, the size and shape of food particles, and mucosal touch. All these sensors have the following main functions—to sense what was eaten, prepare the gut for digestion, create a gastro-sensory memory, and alter food selection in future meals. This is accomplished by direct neural intervention with other body organs and a large number of hormonal signals released by gut tissue. For example, the stomach and intestine may "taste" glucose and amino acids and relays this information (via nerves) to the pancreas and the liver to increase blood insulin and other post-digestive hormones.[32]

Gut-Brain Axis[33,34]

The gastrointestinal tract and nervous system, both central and enteric, are involved in a complicated, two-way communication by both parasympathetic and sympathetic nerves, cholinergic fibers, and dozens of peptides and hormones. We will not deal with details here, but suffice it to say that sensors in the gut relay information during food digestion via vagal and sympathetic spinal nerves to the central nervous system. This input is affected by the nature of the food stimuli (protein, fat, and carbohydrate) and neurohormonal stimuli such as gut hormones, neurotransmitters, and modulators as well as cytokines and microbial end products. The stomach and intestine, therefore, are the body's second chance to evaluate the taste, volume, osmolality, and nutrient composition of chewed food and relay this information to the brain. In addition, the stomach secretes hormones such as *ghrelin*, a powerful appetite stimulant that slows metabolism and inhibits fat burning as well. Dieting causes a rise in this appetite-stimulating hormone, and the more weight you lose the greater the rise. The body doesn't want you to lose weight; this is just one protective mechanism against starvation.

Importance of Stomach Sensing

For years food scientists have created a whole new category of foods that are light in fat, salt, or sugar (or all three). Despite the unpopularity of some of these foods, they still proliferate in the marketplace. And they certainly have their place in our society, as healthier alternatives to junk food. But making a light version of a nutrient-dense food is sensorially difficult, due to the ability of the stomach and intestinal to sense calories. Once you eat a food, the vast array of sensors in the intestine calculate the taste and macronutrient content and relays that information to the brain via vagal afferents to the nucleus of the solitary tract (among others) and then to higher-order brain centers. In essence, the gut-brain axis knows the nutrient density of that food; and if you try to fool the stomach by creating the exact same taste but with reduced calories, the body's natural reaction is to lower food hedonics and, over time, food selection. Remember the craze over low-fat yogurt? Shops popped up everywhere, until the stomach-learning mechanism dropped the food preference and forced us back to ice cream (read that: Cold Stone!). Of all the nutrients that condition food preference, the strongest associations are made from fat- and sugar-containing foods, preferably in the emulsified form.

A number of years back, I was giving a lecture on food preference, and a food scientist in the audience asked what I thought about the new Border Lights menu, developed to great fanfare at Taco Bell in 1995. In a move that made the food police happy (including Michael Jacobson, Center for Science in the Public Interest), the taco giant, owned by PepsiCo, introduced fat- and calorie-reduced versions of tacos, burritos, and taco salads, a healthy alternative for more than half of all their offerings. Two years of development and $75 million in advertising went along with the food revisions. At the time, John Martin, the chairman and chief executive of Taco Bell, suggested the move would transform the fast-food industry. He even suggested that the menu would become a $5 billion opportunity in ten years (quite the optimist).[35]

So what did I think? Well, I visited the local Taco Bell and tried each one of the foods; I noticed that they were good copies of the regular menu items, but in each and every case, the foods were lower in dynamic contrast and hedonic solutes.

The company made three very serious mistakes. First, the brain and gut have a memory of the foods eaten in the past, including the taste *and* the calories. Second, by removing the fat and modifying the ingredients, there was less meltdown, less aroma, less flavor, and increased rubberiness and cardboard notes. (For example, starches replaced milk fat, cheese became nonfat, and the tortillas were baked—ugh!) Finally, I could not find any increased sensation to make up for the calories lost, as should occur based on the food pleasure equation. I told the audience that Taco Bell would lose 50 million bucks. I was wrong; it was double that. Now, don't get me wrong; I like Taco Bell food (it sustained me in college), and I don't wish to be too harsh (their Mexican pizza is high in dynamic contrast and quite tasty). But an awareness of the basic principles of food perception, appreciation, and digestion would have helped enlighten the product development process and increased the probability of success.

Summary: The Big Six

Foods that are considered delicious and desirable have the following characteristics; look for the application of these pleasure qualities in the chapters that follow. Our favorite foods usually combine most, or all, of the following in a single food.

1. Taste Hedonics. Foods must contain salt, sugar, MSG, and flavor-active compounds. Preferably all of the above at the physiologically correct amounts: salt at 1.0–1.5 percent, MSG at 0.15 percent, and 5'-nucleotides at 0.02 percent. In sugar systems, salt will always improve the overall taste hedonics; 0.25 percent salt is usually sufficient. Taste is a major driver of ingestion and pleasure in food, but it only accounts for less than 10 percent of all the *sensation* from the mouth to the brain. Food must also excite thermal (hot and cold), tactile, texture, fatty acid, and pain receptors. And there are many lesser known hedonic solutes yet to be discovered.

2. Dynamic Contrast. Tastiest foods must contain texture and/or flavor contrasts; the more the merrier—rapid food meltdown with snap, crackle, and pop. Next to taste hedonics, this is the most important contributor to food pleasure. Since humans are visual animals (almost 40 percent of the brain cortex is devoted to vision), contrasts must include color and appearance as well.

3. Evoked Qualities. Food must evoke or bring forth previously conditioned pleasure memories—food content, environs where ingested, and prior physiological state. Emeril's "BAM!" blend is a good example: the spices (garlic, onions, etc.) evoke memories and pleasures of past meals. The key is to add these "qualities" in a subtle and balanced way.

4. Food Pleasure Equation. Food pleasure is a function of sensation and macronutrient stimulation. The tastiest foods maximize both dimensions. For example, if a food is lowered in calories, to increase the pleasure, you must add more sensation.

5. Caloric Density. The gut-brain axis senses CD and makes it *good*. A CD of 4–5 is most preferred, often found in junk foods. (0 is the score for water and 9 is for pure fat.) Exceptions to this preference rule are those foods with big volumes that melt down quickly in the mouth (vanishing caloric density), such as popcorn.

6. Emulsion Theory. Taste buds like emulsions, especially salt-fat or sugar-fat combinations. Many of our tastiest foods are in liquid or solid phase emulsions, whether they are butter, chocolate, salad dressings, ice cream, hollandaise sauce, mayonnaise, or *crème*. The making of an emulsion concentrates the hedonic taste solutes (salt, sugar, and MSG) into the water phase. We have discussed that butter is about 2.5 percent salt, but in the emulsified state, the actual salt content presented to the taste bud is 10 percent salt because all of the salt is in the 18 percent water phase. Ice cream is a frozen emulsified "foam" that concentrates the sugar (sucrose) in the water phase, enhancing the perception of sweetness.

Glossary

Caloric Density: Calculated by calories of food divided by weight in grams
Casomorphins: Psychoactive digestion products of the cow milk protein, casein
D1 receptors: Receptors in brain associated with dopamine activation and pleasure or movement
Dopamine: Neurotransmitter in brain associated with arousal, movement, and pleasure response
Emulsion: A mixture in which fats and water are dispersed evenly in a solution
Engram: The brain memory of the sensory and calorie properties of a food
GABA: Neurotransmitter in brain involved with reward and inhibiting actions
Galanin: Brain neuropeptide that increases hunger, especially for fat
Gluteomorphins: Psychoactive compounds formed from wheat digestion
Gustation: The sense of taste
Hedonics: Derived from a Greek word that means the study of pleasure

Hyperphagia: Overeating caused by a tasty or calorically dense food

Leptin: Fat cell hormone that can reduce appetite; the obese are resistant to its effect

Macronutrients: The big three—fat, protein, and carbohydrate

MSG: Monosodium glutamate, a flavor enhancer and stimulator of "umami" taste

Mu-opioids: Brain neuropeptides involved in food pleasure

Nucleus Accumbens: Part of the pleasure center

Olfaction: The sense of smell

Orosensory: All other sensation from the mouth besides basic tastes (pain, heat, cold, and touch)

Palatability: A feature of food; high palatability food is tasty and calorically dense

Solutes: Particles in solution that can be tasted by the tongue

Taste-Active: Solutes that are innately pleasurable, such as salt, sugar, MSG, and the 5'-nucleotides

Trigeminal: Cranial nerve that carries sensation from the mouth to brain and vice versa

Umami: Means "deliciousness" in Japanese; the taste of MSG

Vanilloid Receptors: Ingesting hot and black pepper stimulate these receptors and create a burning sensation

References

1. Wuetcher, S. Capaldi explores preferences for tastes. *University of Buffalo Reporter*, vol. 32, May 10, 2001. http://www.buffalo.edu/reporter/vol32/vol32n31/n4.html

2. Kelley, A. E., Bakshi, V. P., Haber, S. N., Steininger, M. J., Will, M. J., and M. Zhang. Opioid modulation of taste hedonics within the ventral striatum. *Physiol. Behav.*, 76:389–95, 2002.

3. Parker, G., Parker, I., and H. Brotchie. Mood state effects of chocolate. *J. Affect. Disorders*, 92:149–59, 2006.

4. Rozin, P. Why we're so fat, and French are not. *Psychol. Today*, Nov./Dec. 2000.

5. Cota, D., Tschop, M. H., Horvath, T. L., and A. S. Levine. Cannab-inoids, opioids and eating behavior: the molecular face of hedonism? *Brain Res. Brain Res. Rev.*, 51:85–107, 2006.

6. Yeomans, M., Blundell, J. E., and M. Leshem. Palatability: response to nutritional need or need-free stimulation of appetite? *Br. J. Nutr.*, Suppl. 1:S3–S14, 2004.

7. Leigh, R. Cauliflower comes into bloom. *Financial Times USA*, July 8, 2006.

8. Temple, J. L., Kent, K. M., Giacomelli, A. M., Paluch, R. A., Roem-mich, J. N., and L. H. Epstein. Habituation and recovery of salivation and motivated responding for food in children. *Appetite*, 46:280–4, 2006.

9. Biederman, I., and E. Vessel. Perceptual pleasure and the brain. *Am. Sci.*, 94:247–53, 2006.

10. Child, J. 2001. *Mastering the Art of French Cooking*, vol.1, New York: Alfred A. Knopf.

11. Rolls, E. T. Brain mechanisms underlying flavour and appetite. *Phil. Trans. R. Soc. B. Lond., Biol. Sci.*, 361:1123–36, 2006.

12. Keller, T. 1999. *The French Laundry Cookbook*. New York: Artisan.

13. Wansink, B. 2006. *Mindless Eating: Why We Eat More Than We Think*. New York: Bantam Books.

14. Collin, F. Sarah Leibowitz, interview, neuroscientist. *Omni Magazine*, May, 1992. via Looksmart, http://www.findarticles.com/p/articles/mi_m1430/is_n8_v14/ai_12180349/pg_1

15. Yeomans, M. R., Mobini, S., Elliman, T. D., Walker, H. C., and R. J. Stevenson. Hedonic and sensory characteristics of odors condi-tioned by pairing with tastants in humans. *J. Exp. Psychol. Anim. Behav. Process*, 32:2215–28. 2006.

16. Pliner, P. The effects of mere exposure on liking for edible substances. *Appetite*, 3:283–90, 1982.

17. Garcia, J., Lasiter, P. S., Bermudez-Rattoni, F., and D. A. Deems. A general theory of aversion learning. *Ann. N. Y. Acad. Sci.*, 443:8–21, 1985.

18. Rozin, P., Lowery, L., and R. Ebert. Varieties of disgust faces and the structure of disgust. *J. Pers. Soc. Psychol.*, 66:870–81, 1994.

19. Drewnowski, A. Energy density, palatability, and satiety: implications for weight control. *Nutr. Rev.*, 56:347–53, 1998.

20. Levine, A. S., Kotz, C. M., and B. A. Gosnell. Sugar and fats: the neurobiology of preference. *J. of Nutr.*, 133:831S–34S, 2003.

21. Lambert, C. The way we eat now. *Harvard Magazine*, May–June, 2004. http://www.harvardmagazine.com/on-line/050465.html

22. Finch, C. E., and C. B. Stanford. Meat-adaptive genes and the evolution of slower aging in humans. *Q. Rev. Biol.*, 79:3–50, 2004.

23. Lucas, P. 2004. *Dental Functional Morphology*. Cambridge: Cambridge University Press.

24. Mayell, H. Evolving to eat mush: how meat changed our bodies. *National Geographic News*, Feb. 18, 2005. http://news.nationalgeographic.com/news/2005/02/0218_050218_human_diet.html

25. Morris, D. 1967. *The Naked Ape*, New York: Dell Publishing.

26. Goff, S. A., and H. J. Klee. Plant volatile compounds: sensory cues for health and nutritional value? *Science*, 311:815–19, 2006.

27. Berridge, K. C. The debate over dopamine's role in reward: the case for incentive salience. *Psychopharmacology (Berl.)*, Oct. 27, 2006.

28. Mela, D. Eating for pleasure or just wanting to eat? Reconsidering sensory hedonic responses as a driver of obesity. *Appetite*, 47:10–17, 2006.

29. Pecina, S., Smith, K. S., and K. C. Berridge. Hedonic hot spots in the brain. *Neuroscientist*, 12:500–11, 2005.

30. Shimura, T., Kent, K. M., Giacomelli, A. M., Paluch, R. A., Roem-
    mich, J. N., and L. H. Epstein. Neurochemical modulation of inges-
    tive behavior in the ventral pallidum. *Europ. J. Neurosci.*, 23:1596–
    1604, 2006.

31. Mei, N. 1987. Metabolic effects of nutrient ingestion: consequences
    for body weight regulation in man. In *Food Acceptance and Nutrition*,
    221–28. London: Academic Press.

32. Bezencon, C., le Coutre, J., and S. Damak. Taste-signaling proteins
    are coexpressed in solitary intestinal epithelial cells. *Chem. Senses.*
    32:41–9, 2006.

33. Konturek, S. J., Konturek, J. W., Pawlik, T., and T. Brzozowki.
    Brain-gut axis and its role in the control of food intake. *J. Physiol.
    Pharmacol.*, 55:137–54, 2004.

34. Korner, J., and R. L. Leibel. To eat or not to eat—how the gut talks
    to the brain. *New Engl. J. Med.*, 349:926–28, 2003.

35. Collins, G. Company news; From Taco Bell, a healthier option. *The
    New York Times*, Feb. 9, 1995. http://query.nytimes.com/gst/full
    page.html?sec=health&res=990CE7D81F3FF93AA35751C0A96395
    8260

Now let's get to some of the most preferred foods and the physiological and neurochemical explanations behind their popularity.

CHAPTER 2

▼

WHY WE LIKE CORN CHIPS

Americans spent over $60 billion on snack foods in 2005.[1]

Doritos® (*little bits of gold* in Spanish) is a hugely popular $2+ billion worldwide brand. Launched in 1966, it was an immediate hit with the consumers in the United States. Doritos continues to be the most popular snack food yet invented so I created the term "Doritos Effect" in my lectures as an example of a food high in pleasure. Now let's deconstruct the ingredients, tastes, and textures to learn important principles of (just about) the perfect snack food.

First, let me list the ingredients in order from my bag of Doritos Nacho Cheese:

Whole Corn, Vegetable Oil, Salt, Cheddar Cheese, Maltodextrin, Wheat Flour, Whey, Monosodium Glutamate, Buttermilk Solids, Romano Cheese, Whey Protein Concentrate, Onion Powder, Partially Hydrogenated Soybean and Cottonseed Oil, Corn Flour, Disodium Phosphate, Lactose, Natural and Artificial Flavor, Dextrose, Tomato Powder, Spices, Lactic Acid, Artificial Color (Including Yellow 6, Yellow 5, Red 40), Citric Acid, Sugar, Garlic Powder, Red and Green bell Pepper Powder, Sodium Caseinate, Disodium Inosinate, Disodium Guanylate, Nonfat Milk solids, Whey Protein Isolate, and Corn Syrup Solids.

1. Loaded with Taste-Active Components

The Doritos formulation actually excites taste buds with every pleasurable hedonic solute! Since taste is the major pleasure system in food perception that drives ingestion, it is important to include both major pleasure solutes—salt and sugar—and the ingredients that boost their perception—5'-nucleotides and garlic.

a.   Salt (listed as the fourth ingredient!). The actual number will amaze you. Nacho Cheesier has 200 mg sodium per serving, which calculates out to 1.7 percent salt by weight. This beats my 1 percent rule for preferred foods—a little saltier might just be a little better since saliva does dilute down the chip in the mouth.

b.   Sugars (including lactose, corn syrup solids, and sugar).

c.   Umami tastants (5'-nucleotides, MSG, garlic, and certain amino acids) are pleasurable.

2. Creates a Salivary Response

Acids keep the saliva flowing so that the food never dries out in the mouth (buttermilk solids, lactic acid, and citric acid). The induction of saliva may be rewarding in and of itself. Studies on the ingestion of food reveal that dopamine spikes in the brain are highest in *anticipation* of eating! And the term *mouth-watering* has hedonic overtones, similar to the Colonel's "finger lickin' good." Hence, the continued and consistent salivation to a food is a very important aspect of good food construction.

3. High Dynamic Contrast

Thin Doritos chips rapidly melt in the mouth—which create high dynamic contrast is very pleasurable. Lay's potato chips, which are quite thin, share this same oral property. In our food pleasure equation, dynamic contrast plays a major role in food perception and palatability. The contrast here is the hard chip and the powdery coating that disappears quickly in the mouth during mastication—an oral food surprise, or the unexpectedness of rewarding stimuli. Neuroscientist Read Montague and his colleagues (2001) reveal that oral surprise (unexpected pleasure) was more rewarding than expected rewards.[2]

4. Nonspecific Aroma Quality

Doritos' aroma profile is complex, and not one particular aroma dominates. This lack of specific aroma identity allows a person to eat many chips without sensory burnout. This is very important in reducing sensory specific satiety (SSS)—if one can identify the aroma, it is easier to become bored with it. For example, if the chip is distinctively flavored with rosemary or thyme, SSS kicks in with more force, and one is less likely to eat it every day. And very light, non-trigeminal aromas do not activate SSS at all, and can be eaten every day. Michelle Peterman, VP of marketing at Kettle Foods, noted in *Food Product Design* that the best-selling flavor has always been, and continues to be, the lightly salted original flavor potato chips.[3]

5. High Evoked Qualities Effect or Emeril's BAM! Effect

Doritos contains many of our favorite flavors on one chip; this allows us to experience all the foods we love without consciously knowing it. For example, Doritos has corn, cheese, garlic, and tomato flavors; many of these food ingredients are inherently tasty; as you will learn in the chapter on super pleasure foods. Neurophysiologic evidence is now revealing that every eating experience lays down another food engram (memory) in parts of the brain that control our perceptions of taste, texture, aroma, and calorie content. When Emeril adds his BAM! spice blend to a dish (note he adds it to just about everything except ice cream) he is also adding food pleasure gestalt—a very clever hedonic booster. (The original BAM! flavor is quite good and next to Aji-Shio salt, [MSG coated salt], I use more of it than any other flavoring complex.) Hence, the addition of a familiar flavoring system in Doritos brings back or evokes past memories of *all* your favorite foods.

6. Contains 50 Percent Fat Calories

Recall that the brain *prefers* fat and fat-based flavors. Hence, Doritos must really light up the brain for fat perception. In fact, most snack foods are very close to this magical 50 percent fat calorie content. Fat ingestion activates the two types of fat recognition receptors in the mouth (fatty acid and textural), increases levels of gut hormones linked to reduction in anxiety (CCK), activates brains systems for reward, and enhances ingestion for more fat (galanin). Noted brain neuroscientist Ann Kelley says that foods high in sugar and fat change the brain the same way that drugs of abuse can cause addictive behavior—obesity may be an addiction to junk or highly palatable food.[4]

7. A "Cookivore" Food

These tortilla chips contain many cooked, roasted, and fermented food ingredients. Anthropologist Richard Wrangham suggests, in a 2004 *Harvard Review* article, that human beings are cookivores; we evolved to eat cooked food.[5] Cuisine has always been a high art and human obsession—and it has physiological survival value as well. The aromas of fire, fermented foods, and sugar-rich fruits are, at the very least, hedonically imprinted over many thousands of years of selection. Doritos start with corn that is shaped and toasted before being fried in oil. This increases certain aromas, like pyrazines, which many find pleasant, even in very low concentrations. In fact, some scientists believe that liking these aromas (pyrazines) is the innate result of a five hundred thousand year association of fire, food, and survival.

8. Contains Natural and Added MSG

Corn is high in bound and free glutamic acid. MSG is the fifth taste sense and is very pleasurable in the presence of salt. Many believe it is an oral signal identifying the presence of protein in the environment. Corn, among the common vegetables, ranks near the top (the highest being peas) in this hedonic taste solute.

9. High Caloric Density

Many neurobiologists now believe the gut and brain prefer to eat high-density foods—it's just more pleasurable. Doritos certainly qualifies, with a caloric density of 5.0! In fact, many snack foods have a caloric density of 4–6 and the contribution comes mostly from fat in a dry or low moisture food system. The good news is that Doritos has only 1.5 grams of saturated fat per serving (8 grams total). Studies indicate that saturated fat (and probably trans fat as well) upregulates neuropeptide Y (a bad thing)—this increases the consumption of sugar in animal models.[6]

10. Long Hang-Time Flavor System

I have suggested that flavors that are more fatlike (lipophilic) than water-loving have a tendency to hang around a long time in our sensory systems, thus allowing a very strong flavor conditioning acquisition. Doritos' flavor system is so powerful that if one kid in the back of the classroom eats just a few chips, the kids in the front seats will detect the food within minutes! When mixed with saliva and warmed up in the mouth, Doritos has an amazing propensity for volatilization. And Doritos contains many long lasting and lipophilic aromatics from garlic, onions, and cheese. Fat calories combined with long hang-time (lipid) odorants form strong food memories.

11. High Glycemic Starch

Carbohydrates that are quickly broken down (high glycemic) into glucose in the gut elevate blood levels of both glucose and insulin. Studies show that rapid absorption of sugar (glucose) is more rewarding than lower glycemic starches. The rapid reduction of hunger is also more rewarding. In addition, the more rapid insulin increase acts on the brain in a complex manner that encourages a hyperphagic (overeating) response.[7] And through insulin's complex interaction with leptin, serotonin, and other neurotransmitters, a very potent food memory *engram* is formed. (Fat and carbohydrate have separate systems for memory formation.) The brain *wants* to remember junk food since it has greater survival value than other foods. A cast member on "Survivor" could live quite comfortable with a few cases of Nacho Doritos.

12. Doritos Contain Casomorphin Precursors

Cheese contains casein protein and, when digested by the gut proteases, turns casein into morphine-like compounds called *casomorphins*. Some scientists think that these casein derivatives act like morphine and are addictive by themselves—although this is still a controversial hypothesis. (Endogenous opiates, which are widely distributed in the gastrointestinal tract, are grouped into three major families according to their precursor proteins: proopiomelanocortin [endorphin], proenkephalin [enkephalin], and prodynorphin [dynorphin].[8]) Dr. Barnard, in *Breaking the Food Seduction,* believes that casomorphins have about 1/10 of the narcotic activity of morphine. Casomorphins have many interesting properties, and one of them may be that they make a food more memorable. They slow the digestion (cheese is constipating) and lengthen the contact time between inges- tion and food memory formation, that is, the macronutrient content and the sen- sory properties of that food have a longer time to develop a relationship. Casomorphins may also stimulate fat intake via inhibition of the gut hormone enterostatin.[9] Regardless of the controversy, there is no doubt that cheese sells. Tom Rieman, senior business marketing executive at Kraft Foods, has noted that in traditional salty snacks, *cheese* is the number one flavoring system.[3] Now you know why they call Doritos—Nacho *Cheesier*! For a review of casomorphins see Teschemacher, H. (2003).[10]

13. Doritos Has a Nondescript Aroma Complex

The Doritos aroma is a complex mixture of many different ingredients from cheese to onion to garlic to tomato solids. But not one flavor stands out; this reduces the ability of Doritos to initiate sensory specific satiety. Strong and dis- cernable aromas tend to cause food burnout faster than those that are more subtle and not really recognizable. It is very hard to actually pinpoint or name any aroma in the chip if you smell it blindfolded. Give it a try and see. In contrast, if you were given rosemary-flavored chips, you would like them, but rosemary is a powerful and easily recognized trigeminal odorant, and you will burn out on the rosemary flavor fairly quickly.

My wife conducted research that revealed when two or more spices or herbs were mixed together, it greatly diminished the ability to tell what is in the mixture. The exceptions were onions and black pepper—they are always distinguishable in the spice blend. Although name recall of the mixture is lost, the brain activation of the olfactory cortex and associated hedonic interactions still occurs. This phe- nomenon suggests that in humans, perceiving the aroma is much more important than the ability to recall the aroma name.

The Doritos spice complex has some interesting additional properties:

a. Doritos Breath. Although the aroma of Doritos is very complex, it is also very aromatic. When I was younger, we used to notice that when a person ate Doritos in the classroom (usually against the rules), the odor permeated quickly—and we didn't find it as pleasant as the one doing the eating. We had a term for this—Doritos Breath. Rumor has it that Frito Lay was concerned about Doritos breath and lowered the garlic powder in the chip in the mid-1990s. This term is still popular, and one can find many stories on Doritos breath on the Web: http://healthresources.caremark.com/topic/olestra.

b.   Doritos Feet. Bacteria and fungi (yeast) are normal inhabitants of moist feet and can generate aromas similar to the smell of Doritos. In fact, the aroma of smelly, stinking feet (bromhidrosis) is surprisingly like Doritos breath. These aroma compounds are probably sulfur based, and Doritos certainly is loaded with the allium family (garlic, onions) and cheese powders as well. Cheese aroma is based on fatty acid fermentation, and our feet also secrete fatty acids—the metabolic fuel for the bacteria and fungi inhabitants. Here are two examples from the Web:[11]

- "True, some cheese does stink. Doritos smell like stinky feet but I like them."

- "Oh man you are right about Doritos. I like them a lot, but a friend once said Doritos smell like socks … that is just too delicious …"

14. Doritos Taste Absolutely Fresh

Like the rest of the family of snacks at Frito Lay, you will never find a burnt chip or off-taste in any of their product line. Food scientist friends tell me that the founder was a fanatic on this principle of a fresh-tasting product as a differentiation point from all the competition. Bags of Doritos, with high-quality ingredients and excellent barrier packaging, really don't spend much time in the store; they are pulled off the shelf in less than two weeks if they are not sold—which is probably fairly rare for most foods. Eating a poor-quality chip (burnt or oxidized) can induce a preference aversion for a (food) brand that can last a lifetime. I've even had competitors' potato chips that had a green ring around the outside rim, signaling that solanine was present! (Light during storage induces the cogeneration of the alkaloid poison, solanine, and chlorophyll.)

In the losing battle over obesity (thus far), the snack- and junk-food purveyors have come under intense scrutiny and have even been subject to class action lawsuits.[1] Although I am not an apologist for the snack-food companies, Frito Lay has introduced a few healthy trends. Frito Lay has eliminated the nasty trans fats from all of its products, and the company now has a number of calorie-controlled products for those who don't want all the calories—and they actually taste quite good—like *Baked!* Lay's. There is even a Web site dedicated to those addicted to baked Lay's: http://www.worldvillage.com/wv/feature/bakedlay.htm.

I was once asked in a lecture which is tastier, based on my theories: *crunchy* or *puffed* Cheetos (my all-time favorite snack); the follow-up question was, "Why do they have both?" I laughed, because I had this same argument with a friend in Loyola High School many years ago! Well, the crunchy is higher in cheese flavor and hedonic solutes, but puffs are higher in vanishing caloric density, the fun sensation of eating calories but not feeling full. So which one is better? From a pure pleasure standpoint, I think it is a wash. (If Frito Lay is listening, please bring back the black pepper and Monterrey Jack Doritos, a nice blend of black trigeminal spice with subtle cheese flavors.)

Can Doritos Be Improved?

Doritos may be at a hedonic pinnacle, but there are additional structural changes that may add pleasure. Frito Lay has already discovered one of them. The product is called Doritos 3-D's, which are spherical shaped Doritos in a variety of flavors. Lots of fun to eat, actually! Although the caloric density went down a bit (4.6 versus 5.0 for regular Doritos), the large volume and thinness of the sphere went up. In the theory of vanishing caloric density, foods with rapid meltdown and lots of air fool the stomach into reducing the satiety response—this allows repeated oral stimulation without all the fullness. This contributes to the magic of popcorn: non-satiation with repeated ingestional bouts. The 3-D also increases the amount of dynamic contrast; instead of a one-dimensional oral bite, it is now three-dimensional, greatly increasing the surprise factor.

But as advanced and creative as this shape may be, it is not quite original. In French cuisine, there is a potato dish that, when done correctly, creates—instead of a 1/8-inch round chip—a zeppelin-shaped potato crisp. This dish is called *pommes de terre soufflés* and was developed by accident on a train by Head Chef Maître Colînet. He twice cooked radial slices of potatoes and finished them in very hot fat (on the second immersion), which made them puff up, to everyone's astonishment. It were the hit of the meal and were relished by Queen Marie Amélie and her two sons.[12] I have been able to duplicate this potato zeppelin, but the intensive preparation, messiness, and dangerously hot oil make this dish more suitable as a food-science experiment.

How to Calculate Percent Sodium Chloride (Salt) in Foods

To calculate the salt content, find the sodium content in milligrams (mg) found in the nutritional facts box. Then divide this mg amount by 0.4 (salt is 40 percent sodium) and then multiply by the weight (grams) of the food per serving. Finally, multiply this number by 0.10 (conversion factor) to get the percent salt. For example, Nacho Cheese Doritos contains 180 mg sodium, divided by 0.4 equals 450 mg of sodium chloride; then 450 mg is divided by the weight of a serving or 28 grams (1 oz.) which equals 16. Finally, multiply by 0.10, giving us 1.6 percent sodium chloride.

References

1. Obesity concerns change focus of America's $61 billion addiction to munchies. *Medical News Today,* July 13, 2006. http://www.medicalnewstoday.com/medicalnews.php?newsid=47036

2. Berns, G. S., McClure, S. M., Pagnoni, G., and P. R. Montague. Predictability modulates human brain response to reward. *J. Neurosci.,* 21:2793–98, 2001.

3. Decker, K. Getting serious about snacks. *Food Product Design,* April, 2006. http://www.foodproductdesign.com/articles/463/463_641 concepts.html

4. Newcombe, R. Is junk food addictive? BUPA. July 19, 2003. http://www.bupa.co.uk/health_information/html/health_news/190703 addic.html

5. Lambert, C. The way we eat now. *Harvard Magazine,* May–June, 2004. http://www.harvard-magazine.com/on-line/050465.html

6. Huang, X. F., McLennan, P., and L. Storlien. Role of fat amount and type in ameliorating diet-induced obesity: insights at the level of hypothalamic arcuate nucleus leptin receptor, neuropeptide Y and pro-opiomelanocortin mRNA expression. *Diabetes Obes. Metab.,* 6:35–44, 2004.

7. Ludwig, D. S., Majzoub, J. A., Al-Zahrani, A., Dallal, G. E., Blanco, I., and S. B. Roberts. High glycemic index foods, overeating, and obesity. *Pediatrics*, 103:e26, 1999.

8. Trompette, A., Claustre, J. Caillon, F., Jourdan, G., Chayvialle, J. A., and P. Plaisancié. Milk bioactive peptides and ß-casomorphins induce mucus release in rat jejunum. *J. Nutr.*, 133:3499–503, 2003.

9. Berger, K., Winzell, M. S., Mei, J., and C. Erlanson-Albertsson. Beta-casomorphins stimulate and enterostatin inhibits the intake of dietary fat in rats. *Physiol. Behav.*, 83:623–30, 2004.

10. Teschemacher, H. Opioid receptor ligands derived from food proteins. *Curr. Pharm. Design*, 9:1331–44, 2003.

11. Calbee Shrimp Chips: Cheap Eats. Sept. 14, 2005. http://www.bloglander.com/cheapeats/2005/9/14/shrimp-chips-calbee/

12. Amé-Leroy Carley, E. 1983. *Classics from a French Kitchen*. New York: Crown Publishers.

CHAPTER 3

▼

WHY WE LIKE SANDWICH COOKIES

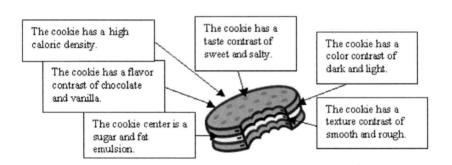

The cookie has a high caloric density.

The cookie has a taste contrast of sweet and salty.

The cookie has a color contrast of dark and light.

The cookie has a flavor contrast of chocolate and vanilla.

The cookie has a texture contrast of smooth and rough.

The cookie center is a sugar and fat emulsion.

Studies on snack foods suggest a narcotic-like effect on the brain.[1]

"Food and Sin are two words that—in the English-speaking world, anyway—have long been linked."
Anthony Broudain[2]

The Oreo cookie is a standard fixture in many a household pantry, including mine, as my daughter has a fondness for the "mini" ones. According to a 2006 editorial by Lynn Kuntz, more than 450 billion Oreos have been sold since their inception in 1912, making this cookie the best seller of any cookie in the twentieth century.[3] The pertinent question is: What sensory or nutritional attributes contribute to the most successful cookie ever developed?

1. Oreos Are High in Fat and Sugar

These are the big two ingredients that really "light up" the brain in brain bioscans of people eating tasty foods. With most of the calories coming from fat (37 percent) and carbohydrate (60 percent), the cookie is basically a vehicle to supply the emulsified interior icing. With most sweet foods, a little added sodium boosts the overall pleasurable response—about 0.5 percent NaCl by weight—the typical level found in many sweet foods like chocolate and ice cream.

    a.   The first ingredient found in Oreos is sugar or sucrose—the most pleasurable of the sugars since it combines a clean, sweet taste with added mouthfeel.

    b.   Commenting on the primal pull of sweets, neuroscientist Ann Kelley noted that the attraction to sugar is very ancient; even bacteria will move toward it.[1]

2. Oreos Are High in Dynamic Contrast

I use this cookie as an example of the Witherly/Hyde theory of food pleasure equation. Let's quantify some of the contrasts in the cookie:

    a.   Visual: Dark cookie and bright white icing

    b.   Visual: Rough cookie top and smooth cookie interior

    c.   Olfaction: Chocolate aroma versus vanilla icing aroma

    d.   Olfaction: Trigeminal aromas (chocolate) versus purer aromatic aromas (vanilla)

    e.   Taste: Salty in cookie versus sweet in icing

    f.   Texture: Rough cookie top versus smooth interior

    g.   Texture: Hard cookie versus soft icing

3. Oreos Allow for an Optional Eating Pattern

Personalizing the eating experience increases food pleasure. Many people manipulate the cookie before ingestion. Your personality may be based on how you eat an Oreo.[4] Men tend to bite through the cookie, and women tend to pull apart the cookie and eat the filling first. The reason? One colleague explained to me that men like excitement, and biting through the cookie is thrilling (lots of dynamic contrast); women tend to prefer fat textures (emulsions) like ice cream, butter, and other high-fat foods and eat the valuable core first. The number one preferred food by women is the French fry, and for men it is the hamburger.[5]

4. High Energy Density

An Oreo with the added icing in the center (mostly fat) amps up the caloric density close to a level we see with many snack foods (4–5). With an energy density of 4.7, Oreos are one of the denser cookie-like foods—even surpassing chocolate chip cookies. Double-Stuf Crème chocolate Oreos are a bit higher at 4.9, but the chocolate-fudge covered top out at almost 5.3 caloric density! The next highly calorically dense cookie that tastes great is the Nestlé Tollhouse, sold at Burger King, at 4.6. Neuroscientist Ann Kelley says that high caloric density mixtures of sugar and fat are very appealing and pleasurable—possibly approaching the "addictive" status.[1] In a 2003 paper, Will, Franzblau, and Kelley say that intake of energy-dense and tasty food is controlled by activity in the pleasure center linked with feeding centers and the more primitive brain stem.[6] Another scientist, Bartley Hoebel (2002), notes that when a high-sugar diet is withdrawn from a rat, the animal exhibits drug withdrawal symptoms.[6] Sucrose is the first ingredient in an Oreo, and fat is the third! Speaking of dependency, Callahan, writing in the *Chicago Tribune*, suggests that Kraft used high-powered brain imaging research from their parent company (Phillip Morris) to make the cookie more addicting (consumer dependency), a charge denied by company officials.[1]

If the regular cookie is not tasty enough, you can always buy them *double stuffed* with icing, top-coated with even *more* icing, and in a bewildering array of flavors and textures: Oreo Big Stuf (twice as big), Double Stuf Peanut Butter Oreo (filling), Mystic Mint flavored, White Fudge Oreo, Chocolate Cream Oreo, Double Delight Oreo (two different fillings), and the Golden Oreo (cookie is yellow).

Fun Oreo Cookie Facts

- Over 450 billion have been sold, making the Oreo the most popular cookie ever invented.

- Placed side by side, the number of cookies sold would encircle the world at the equator 381 times.

- The cookie surface pattern is twelve, four-petaled flowers and ninety radial ticks on the outside.

- Sunshine's Hydrox cookie, after Oreos introduction, kept losing market share and was dropped in 1996.

- There are dozens of Oreo variations (thirty-seven listed on the Web site), including double icing, different flavors (peanut butter, mint, coffee, mocha, and caramel), and different colored icings (red, yellow, green).

- South Park has an episode with a "quadruple stuff" cookie.

- Oreo cookies no longer use hydrogenated oils, but the calorie content is the same.

Numbered References

1. Manier, J., Callahan, P., and D. Alexander. OREO. Craving the cookie. *Chicago Tribune*, Aug. 21, 2005. http://www.chicagotribune.com/news/specials/chi-oreo-1,1,7603329.story

2. Bourdain, A. 2006. *The Nasty Bits*. New York: Bloomsbury USA.

3. Kuntz, L. Alas poor Oreo. *Food Product Design*, June, 2006.

4. Funnyjunk. The great Oreo cookie psycho-personality test. http://www.funnyjunk.com/pages/oreo.htm

5. Sloan, E. A. What, when and where America eats. *Food Tech.*, Jan., 2006.

6. Will, M. J., Franzblau, E. B., and A. E. Kelley. Nucleus accumbens μ-opioids regulate intake of a high-fat diet via activation of a distributed brain network. *J. Neurosci.*, 3:2882–88, 2003.

7. Colantuoni, C., Rada, P., McCarthy, J., Patten, C., Avena, N. M., Chadeayne, A., and B. G. Hoebel. Evidence that intermittent, excessive sugar intake causes endogenous opioid dependence. *Obes. Res.*, 10:478–88, 2002.

References, General

- Poundstone, W. 1986. *Bigger Secrets*. Boston: Houghton Mifflin Company.

- http://www.technospudprojects.com/Projects/Oreo/ oreo2002_facts.htm

- http://en.wikipedia.org/wiki/Oreo

▼

CHAPTER 4

WHY WE LIKE VANILLA ICE CREAM

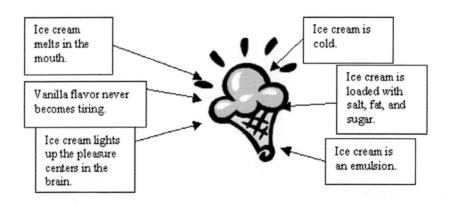

Ice cream melts in the mouth.

Ice cream is cold.

Vanilla flavor never becomes tiring.

Ice cream is loaded with salt, fat, and sugar.

Ice cream lights up the pleasure centers in the brain.

Ice cream is an emulsion.

Ice-cream eating is fun and fires up brain's pleasure center. Every ingestion brings back one's childhood memories.[1]

Adam Drewnowski (nutrition and sensory expert) speculated that there might be a relationship between opioid addiction and ice-cream craving.[2]

Americans love ice cream, and, next to the Australians, consume more of it than people from any other country. The $20 billion ice-cream industry is dominated by Nestlé and Unilever, although there are over five hundred regional mom-and-pop shops that make and distribute America's favorite dessert (or treat). And what is America's favorite flavor? By a long shot, it's vanilla (as high as 50 percent preference), followed by chocolate, butter pecan, and strawberry. (My daughter will only eat cookies and cream Häagen-Dazs, a preference I still find puzzling.)

Why do we like ice cream? Well, my fellow colleague in food science, Dr. Robert Hyde, has developed a comprehensive principle of food pleasure called the "Ice Cream Effect." Later, as we refined our thoughts, we developed the "Dynamic Contrast" theory. Ice cream is the perfect food that lights up the pleasure centers of the brain due to its sensory and caloric properties. In fact, neuroscientists at the Institute of Psychiatry in London scanned the brains (MRI) of people eating vanilla ice cream. They found that the orbitofrontal cortex, the "processing" area at the front of the brain, was activated during ingestion. The researchers conclude by commenting that ice cream makes you a happier person![1]

1. Ice Cream Melts

Ice cream, in the oral cavity, undergoes a phase change from solid to liquid within seconds—dynamic contrast at its best. The mouth has abundant receptors for texture detection and a special area in the brain to perceive it. We like foods that melt down rapidly in the mouth, and ice cream fits this just about as perfectly as any food except popcorn and chocolate. The making of ice cream incorporates almost 50 percent air in the mixing process, which amplifies the rapid melting properties.

2. Ice Cream Is Cold

Another dynamic contrast component to food is the change in oral temperature. The mouth is loaded with trigeminal receptors for both heat and cold, but cold may be a greater stimulator of sensory sensation. Cold perception in the mouth is a huge trigeminal blast, and when the food warms up again, it produces dynamic contrast and increases food pleasure. Dr. Robert Hyde noted in his work on dynamic contrast that oral temperature changes excite neurons at a high level; in fact, our physiology, in general, was designed to detect and respond to minute changes in cellular chemistry, whether they are temperature, oxygen levels, pH, or extracellular sodium levels.

a. Ice-cream coldness excites water receptors in the mouth, which is also inherently pleasurable.[3] This is one reason why, after eating ice cream, you become thirsty; you activate the water receptors for thirst but don't actually drink any water, so the dehydration becomes worse and your brain creates a water thirst.

b. Cold temperatures in the mouth actually activate taste receptors directly.[4]

3. Vanilla Ice-Cream Flavor Never Grows Old

Brain studies have proven that the mostly pure aromatic aroma known as vanilla does not cause flavor burnout in the brain. This is why people prefer it, three to one over chocolate! In addition, vanilla acts as a background flavor base allowing infinite "inclusions" or ice cream add-ons to maximize multidimensional flavor (Cold Stone Effect).

4. Ice Cream Is An Emulsion

In many taste experiments with both rats and humans, preference increases for food if presented in an emulsified form. In fact, this is an important structural element of good food construction, called the Emulsion Preference Theory. Many of our favorite foods are emulsions—some fat in water (milk, cream, ice cream, salad dressings, cake batters, flavor emulsions, meat emulsions, and cream liqueurs), and some water in fat (butter, margarine, and mayonnaise). In making ice cream, the whipping process incorporates air into the emulsion, concentrating the sugar solution into a complex emulsion called "foam." Ice cream, as an emulsion, during melting, delivers small fat globules, and the concentrated sugar explodes on the tongue. Drs. Drewnoswki and Greenwood note in 1983, that preference for sweetened, high-fat foods may contribute to obesity in people.[5] Humans strongly prefer sugar and fat emulsions, and will make the extra effort to find and consume these foods.

5. Ice Cream Is Loaded with Salt, Fat, and Sugar

The "big three" are very pleasurable ingredients, and ice cream has them in abundance. The typical fat content of premium Häagen-Dazs is approximately 16 percent butterfat (by weight), the salt content is about 0.5 to 1.0 percent, and the remaining ingredients being sugar and protein. Baskin-Robbins vanilla has 54 percent of its calories from fat and 40 percent from carbohydrates—which is very similar to most salty snack foods as well. Emeritus Professor of Food Science (an ice-cream expert) Robert Marshall suggest that people like ice cream for three reasons:[6]

a. Contains fat for flavor explosion and smooth mouthfeel.

b. Contains air for rapid meltdown.

c. Contains ice, which people really like due the cold sensation.

6. Ice Cream Has Vanishing Caloric Density (R. Hyde, PhD)

Despite the abundance of salt, fat, and sugar, Baskin-Robbins vanilla ice cream has a surprisingly low caloric density of 2.3, due to the whipping process. The amount of air incorporation can be near 50 percent; but much less for premium brands like Häagen-Dazs (higher butterfat, less air).[7] Dr. Hyde has suggested that foods with an airy structure and a rapid oral meltdown allow repeated self-stimulation without a strong satiety feedback from the stomach. Another classic example is popcorn—all the fun of eating without all that satiety. Popcorn may have a caloric density of 3.0 un-popped, but it's in a volume of one cup popped. Ice cream's (and popcorn's) vanishing caloric density fools the mouth, stomach, and brain into thinking this food is lower in calories that it actually is—and this encourages overconsumption.

I had a roommate in college who once ate a whole half gallon of vanilla ice cream for dinner—and lived. Similarly, many people often substitute popcorn infused with butter and other additions as a substitute for dinner or lunch because of the powerful hedonic combination of orosensation (dynamic contrast) with the satiety reducing effect of vanishing caloric density.

7. Ice Cream Contains Casomorphins

The major milk protein in ice cream is casein, and upon digestion it creates morphine-like molecules called casomorphins. Some scientists believe these compounds can make food more addicting.[8,9] These molecules may also affect pain sensitivity, locomotion, anxiety, and learning.[10] In addition, Lin et al. (1998), note that fat ingestion, through its action on enterostatin (a peptide released by the gut upon fat digestion), *reduces* fat reward by actions on mu-opioids.[11] Beta-casomorphin *inhibits* enterostatin and encourages overeating of fat. In layman terms, the milk proteins in ice cream can override our fat satiety system. It really does seem that casein ingestion, whether in ice cream, milk, or cheese, or as a topping on pizza—encourages food intake via direct and indirect pleasure generation.

8. Final Thought—Turning Ice Cream into a Starbucks Model

Part of Starbucks' success is the infinite variety of personalized drinks. It allows people to maximize multidimensional pleasure—a very important principle in sensory hedonics, developed by the pioneering Canadian sensory scientist Michel Cabanac. Bruce Horovitz, food business writer for *USA Today*, notes that Americans have become picky and want food their own way; this is why Starbucks has over 19,000 variations on the coffee drink.[12] And how would one do this with ice cream? Very simple, actually; go to the nearest Cold Stone Creamery ice cream store and witness the infinite variety of "inclusions" that allows each of us to stimulate our palate exactly as we wish. Although the founders believe that their stores' success is due to entertainment value, the physiological reality is quite different: this candy and ice cream shop allows almost instant personal gratification with any craving that exists *a la moment*; a terrific example of the principle of Cabanac's multidimensional pleasure coupled with dynamic contrast. Because of the huge, almost infinite, variety of possible ice-cream inclusions and flavor combinations, the consumer's palate never tires and the ice cream never fails to be arousing.[13] In addition, the inclusion of solid candies and fudge pieces increases the caloric density of the final ice-cream creation—and this is, we have learned, a particularly pleasurable human culinary activity.

References

1. Adam, D. How ice cream tickles your brain. *The Guardian*, April 29, 2005. http://www.guardian.co.uk/uk_news/story/0,3604,1472620, 00.html

2. Manier, J., Callahan, P., and D. Alexander. OREO. Craving the cookie. *Chicago Tribune*, Aug. 21, 2005. http://www.chicagotribune.com/news/specials/chi-oreo-1,1,7603329.story

3. de Araujo, I. E., Kringelback, M. L., Rolls, E. T., and F. McGlone. Human cortical response to water in the mouth and the effect on thirst. *J. Neurophysiol.*, 90:1865–76, 2003.

4. Breza, J. M., Curtis, K. S., and R. J. Contreras. Temperature modulates taste responsiveness and stimulates gustatory neurons in the rat geniculate ganglion. *J. Neurophysiol.*, 95:674–85, 2006.

5. Drewnowski, A., and M. Greenwood. Cream and sugar: human preferences for high-fat foods. *Physiol. Behav.*, 30:629–33, 1983.

6. Marshal, R. T., Goff, H. D., and R. W. Hartel. 2003. *Ice Cream.* 6th edition, New York: Plenum Publishers.

7. Goff, G. Finding science in ice cream. University of Guelph. http://www.foodsci.uoguelph.ca/dairyedu/findsci.html

8. Teschemacher, H. Opioid receptor ligands derived from food proteins. *Curr. Pharm. Design*, 9:133–44, 2003.

9. Dubynin, V. A., Ivleva, I. A., and A. A. Kamenski. The neurotropic activity of food-derived opioid peptides beta-casomorphins. *Usp Fiziol. Nauk.*, 35:83–101, 2004.

10. Lin, L., Umahara, M., York, D. A., and G. A. Bray. Beta-casomorphins stimulate and enterostatin inhibits the intake of dietary fat in rats. *Peptides*, 19:325–31, 1998.

11. Wang, W., and E. G. de Mejia. A new frontier on soy bioactive peptides that may prevent age-related chronic disease. *Comp. Rev. Food Sci. F.*, 4:63–78, 2005.

12. Horovitz, B. You want it your way. *USA Today*, Money sec., March 5–7, 2004. http://www.usatoday.com/money/industries/food/2004-03-04-picky_x.htm

13. Horovitz, B. Ice cream shops thaw sales with scoops of fun. *USA Today*, Money sec., June 9, 2006. http://www.usatoday.com/money/industries/food/2006-06-09-ice-cream-usat_x.htm

CHAPTER 5

▼

WHY WE LIKE BUTTER

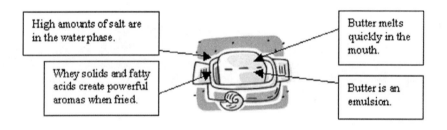

High amounts of salt are in the water phase.	Butter melts quickly in the mouth.
Whey solids and fatty acids create powerful aromas when fried.	Butter is an emulsion.

"Often overlooked, though, is the fact that butter is a ready-made sauce base."
Thomas Keller[1]

"Hunger is the best sauce in the world."
Cervantes (1547–1616)

Julia Child suggests that in French cuisine nothing can be accomplished if one cannot use butter and cream. And Fernand Point, a famous French chef, is known for his maniacal use of butter in recipes. For example, he cooks eggs *very* slowly in butter, and then tops it with more butter just before serving. Certainly, both French and European cuisines use copious amounts of butter in main dishes and dessert courses. And since most Europeans are milk drinkers and are not lactose intolerant, like the rest of the world, their use of dairy derivatives is very high—in cream, cheeses, and ice cream. The fact remains that in French haute cuisine, butter, in salted, unsalted, and clarified forms, is used extensively in frying, basting of meats, and in many vegetable preparations. Just take a look at some of the recipes in Thomas Keller's complex but insightful cookbook, *The French Laundry*, for the extensive use of a novel butter emulsion he calls *beurre monté*.

1. Butter Is an Emulsion

As mentioned above, humans (and rats and mice) tend to prefer many foods in the emulsified form. The reason may be due to the concentrating effect emulsions have on tastants or the fact that taste buds like fats and fatty acids. Liquid and solid emulsions are a huge part of cuisine development and modern cookery. French sauces are basically emulsions, some simple like butter or complex like a hollandaise sauce. Sauces also contain water, and we have seen that the brain has specific areas devoted to water taste (E. T. Rolls) and its built-in pleasure property. Butter is approximately 80 percent fat by weight; 16–17 percent water, and the remaining is the milk protein called whey solids.

2. Butter Is High in Fat

The mouth has the ability to sense fat (perhaps two separate taste mechanisms), and its presence lights up the brain in a pleasure response. This has been confirmed for ice cream. Butter has the same butterfat structure, although it is much lower in sugar. Fat also activates intestinal rewarding peptides CCK and enterostatin (F1-ATPase-mediated pathway), upregulates its own pleasure response (galanin and insulin), and releases mu-opioids in the brain.[2]

3. Butter Is High in Salt

Most salted butters contain 1–3 percent salt by weight. This amount, however, is concentrated in the water phase, which is only 15 percent of the butter weight. This means that the effective salt concentration is almost 10 percent w/v. Now if you tried to taste a 10 percent salt-in-water solution you would probably gag very quickly; this is like drinking the water in the Dead Sea! Since the preferred amount in food is just about 1 percent w/v, the fat emulsion must dilute this high salt level (somehow) to make it more palatable. This effect also applies to the sugar perception in ice cream.

4. Butter Melts Down

This texture property of melting is a huge reason why butter is so pleasurable; this is yet another tasty food with high dynamic contrast. People will not prefer butter substitutes that don't meltdown in the mouth. I know; in my food-science days, I was asked to create a shelf stable whipped topping–the project was a success–but the concoction would not melt in the mouth and was rejected by the taste panelists. Margarine substitutes taste best when they perfectly mimic the meltdown properties of butter.

5. Butter Aroma Is Resistant to Sensory Specific Satiety

For reasons yet unknown, butter aroma, like vanilla, is highly resistant to pleasure or sensory extinction. Perhaps the aroma volatiles are mostly of the pure aroma type, versus a more trigeminal or a "feel" aroma like rosemary.

6. Butter Is High in Caloric Density

As noted earlier, high caloric density foods can release endorphins and/or enkephalins from the brain. Butter stands out as one of the highest caloric density foods ever created, at 7.2! No wonder Chef Point sings the praises of *buerre*!

7. Butter Contains MSG and Nucleotides

Milk and dairy products are a rich source of glutamates and the flavor-boosting nucleotides.[3] When salt is added, glutamates rapidly form MSG, the prototypical taste of "umami"—or, as translated from the Japanese, "deliciousness." Nature put nucleotides in milk not only for their immune-boosting properties, but they also increase the binding of MSG to the glutamate taste receptor–encouraging consumption. Thus, small amounts of these nucleotides (IMP, GMP, and AMP) boost overall umami taste and flavor.

Milk solids in the butter contain whey protein, the most nutritious of all common proteins and unusually rich in the sulfur-containing amino acid "cysteine."[4] This uncommon amino acid gives butter that special flavor when heated in a preparation called *beurre noisette*, or hazelnut butter. Thomas Keller, famed chef and restaurateur, writes about the importance of butter and the exquisite brown butter sauce it can create in his cookbook *Bouchon*. (Easier to cook from than *The French Laundry Cookbook*.[1]) With the addition of an acidic element, butter, being an emulsion, becomes the simplest (and tastiest) of sauces *à la minute* (done in a snap).

References

1.   Keller, T., 2004. *Bouchon*. New York: Artisan.

2. Erlanson-Albertsson, C. How palatable food disrupts appetite regulation. *Basic Clin. Pharmacol. & Toxicol.*, 97:61–73, 2005.

3. Marcus, J. Culinary applications of umami. *Food Tech.*, 59:24–30, 2005. http://members.ift.org/NR/rdonlyres/7A592460-1C4C-4066-B562-26567D2FDEEE/0/0505marcus.pdf

4. Explore the history and making of butter. http://webexhibits.org/butter/index.html

CHAPTER 6

▼

WHY WE LIKE GOURMET COFFEE AND ICE-BLENDED SHAKES

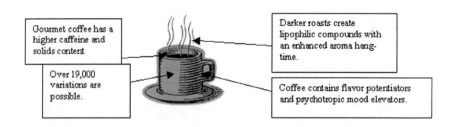

Gourmet coffee has a higher caffeine and solids content

Over 19,000 variations are possible.

Darker roasts create lipophilic compounds with an enhanced aroma hang-time.

Coffee contains flavor potentiators and psychotropic mood elevators.

"Like it or not, Starbucks has changed expectations of how coffee should taste."
Bruce Horovitz (*USA Today*, 2006)[1]

Starbucks over roasts their coffee, they should be called 'Charbucks.'
Anonymous R & D comment

Coffee *aroma* contains powerful antioxidants.
UC Davis Study[2]

Gourmet coffee houses like Starbucks seem to spring up everywhere, as the consumption of coffee and coffee beverages by adults (and kids) shows no signs of abatement. In Valencia, CA, where I live, there is a Starbucks (named after a character in *Moby Dick*) on just about every corner in the northern section of town. Starbucks is the largest retailer and roaster of specialty coffee in the world, with new stores opening up at almost five a day—so far it has over 11,225 locations! Besides the obvious genius of Schultz in marketing the brand and real estate locations, is there an underlying physiological reason behind the $6.4 billion success?

1. Infinite Variety

One of the reasons behind Starbucks' success is the infinite amount of variety in the possible combinations of drinks that one can order. Bruce Horovitz of *USA Today* reports that the number of variations in blended drinks could reach over 19,000, and Starbucks has "five kinds of milk to stir into it: whole, nonfat, half & half, organic, and soy!"[3] In fact, Starbucks, has in the past, clarified drink ordering with a small store brochure (and mailer) that contained twenty-two pages on how to order your favorite coffee drinks. Starbucks' variety selections are often the butt of jokes in movies and in print. I was in a store recently and someone ordered a drink with *five* "adjustments"—and much to my amazement, the coffee *barista* didn't even seem confused or flustered (he made cryptic notes on the cup). Variety, then, assures that everyone gets exactly what he/she wants, which maximizes the pleasure one can extract from their selection—this is a major stroke of physiological genius. Researcher Michel Cabanac (1992) first put forth a theory that physiological systems regulate behavior through "pleasure" response—a term he calls the "simple maximization of pleasure."[4]

Dunkin' Donuts noticed the popularity of the consumers' varieties response and has upgraded its operation in response. It now offers numerous foods and coffee drinks in addition to the standard donut fare: smoothies, nine coffee flavors, breakfast options, and sandwiches. Dunkin's Web site also states that it is the largest retailer of coffee by-the-cup, using only 100 percent Arabica beans. You can download a cute flavor-matching game and earn your PhD in "flavorology."[5] The Web site also has some interesting facts about the flavor additions that make it worth a visit. One factoid states that marshmallows' sweet flavors and aromas often trigger childhood memories. One possible explanation relates to the vanilla aroma nature of marshmallows that may be imprinted soon after birth (vanilla is the main flavor of breast milk and infant formula). In addition, vanilla is often used as a flavorant in many dessert items and chocolate as well, all of which are high in salt, fat, and sugar. Fat and sugar combinations make very strong food-memory imprints, and not only to the food. When you eat high-energy, dense foods, the gut-brain axis also memorizes who was with you, the surroundings, and your metabolic state. Why? So you can *find* that food again. This is the basis of food craving—sights, sounds, even the feel and look of a food can retrigger that memory when a person is hungry, especially when food is presented in a similar environment. The biological mechanism involves the nucleus accumbens (reward center) and the limbic-motor interface, linking environmental cues, past experience, and the movements leading to eating.[6]

2. Starbucks Offers Variety in Coffee Beans—Similar to Fine Wine

In my casual sensory evaluation of the dozen or so types of single and blended whole beans, I find that a person is actually able to distinguish the bean varietals in both taste and aroma profiles—but this may take additional sensory training. Although coffee tasting may be similar to wine tasting, I must admit that most individuals probably couldn't tell the difference between a merlot and cabernet if given a chance to distinguish the two using modern sensory techniques. In a sensory science principle, you must be able to prove that tasters can tell a difference before you ask hedonics (or liking). For example, I've conducted the Coke versus Pepsi challenge many times over the years, using the scientifically valid sensory technique called triangle testing. In this test, panelists are given three number coded samples that are undistinguishable, or "blinded." One of the samples is one cola and the other two are the alternate cola. Everything is randomized so there is no bias in the testing. The panels are then asked to pick out the odd sample. In the hundreds of taste tests I've conducted, only about 5 percent of the cola drinking population can really select the odd sample. If most tasters can't tell a difference, there is no point in asking how much they "like" the colas because the information has no statistical validity or meaning.

But getting back to coffee—do the varietal offerings of whole beans actually help maximize preference and overall pleasure? The two dozen or so coffee varieties found in the gourmet coffee stores have striking differences in taste, body, and aroma. Coffee differences, like fine wine, are also based on the type of soil (*terror*), the amount of shade, the altitude of the plantation, and the drying techniques after harvest. Of course, the degree of roast, sometimes unique to each varietal, also influences the final sensory character. Coffee beans with lighter flavors (Colombian Nariño) often receive a lighter roast to maintain the sensory signature of the bean. Heartier and more flavorful varieties (Ethiopian Harar) undergo more extensive roasting to maximize flavor. Customers given such variety, freely choose their favorite coffee been and roasting level that maximizes their pleasure.

Although the average coffee lover can probably distinguish the flavors of the bean varietals, published literature on the sensory differences among varietals by trained coffee tasters is quite scarce. Although mega-chains' sensory descriptions of their coffee varietal blends appear surprisingly accurate (floral aromas, cocoa undertones, lemony flourish, etc ...), they are more poetic and romantic than scientific.

If I was a professor in sensory evaluation, an excellent student's master thesis would be to compare the sensory profiles of the different bean varietals by using a method known as qualitative descriptive analyses (QDA). One could compare and contrast the taste and aroma profiles of such well-known varieties as Brazil Ipanema Bourbon versus Kopi Kampung or Columbia Nariño Supremo. The goal is to identify the significant sensory differences and analyze how they contribute to taste and flavor. Additional studies on the sensory profiles of roasted arabica versus robusta bean would provide valuable blending information as both species have individual differences and possible complementaries taste. Studies on the roasting process itself (time and temperature) may make it possible to optimize conditions for the perfect cup of Java—one with lower bitterness (trigonelline), high concentrations of taste active compounds (chlorogenic acid), and optimal generation of complex and long hang-time aromas.

Coffee connoisseurs interested in the sensory evaluation techniques of QDA, as applied to coffee evaluation should start with the article by Tom on the Sweetmarias Web site.[7] Using a technique he calls "Flavor Quality Analysis," individuals use rating scales to score coffee attributes, given specific coffee terminology (body, sweet aftertaste, lime flavor, etc.). Each coffee is then graphed into a "spider plot" that provides an overall picture of quality attributes for easy comparison. Although this technique is complex and requires training and experience using rating scales, it is infinitely better than "cupping," the more primitive and highly subjective method of evaluating individual coffees, by writing down *impressions* of body, flavor, acidity, and aftertaste.[8]

3. Highest Level of Caffeine

Caffeine is on the menu at Starbucks (and many gourmet coffee shops), and it's not just for adults—kids and teens can get their buzz via a frozen or whipped concoction of their choosing. This coffee store is actually a modern malt shop catering to caffeine and sugar/fat *fanatiques*. Caffeine in espressos, cappuccinos, mochas, or as shots added to Frappuccinos are now available in an infinite variety of forms without an ID. This is the second physiological secret to Starbucks' success. A recent study analyzed Starbucks' coffee, and the authors were astounded at the high levels of caffeine in a regular coffee venti—almost 500 mg per cup (study by CSPI).[9] A *Wall Street Journal* (*WSJ*) study quoted a Starbucks spokesperson as claiming an average of 325 mg per cup.[10] A coffee venti has over three times as much caffeine as a No-Doze! According to the *WSJ*, the gourmet coffees can contain up to twice the caffeine as the canned brews in the grocery stores (for example, Folgers). The article further reveals that Gloria Jean's coffee was actually higher in caffeine than Starbucks (228 versus 223 mg/10 oz. cup). *WSJ* cited the appropriately named beverage consultant, Tom Pirko, who says that gourmet coffee has more caffeine and this makes people happy. Studies report that the higher the caffeine, the greater the food reward (and possible mild addiction).[11] (See below.)

Caffeine and Beverages:

- Starbucks Venti (20 oz.) coffee   500 mg
- Starbucks Grande (16 oz.) coffee   375 mg
- Starbucks Short (8 oz.) coffee   250 mg
- Starbucks Coffee Frappuccino   98 mg
- Double espresso   70 mg
- Non-gourmet coffee   120–180 mg
- Instant coffee, 1 cup   80 mg
- Red Bull Energy Drink   80 mg

It's little wonder that the soluble coffee market (instant) is declining in the United States—it doesn't have enough phosphodiesterase inhibition: that is, jolt.

Caffeine as a Reward Chemical

Caffeine is the most-ingested natural drug, and it may indirectly activate reward centers in the brain. Although most scientists hesitate to label caffeine as an example of an addictive substance, some hospitals actually studied the value of putting caffeine into the IV solutions of (caffeine-dependant) surgical patients to facilitate their awakening! Caffeine actually can excite the mesolimbic pleasure center via adenosine receptor antagonism. Adenosine is a calming neurotransmitter and when caffeine pushes adenosine from its receptors, the neuron won't fire or activate as per normal (called antagonism). Adenosine receptors are also found in other areas of the brain, and when the caffeine molecule displaces adenosine one feels more alert, alive, and much less sleepy.

Neuroscientist Kent Berridge's experiments revealed that caffeine is rewarding, but the neurochemical mechanism is not dopamine related, as many had expected.[12] And the higher the caffeine level, the greater the activation. Caffeine becomes more rewarding and induces its own pleasure buzz as the level approaches 300 mg. (This is the magic pleasure-activation level; now what was the *average* level at Starbucks?) Activation of reward centers with high caffeine may create a greater liking for the food ingested (taste, aroma, texture, and temperature) and a bonding with the environment where the food was found. It is in the best interest of all food purveyors to keep the customer in the café long enough for this conditioning to take place. Even more interesting, in animal experiments (with genetically low levels of dopamine), a little shot of caffeine could actually substitute for the neurotransmitter, dopamine, which controls locomotion and motivational activation. Researchers at the Seattle's Howard Hughes Medical Institute hint that caffeine could be useful in Parkinson's patients.[12]

The *leçon* here is clear. Starbucks competitors must amp up the caffeine in their beverages just to keep even. The higher caffeine is mostly due to the higher solids content (more coffee grounds); *WSJ* reports that gourmet coffee houses use *two* tablespoons of coffee per cup versus *one* for the supermarket blends like Folgers.[10]

Caffeine and Food Conditioning

An interesting question is whether the caffeine in coffee (or foods in general) can help condition a liking for that food. Since caffeine is rewarding, in theory, foods with caffeine should demonstrate enhanced palatability or greater pleasure than those without. Some of our favorite foods are loaded with caffeine—cola, chocolate, energy drinks, and, of course, coffee drinks, espresso, and their variations, like Frappuccino. Yeomans et al. (2005) studied this concept by giving consumers drinks with and without caffeine over eight conditioning trials.[13] The results reveal that simple exposure to foods does increase liking, but the caffeine-food group increased liking just a bit more. The post-ingestional effects of caffeine, therefore, are rewarding and can help condition a food preference. The effect may be seen most in those suffering from caffeine withdrawal!

4. Unique Aroma and Taste Profile

The sensory epiphany occurred in 1981 when Mr. Schultz, a plastic salesman, wondered why he was selling so many of his trendy Hammarplast Swedish coffee makers to a small Starbucks store in Seattle. When he visited the small coffee, tea, and spice shop, he was "overwhelmed" by the aroma of the coffee in the store. Mr. Schultz then joined the (six store) Starbucks Company as head of marketing. On a business trip to Italy, he fell in love with the Italian-style espresso bars and the camaraderie within. Soon thereafter, a modern-day Starbucks was born and he pursued his dream of serving Italian-style coffee to flavor-deprived US consumers.[14] Few, if any, foods fill the air with such *lasting* impression aromas as dark roast coffee; not chocolate; not tea—only garlic comes close.

Not everyone is a fan of Starbucks coffee's unique flavor. A few of my food-science friends, who work for the world's largest food company, used to joke about the coffee at Starbucks, calling it "Charbucks"—obviously a reference to what they thought was an over-roast, resulting in a "burned" coffee flavor. In contrast, most supermarket coffees, use a much lighter touch, called the "cinnamon or American" roast. Starbucks, however, created a special roasting process that maximizes aroma intensity, reduces coffee's natural acidity and bitterness, and releases taste potentiating compounds such as chlorogenic acid and free glutamates. Coffee experts, who call it simply the "Starbucks roast," consider this roast somewhere between a "full city" roast, (balanced acidity, full body) and the Vienna roast (darker brown, much stronger flavor).

The more intense roasting of coffee beans by the gourmet brands creates a cornucopia of aroma chemicals, these are reduced or lacking altogether in the tinned brands. Darker roasts create higher levels of sugar caramelization and a whole host of Maillard reaction flavors and tastes. Coffee bean oils rise to the surface of the beans, which provide powerful and lingering aromas. Higher roasts not only create more cookivore flavors, but they reduce the bitter compounds (trigonelline) and help release the flavor compounds (nicotinic acid) from the cellulose matrix of the coffee bean, this enhancing both flavor and taste intensity.[15]

Long Hang-Time Odorants

This longer roasting time actually has several physiological effects, all of them positive to the liking of coffee and the unique flavor profile of Starbucks (gourmet) coffee. For example, a longer roast produces more oils in the beans that float to the surface and are more easily volatilized. Loaded with flavor notes, these oils are more lipophilic in nature and produce aromas, which possess "long hang-time." This is a critical aroma-perception event, since aromas that are strong and lingering (usually lipophilic) can form unusually permanent aroma memories. The result is an increased liking for the Starbucks coffee versus, say, the Nestlé soluble coffees or the robusta blends sold in the supermarkets. This is not an insignificant advantage in selling coffee and certainly no laughing matter to marketers. Combine the unique Starbucks flavor profile with high caffeine levels, and you generate a powerful sensory-neuropharmacologic food memory, highly resistant to extinction. I love Starbucks, but I often purchase coffee at Costco made by a local roasting company in Valencia, called the Newhall Roasting Company. The company duplicates the aroma profile quite closely. All I have to do is add more ground coffee to "up" the solids content, and my cup tastes very close to the signature taste of Starbucks.

I have one final comment concerning aroma complexity. R.W. Moncrieff, a renowned sensory scientist, once wrote that, all things being equal, humans prefer more complex aromas than to simple aroma mixtures.[16] I have named this "Moncrief's Observation," and there may be profound implications in creating more pleasurable food aromas. Food flavoring is a huge industry worldwide; most companies try to make an excellent flavor with as few odor compounds as possible. A strawberry aroma may contain a thousand different chemical aromas; coffee has three times this amount, but no company can add them all to a formulation; it's just too costly and complex. Flavor companies, therefore, using advanced gas chromatographic analyses with highly-trained sensory evaluation panels, must design the best flavors possible with the *least* amount of chemical complexity. But the question still remains—is a less complex aroma mixture at a disadvantage in food choice and hedonics? As of this writing, I am unaware of any sensory research directly addressing this issue. In any event, the relationship between aroma complexity and food preference deserves further study.

5. The Darker Roasting Process

The Starbucks roasting process decreases some of the astringent and bitter properties (which is good) compared to other lighter roasted coffees, especially those based on the robusta species, although direct comparisons to Starbucks are not published in any food-science literature I can find. Simply tasting Starbucks side by side with Folgers coffee illustrates the great sensory differences in color, taste, and aroma; similar to the sensory differences of Scharfenberger's dark to Hershey's milk chocolate. Dark roasting of high-quality Arabica beans produces a chocolate-like aroma complex (Maillard reaction products); this is created from the heated reaction of sugar (mostly sucrose), amino acids, phenolic acids, and fatty acid fractions.

I am really surprised that anyone would drink the coffee found in the supermarkets—although I guess these coffees do have caffeine and are less costly. It does, perhaps, take time to appreciate the Starbucks blend, as it is sensorially different than the straw-colored robusta brews. Although my views are just speculation, I think 25 percent of the average coffee drinkers may not appreciate the gourmet brews because they confuse strong flavor with bitterness. Regardless, the specialty coffee market is very hot, with sales at $8.47 billion in 2003 and growing.[17] In this article, the owner of "It's a Grind" commented that, like fine wine, when you've had good coffee, you don't go back to drinking the cheap stuff. There are, then, five main reasons for this:

a.   Quality coffee has fewer bitter and sour flavors.

b.   Quality coffee has a long "hang-time" aroma profile (lipophilic).

c.   Quality coffee has higher caffeine content.

d.   Quality coffee probably has a higher concentration of psychoactive components.

e.   Quality coffee has more mouthfeel since the solids content is higher.

I've tried the new McDonald's Special Brew—and the aroma is surprisingly complex, better than before, but the coffee falls a bit short on taste, solids, and probably caffeine. It is, however, a fine first step, and the other fast-food companies are taking aim or at least using Starbucks as the palate standard. For example, Chick-fil-A has doubled coffee sales since it added premium light and dark roasts.[18] And Dunkin' Donuts' coffee was preferred over the gourmet brews as reported by a top consumer magazine.

Starbucks Frappuccino-Favorite?

Starbucks Frappuccinos are certainly one of the most popular selling drink items beyond the morning coffee fix, and may account for up to 15 percent of all of the company's revenue. Although morning sales appear rare, by midday (from my casual observation), scores of youngsters and adults purchase one after school or work and can be seen sipping them with obvious delight on their way home. (During my research on blended drinks, I counted more than fifty kids packed into a Starbucks after the middle school's final bell at 2:30 PM!)

Who really developed the blended coffee milkshake? Starbucks says its formula originated from Starbucks' acquisition of the Boston-based Coffee Connection, which already served a version of an iced drink. Wikipedia states that coffee ship in Crete, Greece, was selling a beverage called a *Frappecino* as early as 1993. However, based on my research, it appears that the California-predominant gourmet coffee chain, Coffee Bean and Tea Leaf, was selling the "Original Ice Blended Drinks" back in the 1980s. The drinks were so popular that the company created a coffee concentrate and powder mix that duplicate the taste of the "ice blended" for home use.

Let's take a quick look at the composition of the ice-blended Frappuccino (or the "Ice-Blended" Coffee drink) to see what the buzz is all about.

1. Frappuccinos Are Cold.

   The theory of dynamic contrast (DC) states that changing temperature in the mouth is pleasurable, and ice crystals melting down in the mouth is a perfect application of this concept. According to the theory, the smaller the ice crystal, the greater the possible DC in the food, the faster it melts down. Ice cream is the most pleasurable food yet created because of the very small water crystals (emulsion) in a foam solution technically. Some physiologists suggest that a cold drink warming up in the mouth is more pleasurable than a hot drink cooling down in the mouth.

2.   Frappuccinos Are Wet.

Edmund Rolls and his group at Oxford identified a "water taste" in the mouth that lights up a certain portion of the brain comparable to that stimulated by the typical tastants of salt and glucose (cortical taste areas). [19] This implies that water taste is intrinsically rewarding. The reward value may be encoded in the orbitofrontal cortex and, as you would suspect, is much stronger when the subject is thirsty.

3.   Frappuccinos Have Salt, Sugar, and Umami.

We have learned that three tastants dominate the hedonic appreciation of food: salt, sugar, and MSG. Frappuccinos and sweetened coffee beverages contain all three hedonic solutes. Sugar (sucrose) is the predominant carbohydrate found in the beverages, from a low of 44 g (coffee frap) to a high of 81 g (banana caramel frap) per serving. Sucrose is the best sugar to use for both taste and mouthfeel. The beverages also average around 275 mg of sodium, which is in the hedonic "sweet spot"; the best level of added sodium to a sweet-based system (based on my research). Sodium adds additional hedonic pleasure, which is independent from the well-known taste phenomenon wherein small amounts of sodium exert a sweet taste on the tongue. The next hedonic tastant may come as a surprise, but coffee protein contains more than 18 percent glutamic acid; and during roasting and brewing, these free glutamates are increased, released, and provide an umami mouthfeel and taste in coffee—similar to the umami flavor in wine created by the breakdown of the yeast during fermentation and aging.

Bottled Frappuccino

Starbucks' genius extends beyond the brewed bean. In 1996, in partnership with PepsiCo (the North American Coffee Partnership), introduced the bottled coffee experience (Frappuccino) to the mass market—and yes, once again, it was an instant hit with consumers. Howard Schultz, in his book *Pour Your Heart into It*, recalls that demand for this drink was ten times the amount as predicted by sales. [14] The marketplace for bottled and canned coffee drinks is now over one billion in the United States, and the market for portable, drink-when-you-want coffees overseas is exploding. In Japan, such convenience drinks are everywhere in the stores and vending machines. Starbucks followed Frappuccino with the canned Doubleshot in 2002 and Iced Coffee Italian Roast in 2006. All three products are noted for their high-quality taste, good stability, smooth mouthfeel, and the surprising lack of off-flavors that are usually created during the bottling or canning process. As a food scientist, I can attest that these products are in a class of their own, an impressive display of formulation and processing collaboration. Schultz predicts that the bottle Frappuccinos and other ready-to-drink coffee derivatives may bring in over $1.5 billion per year worldwide for Starbucks!

Was Starbucks Lucky?

A food scientist friend of mine once suggested that Starbucks lucked into its amazing fame and food fortune. With six stores being opened (every day!) and competition nowhere in sight, except for the donut shops, its management team seems unusually blessed and almost incapable of making a food *faux pas*. Except for the retooling of Chantico, Starbucks' success has little to do with the divine or lucky stars. Here is a quick review of what they did correctly:

- Starbucks recognized the consumers' need for high-quality coffee.

- Starbucks recreated the Italian-style coffee utilizing a specialized roasting process that created long hang-time odorants, reduced bitterness, and created taste potentiators.

- Starbucks prepared coffee with greater solids—thus flavor.

- Starbucks maximized the hedonic experience by offering almost unlimited personalization of coffee drinks.

- Starbucks helped popularize the ice-blended drinks that appeal to both coffee and non-coffee drinkers alike. Now, both cold and hot food pleasure systems are available to the consumer.

- Starbucks was the first to introduce bottled drinks of high sensory quality.

Perhaps any one execution of the above may have been luck, but not all of them sequentially. *Ce n'était pas chance*! (This was not luck!)

Can Soluble Coffee Be as Good as Ground Bean?

Nestlé spends a lot of effort promoting soluble coffee in the United States. (Instant—they invented it). This powdered extract is actually the dominant form served in many European and Asian countries (and also nourished our troops during World War II). It's quite easy to tell the difference if you know what flavor notes to look for. Now, while I *loathe* the instant coffees in the United States, they do serve a valuable purpose—mostly as flavorants in ice cream and mousses and on the occasional camping trip. The first problem is that instant coffees taste closer to the canned Folgers flavor—not exactly what Starbucks' clientele have bonded with. Second, solubles are lower in caffeine and total solids or mouthfeel than ground and thereby lack the oral and cerebral kick. Now, having said this, during my travels in China, I picked up soluble (Nescafé Gold Blend) coffee in a Wal-Mart, of all places (not quite the colossal store we have in the United States). It was the best soluble coffee I have ever tasted, and I bought several containers to bring home (imagine, I could have brought home expensive *cognac* instead)!

Here is my challenge to the instant coffee scientists. Since gourmet coffees are growing at double-digit levels and solubles in the United States are not, create a soluble Starbucks experience—with boosted caffeine, chlorogenic acids, and solids levels. Make an instant coffee that brings back the memories of the real macoy—a coffee one can feel; and I know it's possible. Unfortunately, most instant coffee processes use robusta and lower quality Arabica beans.[20] A truly high quality 100 percent Arabica instant may be too costly to create.

Reader Note: Although I've compared gourmet coffee with typical supermarket brands (i.e. Folgers) I recently tried Folgers' Special Roast in the big, red, plastic can, and I was surprised at the good quality of the aroma and taste. You can now get Folgers coffee (blend of Arabica and robusta beans) in a Breakfast Blend, Classic Roast, Special Roast, Gourmet Supreme, and many more blends, according to the company's Web site. The gourmet coffee houses must be raising the flavor bar for all brands of coffee. However, most supermarket coffees in cans and tubs still use a lower flavor grade of Arabica and robusta beans.[20]

Coffee and Health

It now appears that coffee antioxidants (chlorogenic acids, caffeic acids, and quinides) and the simple molecule (caffeine) may protect against a whole host of human maladies. Coffee may have the following potential health benefits:[21, 22]

- Reduced suicide rates

- Lower risk of Alzheimer's disease (caffeine?)

- Lower risk of Parkinson's disease (caffeine?)

- Less alcoholic liver damage

- Improved mood and memory

- Improved blood sugar control (delayed absorption)

- Reduced incidence of Gallstones

- Increased fat burning (caffeine)

- Enhanced athletic endurance (caffeine)

- Improved work output (caffeine)

- Less inflammation and increased pain tolerance

And the longer and darker roasting process may produce fat-soluble quinides that help control blood sugar.[22] Ergo, the gourmet coffees are better for you. If caffeine makes you jittery, be advised that decaf contains the same excellent antioxidants; however, caffeine *itself* may have additional health benefits as well.

Although the levels of antioxidant precursors are somewhat higher in robusta (species: *canephora*) versus Arabica beans, darker roasting (of premium arabicas) can *increase* the total antioxidant production.[23] Gourmet coffees' serving suggestion uses *twice* as much coffee per serving than the canned. Thus, gourmet roasted coffees are optimized for both flavor and antioxidant production—and this makes me feel much better about my morning habit.

Coffee Contains Interesting Phytochemicals

Caffeine isn't the only substance in coffee that may have pleasure or reward actions. Coffee contains over a thousand compounds that are created by the roasting of the beans and the interactions of the sugars and protein in the process (Maillard reactions and Strecker degradations). Coffee beans contain several interesting compounds, like chlorogenic acids (CA), that may have psychotropic effects and may even reduce the absorption of sugar in a meal. Sudano et al. (2005) found that coffee stimulates the cardiovascular system independent of caffeine.[24] Coffee's chlorogenic acids also affect taste perception—they make water taste sweet (work by Linda Bartoshuk et al. 1972),[25] which may help mask the bitterness of caffeine and caffeic acid. Chlorogenic acids may also act like naloxone, an opioid antagonist! Dr. Lima states that a cup of coffee has an equivalent opioid-blocking ability as 1/3 of an ampoule of naloxone.[26] Hence, Starbucks' higher caffeine and (probably) CA content may be more rewarding and satisfying cup of coffee. I must admit, when I need a lift, I always seek out a double espresso from Starbucks!

The Ultimate Coffee Shop

Based on the theories of Food Pleasure, what would the ultimate coffee shop look like? Although Starbucks has great coffee, it is plagued by two situations (one operational, the other food related) that reduce its overall ability to be a highly rewarding restaurant experience. First, the production of good, quality coffee, and its numerous variations, takes too much time. And second, the pastries, scones, and croissants, although they look good, taste, well, *pas aussi bon*. What is the solution? Because humans are mildly ketotic (hungry) in the morning, a simple investment in food service equipment that creates freshly baked foods with appealing aromas would instantly signal the brain that our morning cravings for caffeine and calories will be satisfied. Care must be taken to avoid *competing* aromas with coffee as this may lessen their impact and create cognitive dissonance (conflicting sensory desires). I am surprised that the major chains haven't explored this solution—you don't even see a toaster in Starbucks!

Summary

Brewed coffee is a strong flavor enhancer, almost like adding soy sauce to a savory meal. With long hang-time odorants, umami tastants, and a high chlorogenic acid content (which makes water taste sweet), it is little wonder that coffee, with the addition of sugar, sodium, and fat, makes a tasty beverage. Coffee may even be a better flavor enhancer than its food chemical cousin—chocolate!

References

1.   Horovitz, B. Starbucks aims beyond lattes to extend brand. *USA Today*, Money sec., May 18, 2006. http://www.usatoday.com/money/industries/food/2006-05-18-starbucks-usat_x.htm

2.   Yanagimoto, K., Kwang-Geun, L., Ochi, H., and T. Shibamoto. Antioxidant activity heterocyclic compounds found in coffee volatiles

produced by Maillard reaction. *J. Agric. Food Chem.*, 50:5480–4, 2002.

3.   Horovitz, B. You want it your way. *USA Today*, Money sec., March 4, 2004.

4.   Cabanac, M. Pleasure: the common currency. *J. Theor. Biol.*, 155:173–200, 1992.

5.   Flavorology. Dunkin' Donuts talk. Oct. 10, 2005. http://www. flavorology.com/flavorology.html

6.   Kelley, A., and K. Berridge. The neuroscience of natural rewards: relevance to addictive drugs. *J. Neurosci.*, 22:3306–11, 2002.

7.   Owen, T. Our updated 100 point cupping system. http://www. sweetmarias.com/coffee.reference.html

8.   Coffee cupping. http://www.coffeeresearch.org/coffee/cupping.htm.

9.   The caffeine corner: products ranked by amount. *Nutrition Action Health Letter*, Dec., 1996. http://www.cspinet.org/nah/caffeine/caffe ine_corner.htm

10. McCarthy, M. The caffeine count in your morning fix. *Wall Street Journal*, April 13, 2004.

11. Gross, D. Starbucks versus its addicts. Oct., 5, 2004. http:// slate.msn.com/id/2107807/

12. Adelson, R. Dopamine and desire. *APA Online*, 36, March, 2005. http://www.apa.org/monitor/mar05/dopamine.html

13. Yeomans, M. R., Javaherian, S., Tovey, H. M., and L. D. Stafford. Attentional bias for caffeine-related stimuli in high but not moderate or non-caffeine consumers. *Psychopharmacology (Berl.)*, 181:477–85, 2005.

14. Schultz, H. 1997. *Pour Your Heart Into It*. New York: Hyperion.

15. Staub, C. Basic chemical reactions occurring in the roasting process. http://www.sweetmarias.com/roast.carlstaub.html

16. Moncrieff, R. W. 1966. *Odour Preferences*. New York: John Wiley & Sons.

17. Pennington, A. Specialty coffee market getting hotter. Entrepreneur.com, Aug. 9, 2005. http://www.msnbc.msn.com/id/8841941/

18. Chick-fil-A. Chick-fil-A post 38th consecutive year of sales growth. Jan. 26, 2006. http://www.chickfilapressroom.com/press_kit/press_kit.pdf

19. de Araujo, I. E., Kringelbach, M. L., Rolls, E. T., and F. McGlone. Human cortical response to water in the mouth and the effect on thirst. *J. Neurophysiol.*, 90:1865–76, 2003.

20. Coffee contact. http://www.geocities.com/RainForest/Canopy/1290/basics.html

21. Painter, K. Good news, coffee lovers. *USA Today*, sec. 4D, Nov. 6, 2006. http://www.usatoday.com/news/health/yourhealth/2006-11-05-yourhealth_x.htm

22. Fackelmann, K. Can caffeine protect against Alzheimer's? *USA Today*, sec. 4D, Nov. 6, 2006. http://www.usatoday.com/news/health/2006-11-05-caffeine-alzheimers_x.htm

23. Antioxidants in coffee. The Coffee Science Information Center. http://www.cosic.org/coffee-and-health/antioxidants

24. Sudano, I., Spieker, L., Binggeli, C., and F. Ruschitzka. Coffee blunts mental stress-induced blood pressure increase in habitual but not in nonhabitual coffee drinkers. *Hypertension*, 46:521–26, 2005.

25. Bartoshuk, L., Chi-Hang, L., and R. Scarpellino. Sweet taste of water induced by artichoke (*Cynara scolymus*). *Science*, 178:988–90, 1972.

26. Lima, D. R. A. Project coffee and health. http://www.ico.org/event_pdfs/lima.pdf

Starbucks References

- Moore, J. 2006. *Tribal Knowledge: Business Wisdom Brewed from the Grounds of Starbucks Corporate Culture.* Chicago: Kaplan Publishing.

- Schultz, H. 1997. *Pour Your Heart Into It.* New York: Hyperion. Note: book sales go to charity.

- Simmons, J. 2005. *My Sister's a Barista: How They Made Starbucks a Home Away from Home.* London: Cyan Communications.

- Sweet, L. 2007. *The Gospel According to Starbucks: Living with a Grande Passion.* Colorado Springs: WaterBrook Press.

- Michelli, A. 2006. The *Starbucks Experience: 5 Principles for Turning Ordinary into Extraordinary.* New York: McGraw-Hill.

CHAPTER 7

▼

WHY WE LIKE POPCORN

Popcorn has vanishing caloric density (pleasure without satiety).

Popcorn aroma is resistant to extinction.

Popcorn melts down quickly in the mouth (high dynamic contrast).

Popcorn is an excellent excuse to eat butter—a pleasure emulsion.

Popcorn

Popcorn in larger containers increased consumption by 45 percent.
Brian Wansink[1]

Popcorn is one of America's favorite snacks, with sales over $24.5 billion in the United States. The Popcorn Board says that Americans (the greatest consumers of popcorn—and ice cream—worldwide) consume more than 17 billion quarts a year, which translates into 54 quarts per capita. About 30 percent of popcorn is eaten outside the home. Archaeologists have found the Paleolithic beginning of popcorn in Indian caves, dating back more than 5,600 years. What, then, is the physiological basis for popcorn liking, and can any of our theories provide additional insight?

1. Popcorn Melts Down Very Quickly in the Mouth

The highly porous nature of the starch kernel coupled with the high air content allows popcorn to melt down quickly in the mouth upon contact with saliva. In fact, it is one of the quickest of all solid foods to disintegrate upon mastication. Quick meltdown means high dynamic contrast, which increases the pleasure of eating.

2. Popcorn Variety

Popcorn is, by nature, a fairly bland food with potent but subtle aromas. This sensory characteristic allows an endless variety of toppings or additions. The favorite topping, of course, is butter or butter substitutes; the old and very tasty coconut-based topping has largely been replaced by soybean oils.

3. Popcorn Is Resistant to Flavor Burnout

Some aromas are resistant to "flavor burnout"—vanilla, for example. I speculate here that cooked popcorn is yet another aroma, similar to potato that is mostly pure "aroma" as opposed to the "feel" of trigeminal aromas like rosemary. And butter, which we frequently add to our popcorn, is yet another aroma that is resistant to flavor burnout. Together, butter and popcorn create a tasty combination that resists sensory specific satiety and gut satiety (vanishing caloric density). Hence, we can indulge in eating popcorn on a daily basis, because we just don't get tired of the flavor complex and don't fill up that quickly. This "perfect storm" of taste and reduced satiety contributes to the disappearance of huge tubs of popcorn in the movie theaters. Foods with similar properties (pure aroma-type) include milk, vanilla ice cream, potato chips, and bread.

4. Popcorn Is an Excuse to Eat Butter

As the reader surely knows by now, the brain loves salt, fat, and sugar. Popcorn is usually eaten with salt, and the favorite salt source is butter (2–3 percent salt). But the real treat in eating popcorn is the taste sensation of butter itself—the kernels provide a high surface area for the butter (remember that the body loves an emulsion), greatly amplifying the hedonic solutes. Butter, as noted by *célèbre* Chef Thomas Keller, is basically a sauce that is very hedonically active—the butter-making process concentrates the NaCl (salt) into the 18 percent water phase––this produces a strong salt opioid pleasure response.

5. Popcorn Has Vanishing Caloric Density

Barbara Rolls reports that humans tend to eat a certain volume of food per day, and this thesis is the basis of her diet book, *Volumetrics*. We also know that humans like to eat calorically dense foods—like ice cream, chocolate, and many snack foods. If this is true, then why do we like a low-density food like popcorn? Popcorn's airy starch structure, melts down very quickly in the mouth, and is also low in calories and won't fill you up. In the theory by Dr. Robert Hyde, called "vanishing caloric density," some foods are pleasurable when they have initial high volume in the mouth and then simply melt down to nothing—without increasing satiety. Eating salted popcorn excites the palate with hedonic taste and fast meltdown, but the greatly reduced volume of food does not excite the stretch receptors in the stomach; so you just keep shoveling the popcorn in, like coal into a furnace. Activation of stretch receptors in the walls of the stomach can actually decrease the pleasure response of eating. Hence, popcorn activates oral pleasure without activating intestinal satiety too quickly. I'm convinced that this is a major reason we like popcorn—reward without satiation. What about the fat we add to it? Isn't this satiating? Well, calorie for calorie, protein is much more satiating than fat—popcorn dripping with salted butter (low in protein) has just about the most oral reward for the ingested calorie. However, after a trip to see the wonderful movie *Pirates of the Caribbean: Dead Man's Chest*, the price of *cinema popcorn* certainly dampened my gastric enthusiasm.

6. Perfect Popcorn

Here is a recipe for perfect-tasting popcorn that always receives favorable comments from the kids and neighbors, such as: "This is the best tasting popcorn—how do you make it?" The recipe uses all of the principles we have learned so far on how to make food taste good. Some of the ingredients are exotic but are probably available in many Asian supermarkets, such as Ranch 99 in California. The recipe uses the new weight-management oils like ADM's Enova or Nisshin Oillio's Healthy Resetta oils. These designer oils not only taste and look like real vegetable oil but are less likely to be stored as body fat. In addition, these cooking oils may actually *encourage* the fat cells to release fatty acids instead of storing it in adipose tissue. Healthy Resetta is only found in Japan at present. For the best popcorn follow these steps:

a.   Start with at least a 4-quart casserole pan or a large wok with a lid or a Whirlybird popcorn maker (works well, but be careful—the metal lid can get hot).

b.   Pour ½ cup of popcorn into the pan. (I like Orville Reddenbacker brand.)

c.   Pour 1/3 cup of Enova oil into the pan (almost any vegetable oil will work as well).

d.   Cook over high heat with the lid slightly ajar to let steam escape—or the popcorn becomes soggy (steamed).

e.   When the last few kernels pop take the pan off the heat, quickly.

f.   Salt to taste (generally about 1½ teaspoons salt):

   • The best salt to use is AJI-SHIO from Ajinomoto.

   • Popcorn salt is next best with the finer salt grains that stick to the popcorn. Butter-flavored salt has never worked well for me. It has a very artificial note that I find disagreeable (butter flavor is a challenge to duplicate).

   • Table iodized salt is not a good choice. The iodine flavor comes through, and the salt grains are too big to stick to the popcorn.

g.   Add 2 tablespoons of Kraft Parmesan cheese and blend well. The expensive *Parmigiano Reggiano* Italian cheese does not work well in this medium.

h.   For additional flavor (if desired), add 1/2 teaspoon of McCormick garlic powder (or white pepper). Add to the Parmesan first as a dispersion aid, then add to the popcorn and shake well.

This is good, old-fashioned popcorn with added umami tastants (MSG, Parmesan, and garlic powder) that is dispersed, not in butter, but in the healthy oils that coat the kernels in the cooking process. Many consumers have never tasted real popcorn, as 90 percent of all popcorn sold is now in the microwave form. Although microwave popcorn is convenient, it tends to ruin the natural meltdown of the starch pericarp by causing a retro-degradation of the starch—in effect, staling the popcorn as it cooks. This reduces the natural meltdown of popcorn and the overall dynamic contrast. By the way, the AJI-SHIO salt is more powerful than regular salt, so be careful not to add the equivalent amount—use about 20–40 percent less. MSG enhances the taste of sodium ions, and the total pleasure effect is *plus savoureux*!

Reference

1. Lang, S. Big portions influence overeating as much as taste, even when the food tastes lousy, Cornell study finds. *Cornell Chronicle Online*, Nov. 9, 2005. http://research.cals.cornell.edu/entity?home =5&id=15957

<u>Information on Designer Oils</u>

- For ADM's Enova see: http://www.enovaoil.com/

- For Nisshin Oillio's Healthy Resetta see: technicalproductsinc.net/ presentation.htm

▼

CHAPTER 8

WHY WE LIKE DONUTS

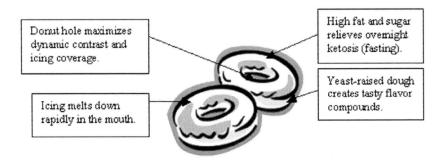

Donut hole maximizes dynamic contrast and icing coverage.	High fat and sugar relieves overnight ketosis (fasting).
Icing melts down rapidly in the mouth.	Yeast-raised dough creates tasty flavor compounds.

Every year Krispy Kreme bakes over 2.7 billion donuts.
Krispy Kreme Web site[1]

Sexual stimuli and very tasty junk foods stimulate the dopamine system (pleasure centers) in a manner close to addictive drugs.
B. Hoebel[2]

Krispy Kreme (KK) appeared on the donut scene in 1937 when Vernon Rudolph obtained a secret, yeast-raised donut formula scribbled from a French chef. In the last few years KK has become a national sensation, although the low-carb boom briefly cut into sales. Franchises bloomed everywhere, as of this writing the icing has cooled on the stock price—but the question remains: are KK donuts better than the rest, and what is the physiological reason behind the rapid rise in popularity?

1. You Can Get KK Donuts Warm

My son had a chance to eat fresh KK donuts (after a very long night of work) hot off the presses and declared, "Dad, these are the most amazing donuts I have ever eaten"—and promptly ate four of the glazed ones, one after another. I tried one and found it quite tasty as well; although my wife noted that these donuts were unusually dense in icing (she could only eat half of one). A warm donut has sensory pleasure advantages due to increases in dynamic contrast. In addition, warm food activates a large percentage of the taste receptors in the mouth for the basic tastes and many of which are hardwired or activate the pleasure center automatically. Warm food just tastes better as a result. Steven Strauss, a business writer, also agrees that a fresh, hot donut is much more tasty.[3] Such is the power of increasing the thermal dynamic contrast in a food!

2. The Donut Is Now Theater

There is strong associative neurophysiology behind letting the customer see the donut-making process: the sights, the smells, and the anticipation. This reinforces the total sensory experience into a strong mental image. Remember, when one eats a food, the brain memorizes the entire experience of where the food was eaten and who was in the store at the time. This is also similar to the Starbucks experience, wherein the store, its colors, and the intense smells become memorized along with the java within. The retro 60s look of a KK donut shop is instantly recognizable. Since humans are visual animals, this distinctive appearance is perfect for a hedonically conditioned linkage (donut plus surroundings). In any fast-food establishment this is precisely what one should do—make the product uniquely good and build a strong, but *distinctive*, sensory experience around it.

3. Donuts Melt Down Quickly

Like many of our most preferred foods, donuts (yeast-raised conglomerate of wheat flour fat and sugar) melt down quickly in the mouth upon mastication. Rapid food meltdown is rewarding, first by exciting dynamic contrast (DC) and food arousal, and secondly by releasing a flood of sugars that incite the sweet taste. The donuts are perfectly coated with thick icing and carefully packaged side by side (they don't touch). There are two big dynamic contrasts in the glazed donut. First, as we have said, if you can get one warm, the activation of taste receptors (due to the heat) and the change in oral temperature (donut to mouth temperature) is a very strong DC pleasure generator. Second, KK donuts appear to be smaller and have a greater icing-to-dough ratio than others; icing, when it melts in the mouth, is another generator of DC and a major inducer of salivation (positive feedback). This double sensory whammy is hard to beat. And KK donuts don't touch each other in the box—this prevents the icing from visual and structural damage, which would reduce the DC. Donuts that touch also cross contaminate flavor systems inducing a type of meatloaf effect where all the donuts start to taste the same. My impression after eating one is that the KK donut is merely a vehicle for ingesting the icing.

Melts in Your Mouth

Food-science professor Massimo Marcone at the University of Guelph, studied the donut melt-in-your mouth phenomenon. He sensory-tested Canada's biggest donut maker, Tim Horton's, versus the newcomer Krispy Kreme.[4] The professor discovers that the fat used in the KK donut actually had a higher amount of liquid versus solid fat at room temperature. From a food-science standpoint, this means that once in the mouth, a KK donut melts down faster (greater dynamic contrast) than the competition. The professor suggested that donut liking is rooted in the fat content that contributes better flavor and a feeling of fullness.

Compared with most of its competitors, KK donuts appear to be richer in fat and calories and have a slightly increased caloric density (which we know the brain finds pleasurable). At 50 percent fat calories, the KK donut is very close to the average of most salty snack foods.[2] Professor Marcone also notes that the KK glazed donut was 25 percent smaller in size than Horton's, but had 10 more calories.

4. KK Donuts Have High Caloric Density

As we have seen, humans like food with lots of calories in small volumes.[5] Consumption of an energy-dense food also stimulates the brain's opioid centers, which in turn releases dopamine and pleasure neurotransmitters. I've calculated the KK glazed donut at 3.8 DC; this puts it close to salami, at 4.2! That this is an energy-dense food is, no doubt, a secret to the company's success. In fact, in my son's purchased box of mixed KK donuts, I noticed that there were additional flavored icings on top of the regular glaze (for example, maple over the regular glaze). A chocolate-glazed donut amps the calories from 200 for a glazed to 350! Enough already! Eating one of these on an empty stomach could be painful with all that icing—I know; I've tried it. In fact, I ate two just to see what would happen on an empty stomach. They were very good while I was eating them, but, during *digestion*, my stomach felt bloated and sent out a high satiety signal—a physiological reaction strikingly similar to the way I felt drinking the fancy liquid chocolate bar, Chantico. And what percent of the population may have the same gut reaction of excessive satiety? If I had to speculate, I'd say 10–15 percent. Excessive satiety forms a food aversion, and these calorie sensitive individuals may dine elsewhere.

5. Donuts Quickly Fix the Nighttime Ketotic Fast

After a long night of sleep, our bodies actually wake up in what Dr. May, a well-known Los Angeles internist, calls a mild ketotic condition; overnight, the body uses up most of the stored glucose in the body (glycogen) and by morning the supply is almost exhausted. In addition, levels of fats in the blood are at their lowest levels. Hence, upon awakening, the body naturally looks for a calorically dense food to restore energy balance. And a donut with lots of sugar and high glycemic starch, coated with icing, and cooked in fat suits the empty stomach quite nicely. Neuroscientist Sarah Leibowitz has also studied the ebb and flow of what we like to eat during the day. She says that when we get up in the morning, we want a glucose and fat blast because insulin is low and glycogen is depleted. At lunch however, the brain neurochemistry starts to look for protein, and then by dinner the brain hormone galanin pushes us toward more fat again.[6]

References

1. History. Krispy Kreme Doughnuts. http:www.krispykreme/
    history.html#

2. Martindale, D. A high with your fries? *New Sci.*, Feb. 1, 2003. http://
    www.newscientist.com/article/mg17723800.100-a-high-with-your-
    fries.html

3. Strauss, S. Sweet success of Krispy Kreme has lessons for all. http://
    biz-eye-view.sbc.com/SBR_template.cfm?document=steve.cfm&arti
    cle=2003Sep.15

4. Meyer, K. The hole story on donuts. *Univ. of Guelph Res. News*,
    Dec.15, 2002. http://www.uoguelph.ca/research/news/articles/2002/
    hole_story_on_donuts.shtml

5. Kelley, A. E., Bakshi, V. P., Haber, S. N., and T. L. Steininger. Opioid modulation of taste hedonics within the ventral striatum. *Physiol. Behav.*, 76:365–77, 2002.

6. Collin, F. Sarah Leibowitz, interview, neuroscientist. *Omni Magazine*, May, 1992. via Looksmart, http://www.findarticles.com/p/articles/mi_m1430/is_n8_v14/ai_12180349/pg_1

General Information

- If you would like to learn more about Krispy Kreme's marketing secrets, pick up *Making Dough: The 12 Secret Ingredients of Krispy Kreme's Sweet Success* by Kirk Kazanjian, 2004, Indianapolis: Wiley Publishing.

CHAPTER 9

▼

WHY WE LIKE GARLIC

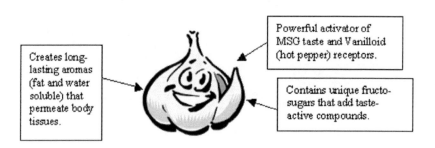

Creates long-lasting aromas (fat and water soluble) that permeate body tissues.

Powerful activator of MSG taste and Vanilloid (hot pepper) receptors.

Contains unique fructo-sugars that add taste-active compounds.

"All you need is fat, some herbs, garlic, salt and pepper."
A. Bourdain[1]

Garlic has been used in food seasoning and medicine for many thousands of years. Mummies were buried with it (perhaps five thousand years ago), and a surprisingly large number of cultures cook with it, even if it was just recently introduced into their food supply (as is the case with the French). The medicinal benefits include positive effects on the cardiovascular system (lower blood pressure), reduced blood viscosity, reduced rates of certain cancers, antibiotic-like effects, and increased response of the immune system to stress. All of these actions are due to the sulfur atom containing compounds when garlic is ingested. Sulfur compounds are highly reactive, not only do they interact with themselves, but they act as both pro- and anti-oxidants in body tissues.

Garlic aroma is created when a garlic compound called *alliin* is broken down by the enzyme *allinase* into *allicin*, which is activated during crushing or smashing of the clove. The enzyme, which is inside certain garlic cells, is suddenly released during crushing and then acts quickly on its substrate, alliin. Allicin is a very unstable molecule and rapidly breaks down into many hundreds of additional organosulfur flavor compounds. Some of them include ajoene, methyl ajoene, dithiins, diallyl disulfide, and diallyl trisulfide (which are strong smelling). This reaction, alliin into allicin, is stopped or greatly reduced by roasting whole garlic, because the enzyme allinase is destroyed by heat. Alliin, by itself, has no aroma whatsoever.

The peculiar nature of the chemical structure of the flavor compounds formed is very important to the flavor and perception of garlic. Many of the sulfur compounds created are powerful aromatics that we can detect in small amounts, such as just a few parts per billion. In addition, many of the flavor compounds are lipid soluble and have what I call a *long hang-time*, not only in the house but the body as well. In fact, ingestion of garlic generates flavor compounds that stay in the bloodstream and are breathed out via the lungs and skin pores. This is the true mechanism of garlic breath and not the residual garlic in the mouth after eating. For the first three hours after eating, a person suffers from some garlic breath, but most of the garlic smell exudes from the lung tissue, which has a huge surface volume for volatiles to exude. Scott believes the garlic compounds last up to twenty-four hours in the body—mainly allyl methyl sulphide, dimethyl sulphide, and acetone.[2] Although breath mints may handle the oral odor, they won't touch the internal—in this case you need a special mushroom that has been shown to reduce garlic body odor—*Agaricus bisporus*.

Infants like the taste of garlic as well. It has been reported that infants will drink more breast milk when it is garlic flavored, probably due to the umami effect, but this is speculation.

1. Garlic Aroma Has a "Long Hang-Time"

Why would this be important? In studies of nutritional-aroma conditioning, strong and long-lasting aromas formed the best food-nutrient conditioning. No one can dispute that garlic aroma lingers around forever. As an experiment, rub you fingers with a cut garlic clove and notice that the aromas will quickly infiltrate the skin mucosa due to the high lipid solubility of the garlic flavorants. In fact, your fingers will smell like garlic for almost forty-eight hours. Hence, during ingestion, garlic aromas permeate body tissues and form very strong aroma-calorie memories. There are other aromas almost as lingering in body tissues as garlic, and based on my personal experience they are in this order: green onions, white and yellow onions, red onions, shallots, chives, leeks, and Maui or sweet onions.

2. Garlic Boosts "Umami" Taste

I first learned of this interaction almost twenty years ago when Japanese researchers reported a strong increase in umami flavor when garlic juice was added to basic food system. Researchers confirm that the odor of garlic boosts the flavor of MSG or umami taste in food.[3] Work by E. T. Rolls illustrates that when a garlic aroma compound was dissolved in water, the umami taste became stronger. Rolls also reports that there are "flavor" neurons in the orbitofrontal cortex when tastes and their aromas are perceived. Umami tastants in onions are especially good at activating these neurons. Remember that umami taste evolved to help encourage humans to detect and ingest proteins, and the use of garlic aromatics in food increases the rewarding tastes of proteins. This is basically neuro-driven cuisine! I encourage the curious food scientist to read the papers by E. T. Rolls and his colleagues; they contain very illuminating information on how the brain integrates and modulates food perception with pleasure.[4]

3. Garlic Is a Special Trigeminal Stimulant

Fresh garlic burns the tongue with its own unique bite. Many of the foods we love—black pepper, hot peppers, and onions—have this burning sensation as well. The addition of this "orosensation" gives more pleasure to the ingestion of food. The nature of this stimulation was identified by the Scripts Institute and is described in *Current Biology*.[5] Raw or slightly cooked garlic activates the TRP (Transient Receptor Potential) channels, TRPV1 and TRPA1, which respond to temperature and chemicals. Orosensation is also called "chemesthesis," also known as the *somatosensory* aspect of taste perception. TRPV1 responds to heat and capsaicin—the hot principle in chili pepper, whereas TRPA1 responds to cold and pungent compounds like cinnamon oil, mustard oil, and wintergreen. Hence, garlic activates both these receptors in the mouth, which contributes to its amazing ability to light up the mouth with both umami flavor and orosensation. Now you know—so be sure to include it whenever you can in your own cooking! You don't have to add much; just a subtle clove or two will do. Note that garlic is one of Emeril's ingredients in his BAM! spice—fourth on the list. And during the *Emeril Live!* cooking show, his liberal use of chopped garlic (he usually says *forty* cloves!) is legendary.

The French use this taste-activation property of raw garlic in the classic preparation of Caesar salad, the initial step requires one to rub a cut raw garlic clove around the bowl. Due to the strong orosensory properties of raw garlic, this light touch provides all the flavor you need—you certainly wouldn't add chopped raw garlic to the salad.

The longer you cook garlic, the less of this burning raw taste property. Baked garlic is almost devoid of the activation of these temperature receptors because heat destroys the enzyme necessary for allicin generation. Roasting garlic, however, creates a creamy sweetness and an unusual aroma complex that is smoky in nature. Recall that in our discussion of cookivore theory, humans have a predilection for smoky and lingering aromas paired with high caloric density foods. Roasted garlic, then pairs well with rich and creamy sauces, mashed potatoes, and vinaigrettes.

TRP Summary

Wikipedia has a nice summary of the TRPs relevant to food intake.[6] Note which food compounds stimulate these receptors. The take-home lesson here is that activation of TRPs creates more orosensation, which is generally related to more pleasure generation. Carl Pfaffman, a noted sensory physiologist, was fond of saying that all pleasure starts with sensation.[7]

1. TRPV1 to TRPV4 can basically be seen as thermometers on a molecular level and are activated by a variety of stimulants. TRPV1 is, for example, activated by potentially noxious stimuli: heat, acidic pH, and capsaicin.

2. TRPM5 is involved in the sensory transduction pathway of taste cells.

3. ANKTM1 is a member of the TRP ion channel family implicated in the detection of tetrahydrocannabinol and mustard oil.

4. TRPM8 is a calcium permeable channel, which can be activated by: low temperatures, menthol, eucalyptol, and icilin (supercooling agent).

Taste Synergism

As a demonstration on how a taste-active compound can interact with temperature, try this simple experiment. Chew a few thin mints, masticate well, and then take a sip of cold milk. You will notice an intense increase in cold oral temperature. Peppermint oils excite cold receptor channels, and the combination of the cold and mint is synergistic—many times stronger than either alone. Gum-makers and shaving-cream companies take advantage of the cooling effect by using synthetic compounds that are tight and long-lasting binders to these TRP receptors. I recently tried a Japanese mint flavored gum, and the flavor persisted for many hours in my mouth and actually interfered with the pleasure of other foods I ate later on; one can go too far in flavor persistence.

References

1. Bourdain, A. 2004. *Les Halles Cookbook.* New York: Bloomsbury USA.

2. Scott, P. Question of taste. *New Scientist,* Aug. 12, 2006. http://www.newscientist.com/backpage.ns?id=mg19125642.800

3. Rolls, E. T. The representation of umami taste in the taste cortex. *J. Nutr.,* 130:9605–55, 2000.

4. Rolls, E. T. Brain mechanisms underlying flavour and appetite. *Philos. Trans. R. Soc. Lond. B. Biol. Sci.,* 361:1123–36, 2006. (This is one of the most important papers ever written on food perception and pleasure.)

5. Macpherson, L. The pungency of garlic: activation of TRPA1 and TRPV1 in response to allicin. *Curr. Bio.,* 15:929–34, 2005.

6. Transient receptor potential. Wikipedia. http://en.wikipedia.org/wiki/Transient_receptor_potential

7. Pfaffman, C. The pleasure of sensation. *Psychol. Rev.,* 67: 253–68, 1960.

<u>Wonderful site for all things flavor and fragrance</u>

• Leffingwell, J. C. Cool without menthol & cooler than menthol and cooling compounds as insect repellants. April 5, 2006. http://www.leffingwell.com/cooler_than_menthol.htm#b

CHAPTER 10

▼

IS TOASTY BETTER?

Toasting creates cookivore aromas: pyrazines and pyrroles.

Toasting increases food temperature and dynamic contrast.

People like grilled foods because they taste good.
Melanie Dubberley.[1]

Quiznos introduced the sensory slogan "mmmm … TOASTY" as part of its major differentiation from the other sub shops. The question is whether toasty *is* better or just marketing hype? Since Quiznos is the most rapid growing new fast-food chain (4,400 franchises worldwide) and the third-ranked franchise, there must be strong physiology behind the toasting. In a recent report, the "toasty wars" in the submarine sandwich business should not be underestimated—companies like Subway are spending millions on fancy, high-tech toasting equipment to keep up with fast-growing rival Quiznos.[2] And why do consumers like a toasted sub sandwich? The sandwiches must taste better that way; up to 1/3 of Subway patrons now ask for the toasty treatment.[2] Let's now delve into the physiology of toasting, flavor perception and the hedonic consequences. After all, isn't it amazing that millions of dollars are at stake on a basic cooking method that modifies food pleasure in ways that are mysterious and unexplained?

1. Toasting Makes the Food Warm

Although this answer at first glance seems obvious, the principle of dynamic contrast is hot at work. The oral cavity prefers temperature changes, and the oral neural response is greatest to *changing* temperature, not static ones. Eighty to 90 percent of all food is consumed either hot or cold. It is this temperature *change* in the mouth upon eating that is very pleasurable. This is the ice-cream effect in reverse (ice cream is pleasurable because it's cold). Most fast food is served hot. In fact, chains like Jack in the Box only cook food when ordered, so the food is as hot as possible (it's my favorite chain, by the way). But sub shops serve their product, unless it is corned beef or a similar hot sandwich, at room temperature. Jersey Mike's, however, a national sub chain started in 1956, has a number of *very* hot sub sandwiches (the chipotle cheese steak is particularly tasty). A room-temperature sub is at a significant sensory disadvantage; however, the addition of sandwich inclusions (pickles, onions, dressing, etc.) compensates in part by greater sensory complexity of the sandwich. This follows the food pleasure equation, where added flavor sensations increase the hedonic response.

Hence, adding heat to a sandwich elevated the food pleasure to newer heights, and Quiznos caught the other sub shops off guard, at least initially. Heating the sandwich may also activate taste cell receptors in the mouth, independent of direct taste stimulation by solutes, and increases food pleasure. Why? Sweet, umami, and salty taste sensations, when activated by heat, have innate or hardwired inputs into the brain circuits for pleasure.[3] Food is better when it's hotter—and this *same* hedonic reaction occurs when a food is cold and warms up in the mouth.

2. Toasty Creates Special Flavor Compounds

Recall the theory that humans are cookivores. Fire invention and manipulation spurred the development of *Homo culinarus* via the great advantages of cooked food—increased digestibility, reduction of pathogens, and increased caloric density. A professor once told me that certain aromas are epigenetic—built-in sensing aroma programs that signal survival. Toasting and fire are one and the same—do they bring back memories of survivals past? Witness the wonderful thoughts and memories of people cooking over hardwood or just heating their homes with a wood burning fireplace. Although the evidence is scientific conjecture, I suspect that certain fire-created aromas (like flame-broiled hamburgers) conjure up genetic memories of successful Paleolithic hunts. It's very possible that our sense of smell, in which the actual receptors have devolved over time, became selectively sensitive to certain environmental aromas of cooked food.

3. Toasting Changes the Dynamic of the Sandwich

Dynamic contrast works through many levels. And the next level is what heat does to the entire sandwich:

a. Many new flavor compounds are created via Maillard reactions or Strecker degradations; for example, the aromatic pyrazines, and the tasty melanoidins.[1] This means increased aroma complexity—and the theory is that aroma complexity is more rewarding than aroma simplicity, also known as Moncrief's Observation. Even McDonald's experiments with a longer toasting time for their hamburger buns to enhance the flavor.[4]

b. The sandwich now becomes more dynamically contrastable. Now what does this mean? Instead of a soft bun on top with little give, you have now changed the starch structure to be harder at the surface, such that it fractures and gives way during mastication and then melts down—similar to the wonderful contrast sensation of breaking through the caramelized top of a *crème brûlée*. Name me a burger that can match this ... There is none—except the grilled panini sandwich.

c. Toasting elevates the volatiles that can be perceived in the sandwich. This increases the chance to bond with those flavors you love most: onion, garlic, and umami-linked aromatics of meat.

d. Grilling also melts the cheese in the sandwich, allowing for quicker and more sustained contact with the taste buds. This enhances the contact of the salt and taste active compounds in cheese with the taste bud epithelium itself.

Now what would be the *ultimate* sandwich-burger combo that excites just about every sensation? It would have the following features:

a. High caloric density must be maintained.

b. It must have a high dynamic contrast in ingredients (like an Italian sub).

c. Meat ingredients should gush umami when chewed.

d. The whole sandwich must be toasted (easy enough) outside with grill marks.

e. The meat should be flame broiled.

f. Cheese must be stuffed in somewhere.

g. The entire ensemble must not be soggy at presentation or the hedonics are reduced.

h. The outside bread should be buttered, as in the classic cheese sandwich.

i. In a perfect world, the sandwich should be a combination of hot and cold elements.

McDonald's tried a version of this concept with the McDLT in 1985, in which the customer actually put together the hot burger with the cooler ingredients, lettuce and tomato, in a specially designed container that separated the foods. This allowed both types of dynamic contrast into play—both hot and cold elements—and was quite forward thinking at the time, never caught on with the customer.

The popularity of toasting sandwiches is now manifest in the panini; the classic Italian sandwich is grilled on both sides—basically a fancy cheese sandwich. The panini process creates Maillard reation flavors, visual contrast and helps melt the cheese for "quicker" activation of hedonic tastes. The key to a great tasting panini is to thinly slice the cheese and meat fillings so that when the crust is ready, the fillings are hot and melted.

Bruce Horovitz, business writer for *USA Today*, uncovered a new food trend in which companies are combining two favorite foods into a single meal.[5] In his article, "Cheeseburger couplings match 2 favorites," he indicates that companies are making cheeseburger pizzas, donuts, and tacos, and even deep-fried cheeseburger sticks. And just imagine a cheeseburger using two Krispy Kreme donut halves instead of a sesame seed bun! These combinations may seem over-the-top, but the best taste elements of familiar foods may create a food with enhanced hedonics. Conversely, many foods are typically eaten during certain times of the day, and combining a breakfast food with lunch or dinner food may be perceptually unsettling (cognitive dissonance).

References

1. Dubberley, M. Seared sandwiches take center stage. *Food Product Design*, Oct. 2003. http://www.foodproductdesign.com/archive/2003/1003FFOC.html

2. Apuzzo, M. Quiznos booms, Subway rolls on as sandwich market heats up. Associated Press, Aug. 1, 2005. http://www.msnbc.msn.com/id/8789466/

3. Breza, J. M., Curtis, K. S., and R. J. Contreras. Temperature modulates taste responsiveness and stimulates gustatory neurons in the rat geniculate ganglion. *J. Neurophysiol.*, 95:674–85, 2002.

4. Gogoi, P., and M. Arndt. McDonald's hamburger hell. *BuisinessWeek online*, March, 3, 2003. http://www.businessweek.com/magazine/content/03_09/b3822085_mz017.htm

5. Horovitz, B. Cheeseburger couplings match 2 favorites. *USA Today*, Money sec., June 23, 2006. http://www.usatoday.com/money/industries/food/2006-06-23-cheeseburger-usat_x.htm

Panini recipes abound on the Web:

*   http://www.mrcappuccino.com/recipe-panini.htm

*   http://www.kraftfoods.com/pollyo/panini.html

*   http://www.jkings.com/recipes/paninis.pdf

*   http://www.backerhausveit.com/pdf/Panini%20Sandwich.pdf

CHAPTER 11

▼

WHY DO PEOPLE LIKE A
HAMBURGER?

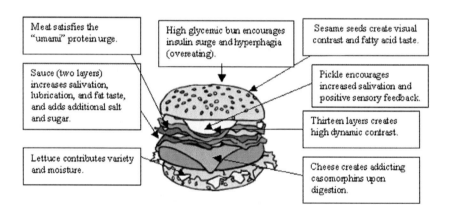

Meat satisfies the "umami" protein urge.

High glycemic bun encourages insulin surge and hyperphagia (overeating).

Sesame seeds create visual contrast and fatty acid taste.

Sauce (two layers) increases salivation, lubrication, and fat taste, and adds additional salt and sugar.

Pickle encourages increased salivation and positive sensory feedback.

Thirteen layers creates high dynamic contrast.

Lettuce contributes variety and moisture.

Cheese creates addicting casomorphins upon digestion.

Tasty foods may change gene expression and create a food addiction.[1]
Humans may have an inherited preference for protein.[2]
Very tasty food improves one's mood, and may cause drug-like brain adaptation.[3]

The McDonald's Big Mac (first developed in 1968) was modeled after the hamburger created by the Bob's Big Boy franchise that started its operations in 1936. In 1968, Jim Delligatti, a 10-store McDonald's franchisee, developed the modern Big Mac.[4,5] The major ingredients in a Big Mac are: two all-beef patties, special sauce, lettuce, cheese, pickles, and onions on a sesame-seed bun. Bob's

Hamburger is similar: a double-decker with 2.6 oz. all-beef patties, grilled sesame-seed bun with shredded lettuce, cheese, and dressing. Of all the hamburgers I've tasted, the Big Mac and the In-and-Out Double-Double are my favorites. Bob's Big Boy is good but a little too dry for my taste. McDonald's has a very informative and interactive nutrition Web site that details the nutritional breakdown with numerous and entertaining "what ifs"—how the calories and nutrients change with ingredient additions and deletions. The Web site is worth exploring. (Get rid of the cheese and secret sauce, and the burger is almost healthy.)

1. Macronutrient Content

Big Macs contain all three macronutrients (25 g protein, 30 g fat, and 47 g carbohydrate), so they excite each physiological system devoted to their detection and assimilation.

High in Salt, Fat, and Sugar

A whopping 1 gram of salt is concentrated in the cheese, pickle, and the bun.

- A Big Mac contains 30 grams of fat (about 47 percent of the recommended daily value) with an unhealthy but tasty 11.5 grams of saturated and trans fat. Some scientists think that people actually prefer saturated fat, since it is found predominately in meat products, suggesting an evolutionary linkage. However, wild game (much more likely to be the type of animal hunted thousands of years ago), is actually much higher in unsaturated fat and lower in fat overall (averaging 4 percent fat). McDonald's used to fry its French fries in beef tallow (very low in trans fat, actually!) before switching to its current vegetable oil plus a flavor additive blend. Beef tallow contains cookivore aromas that humans find innately pleasant; the fatty acid profile (higher saturates) created a crispier surface, which enhanced dynamic contrast. (Note that trans fat is considerably unhealthier than saturated fat—Professor Randy Buddington used to call it cellular sludge!) Luckily for the Fast-Food Nation, evidence suggests that oils with higher levels of essential fatty acids are actually preferred, because they activate taste receptors sensitive to essential *nutrients* (linoleic and linolenic fatty acids). Most cooking oils are now made from vegetable sources, naturally rich in the levels of the good fatty acids and low in saturated fats: canola, safflower, sunflower, corn, olive soybean, peanut, and cottonseed.

- The carbohydrate content comes from wheat and barley starch, high fructose corn syrup, sugar, and corn syrup. All are high glycemic starches and sugars that provide immediate glucose availability, which may be more satiating than slow-release starch. High fructose corn syrup (HFCS) is a particularly problematic ingredient. Fructose is a strong reducing sugar (very reactive) and may encourage fat storage, hyperphagia (overeating), and protein glycosylation (damage to cells).[6] (The actual amount of HFCS is fairly small, and certainly lower than in, say, Smucker's Jams.)

- McDonald's also appears to salt and spice the meat on the grill, because it lists a grill seasoning blend, which adds additional taste-active compounds.

2. Taste-Active Components and Salivation Generation

The Mac is loaded with all the ingredients that make food taste good—including the aptly named "Secret Sauce" (SS). The SS contains vinegar (arousal), egg yolks (emulsifier effect), HFCS, sugar (sweetness and addictiveness), onion and garlic powder (flavorants and umami boosters), hydrolyzed corn, wheat, and soy glutens (natural MSG and the hedonically active amino acid tastants). If you include the pickle, which encourages salivation, the Big Mac has one outstanding property that most burgers do not possess: it is not *dry*! Although discussed elsewhere in this book, all fine cuisines encourage salivation; dry food is sensory death. Without a sauce, French food would be lifeless, and in Asian cuisine, and the vast majority of stir fry dishes are enveloped with a thickened soy sauce glaze.

3. Dynamic Contrast

The Big Mac is a cornucopia of flavor and texture contrasts in, on, and around the buns.

a.   The triple-decker look increases the perceived dynamic contrast (DC); it certainly has more contrast than a single beef patty!

b.   Two thinner patties versus one add more DC and visual interest. For example, eating two 1/4-inch-cut French fries is probably more pleasurable than eating *one* 1/2-inch fry.

c.   Two layers of lettuce add more DC (color).

d.   Sesame seeds on the top bun add visual interest and more DC. Sesame seeds is a rich source (37 percent) of an essential fatty acid called linoleic acid. During mastication, this fatty acid uniquely excites oral receptors for fat (with the help of lingual lipase).

e.   According to William Poundstone in *Big Secrets*, there are thirteen layers in a Big Mac in this order: top sesame bun, onions, meat, pickles, lettuce, secret sauce, middle bun, onions, meat, cheese, lettuce, secret sauce, and bottom bun. Almost like a croissant, this layering effect creates high dynamic contrast—and *this* is the main secret of this burger.

f.   The onion addition to the meat is a centuries-old flavor combination (Middle Eastern). Onion sulfur compounds add trigeminal stimulation along with powerful and long-lasting aromas that signal the taste of flesh and survival.

4. High Caloric Density

Recall that as omnivores, we have a predilection for food high in caloric density (CD) or concentrated calories. The calculation is simple—just divide kcals by grams. Hence, a Big Mac would be 560 kcals/219 g, or 2.6, which puts it into the middleweight category. Heavyweights are foods above 4.0, like most salty snacks, cookies, and chocolates rich in fat. Other middleweight foods (1.6–3.0) are meat and cheese. Diet-friendly lightweight foods (0.8–1.5) include many dairy products such as yogurt. Most vegetables, due to their high water content, are less than 1.0 CD. (See the excellent book *Volumetrics* by Barbara Rolls for more information. One diet tip—she recommends avoiding any food above a 2 CD.)

My son tells me that in Canada they have a double-double Big Mac with *four* meat patties and *two* slices of cheese—close to 700 kcals! And if that doesn't whet your appetite there is always the Hardee's Monsterburger; my comments on why we like it are still on the Web.[7]

For an excellent and hilarious Web site on junk food see http://calorielab.com/news/categories/fast-food-restaurants/.

In-N-Out Burgers

My favorite burger is the freshly made, cooked-to-order, cheese-laden Double-Double at In-N-Out Burger. Although the wait at the store can be as long as fifteen to twenty minutes, I don't mind; I often bike there with my wife (about ten miles round trip, with my daughter happily riding and singing in a bike trailer behind), and we split a number one (Double-Double with fries and Diet Coke). Apparently, this chain is also the favorite of *überchef* Thomas Keller, who said to Russ Parsons that he respects the chain's adherence to the simplified burger menu; if you don't like burgers, there are plenty of other eateries.[8]

Although the burger menu is fairly straightforward (Double-Double, Cheeseburger, and Hamburger), there is a somewhat secret menu that adds additional burger variations (some of them entertaining):[9]

- Double Meat with no cheese (lactose intolerance?)

- 3-by-3: three meat patties and three slices of cheese (trifecta?)

- 4-by-4: four meat patties and four cheese slices (Cardiologist *order spécial*). A *regular* Double-Double is 670 kcals and 55 percent fat calories. I'm guessing the 4-by-4 would weigh-in at 1,000 kcals and 65 percent fat calories! And a Double-Double, Fries and Milkshake contains 1,763 calories and 95 grams of fat. Whoa!

- Grilled Cheese Version (comfort food)

- Protein Style (low carb) with lettuce as the bun (*dans le passé* nowadays)

- Animal (House?) Style: burger with lettuce, tomato, a mustard cooked beef patty, pickle, extra sauce, and grilled onions

- Flying Dutchman: two meat patties and cheese (and that's it)

The French fries, onions, and drinks also receive personalized attention if desired. For example, one can order a Neapolitan Shake (chocolate, vanilla, and strawberry layered in a cup).

Anthropologist David Givens, PhD has written an entertaining description of why we like a Big Mac.[10] Many of his observations (although a bit cryptic and in anthrospeak) are insightful historically interesting, and physiologically correct.

References

1. Martindale, D. A high with those fries? *New Sci.*, 177:3, 27–9, 2003.

2. Breen, F. M., Plomin, R., and J. Wardle. Heritability of food preferences in young children. *Physiol. Behav.*, 88:443–7, 2006.

3. Cota, D., Tschop, M. H., Horvath, T. L., and A. S. Levine. Cannabinoids, opioids and eating behavior: the molecular face of hedonism? *Brain Res. Reviews*, 51:85–107, 2006.

4. Big Mac. Wikipedia. http://en.wikipedia.org/wiki/Big_Mac

5. Adamy, J. For McDonald's, it's a wrap. *Wall Street Journal*, Jan. 30, 2007.

6. Elliot, S., Keim, N. L., Stern, J. S., and K. Teff. Fructose, weight gain, and the insulin resistance syndrome *Am. J. Clin. Nutr.*, 76:911–22, 2002.

7. Horovitz, B. Restaurant sales climb with bad-for-you food. *USA Today*, May 12, 2005. http://www.usatoday.com/money/industries/food/2005-05-12-bad-food-cover_x.htm

8. Parsons, R. Thomas Keller, the chef behind Per Se, takes a distinctly American turn. Blame In-N-Out. *Los Angeles Times*, June 7, 2006.

9. In-N-Out Web site; Wikipedia, http://www.zenlemur.com/inn out.shtml

10. Givens, D. Big Mac. http://members.aol.com/nonverbal2/bigmac.htm

CHAPTER 12

▼

WHY WE LIKE SOUTHERN FRIED CHICKEN

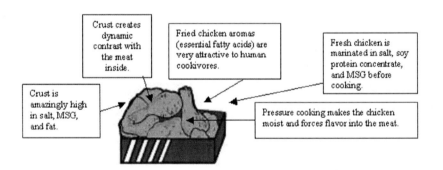

Crust creates dynamic contrast with the meat inside.

Fried chicken aromas (essential fatty acids) are very attractive to human cookivores.

Fresh chicken is marinated in salt, soy protein concentrate, and MSG before cooking.

Crust is amazingly high in salt, MSG, and fat.

Pressure cooking makes the chicken moist and forces flavor into the meat.

Colonel Sanders' eleven herbs and spice blend are found in everyone's cupboard.
W. Poundstone in *Big Secrets*[1]

India found KFC chicken exceeded the levels of MSG allowed in foods.
Source: Wikipedia[2]

Kentucky Fried Chicken (KFC) is a member of the YUM! Brands, which also owns Pizza Hut, Taco Bell, A & W, All-American Food, and Long John Silvers. In the United States, the Colonel has almost 3,500 stores, and worldwide, more than 11,000 restaurants in 80 countries. And it's hard to believe such chicken dominance was started by a 65-year-old gentleman who used his $105 Social Security check to open his first store in 1952! The Colonel is also the most rapidly growing fast-food chain in China, with more than 1,300 stores, and one opening almost every day. Two million Chinese eat at its shops daily.

Since I am a big fan of KFC's (I like the taste of both original and extra crispy), let's take a closer look into the food science and physiology behind one of the most popular foods ever invented. KFC's annual sales are now at $9 billion with a pretax profit of $1 billion—*non mauvais!*[3]

Liking Colonel's Chicken

Let's investigate these primary areas for the answer:

- Investigate the eleven herbs and spices for "magic" ingredients.

- Analyze the crust for fat and salt levels.

- Evaluate the chicken cooking method.

1. Caloric Density

One way to make food tastier is to increase the caloric density. Although humans evolved in a relatively low-density foraging environment, foods with concentrated calories are a special treat, and humans quickly learn to prefer them. Some scientists suggest that as our omnivore diet included more energy-dense foods, our stomach became smaller and our brains got bigger.[4] For example, humans (cookivores) discovers cheese-making many thousands of years ago. Start with a food with low caloric density (fresh milk at 0.6), and, through casein extraction and fermentation, we have a nutritious final product (cheese) with a CD of almost 3.8.

Raw chicken breast meat without the skin has a CD of 1.35. KFC's Original Recipe Chicken Breast has 19 grams of fat and 380 calories, a CD of 2.3. Extra Crispy elevates the CD to 2.9. (Compared to a Burger King Double Whopper with 68 grams of fat and 1,061 calories, the chicken appears a little healthier.) If you remove the skin and breading from the Original Recipe, the fat content drops to 3 grams, 0 grams of trans fat, and only 140 calories. Although it is difficult to know the weight of the crust, I estimate it to be 50 grams. The caloric density of the skin would be 380 minus 140 kcals, or 240 divided by 50 grams; this equals a caloric density of 5.0! This is the average level of snack foods like potato chips. Ergo, the chicken is only a vehicle for eating the skin.

2. Taste-Active Compounds

a. <u>Salt Content</u>. Based upon the nutritional information on the KFC Web site, an Original Recipe chicken breast contains 2.8 grams of sodium chloride or a whopping 50 percent of your requirement in just one piece of chicken; and most of this is in the skin! Sodium chloride is, of course, a major hedonic solute, and I've calculated that the salt in the skin may be as high as 5–7 percent by weight. Compare that to soy sauce at 10–12 percent salt by weight. (KFC used to sell chicken skins as a snack.) Total salt content of the chicken is 1.7 percent, strangely close to the salt content of Doritos corn chips. Perhaps there is something magical with this sodium level in snack and fast foods. But if our preference for salt in food is around 1 percent, why do we like foods with almost double the salt concentration?

   After pondering this contradiction in salt liking, the answer came to me! In foods that are primarily water (soups)—the most preferred levels of salt is similar to the blood saline concentration of 0.9 percent; but in dry food systems (chips, French fries) salt preference goes up because we dilute the food with our saliva.[5,6,7,8] Thus is the wisdom of the body—our most preferred level of salt in foods is osmotically equivalent to our bloodstream sodium levels.

The Colonel did add MSG to his chicken and still does today based on the nutritional information available on their Web site; we just don't know how much. We have seen that MSG enhances salt taste pleasure and increases the salt sensation on the tongue. We know that the brain likes the "umami" taste, and it has its own neural representation. Poundstone discovers, through testing, that the original eleven herbs and spices never existed (although they do add them now, I believe).[1] After one of my many lectures to the food industry on "Food Pleasure," one gracious seasoning company actually showed me the spice processing area for the KFC blend; and yes, they use eleven herbs and spices, and they actually break up the formula so that no one knows the final blend. Based on my research, the ingredients that contribute most to the chicken's great flavor, exactly what Poundstone uncovers, are simply: salt, MSG, and pepper extracts—the most important hedonic tastants. And you can certainly duplicate this at home. Although the herbs evoke some warm memories from past eating experiences, they are not direct hedonic stimulants. KFC continues to add MSG directly and indirectly by using hydrolysates of soybean, wheat, or both. And based upon the evaluation of the aroma profile, I can detect Italian seasonings in the blend—thyme, oregano, and/or rosemary.

3. Chicken Moistness

> The Black Pearl curse on the crew made all food too dry and liquids failed to quench one's thirst.
> Captain Barbossa in *Pirates of the Caribbean: The Curse of the Black Pearl*

a. <u>Increased Salivation</u>. My salivation theory states that we prefer foods that are moist or evoke saliva during the mastication process. Saliva is critical for hedonic solute contact with taste buds; simply put, no taste, no pleasure. Saliva also fosters food lubrication and enhances the entire eating experience. Even dry foods like saltine crackers have salt on top and a flaky texture that fosters salivation. Add a little fat, and you have the perfect lubricator and salivary food (potato chips). Chips have a texture that melts down quickly and stimulates salivary flow. The tastiest foods should evoke saliva or at least provide lubrication and moistness. Many chefs of fine cuisines know this secret. French food utilizes sweet and savory sauces; Chinese and Indian foods are almost entirely finished with a sauce or glaze. Now, the Colonel's unique method of cooking chicken utilizes a pressure cooker, a somewhat unorthodox method for frying chicken, which is seldom used in Southern cooking. This technique cooks chicken quickly under pressure (less than half the time) and keeps or locks the moisture inside the meat. Pressure cooking may also drive some of the salt and MSG into the meat, further adding flavor and taste. But that's not all; it is likely that this method may also create flavor compounds that we home cooks cannot duplicate with the traditional pan frying. This combination of frying and steaming provided the Colonel with his unique flavor signature.

b. <u>Skin Moistness</u>. Pressure cooking not only cooks quickly but increases the moisture content of the food. Regular fried chicken can be fairly dry, especially if it is not brined or soaked in buttermilk (the traditional method). Traditional fried chicken takes a few seconds to activate the taste buds during ingestion since the surface is dry—but not the Colonel's. The crust is very moist and is still filled with oil in a semi-emulsified state. Add to this unique crust lots of salt and MSG (in probably the perfect ratio of ten to one), and you have a powerful hedonic motivation to eat. Although many find eating chicken skin unpalatable, the use of a pressure cooker, a breading rich in hedonically active tastants in a semi-emulsified form, and the generous addition of salt and MSG—transformed eating chicken into eating the chicken *skin*.

c.   <u>Taste and Bioactive Compounds</u>. Restaurants are not compelled to list their ingredients per se, so we have to guess what is in the crust. The KFC Web site does list that there are milk, egg, wheat, and soy ingredients present, but we do not know the exact quantities of each. Soy and wheat ingredients are probably the source of the plant hydrolysates containing MSG and other flavor-active compounds and flavors. Eggs, milk, and wheat flour are the likely base of the chicken coating.

In summary, Mr. Poundstone's investigation into the "secrets" of Colonel Sanders chicken was right on the mark. His research, using a food scientist unmasked the four major flavor active ingredients in the coating: flour, salt, pepper, and monosodium glutamate. The other half of the secret he said, is the cooking technique (pressure cooking) that retains chicken's moistness and juiciness.[1]

Interestingly, wheat flour contains the wheat protein fraction (gliadin), which has the highest concentration of glutamic acid of any plant protein (almost 45 percent). Corn and peas also contain high amounts of natural glutamate; pea puree is popular in French soups, and where would Tex-Mex be without maize?

Duplicating the Colonel

To create great tasting fried chicken at home, all you need is a good recipe with a few tasty hedonic additions. Start with the excellent fried chicken recipe in the cookbook, *The New Best Recipe* by the editors of *Cook's Illustrated*. (This tome contains recipes with food-science explanations to create great tasting food.[8]) Moist and flavorful chicken begins with a brining solution; follow their instructions on creating a chicken soak of salt, sugar, buttermilk, garlic, bay leaves, and paprika. To closely duplicate the Colonel's formula, in the *Cook's Illustrated* coating mix recipe, add an additional 2 teaspoons popcorn salt, 1/3 teaspoon MSG (Accent), and 1 teaspoon of white pepper. Remember that MSG is used in smaller amounts than salt, adding more does *not* improve the taste measurably.

Use the 10:1 rule—ten parts salt to one part MSG. When I make this dish, I add 1 teaspoon of Emeril's original seasoning to the batter mix just before frying.

KFC and Trans Fat

The Colonel has announced the use of a trans fat-free soybean oil (low linolenic) in its cooking fryers in over 5,500 U.S. restaurants. Michael Jacobson, the director of the Center of Science in the Public Interest, hailed the change and said KFC deserves a "bucketful of praise." The chicken, however, contains the same amount of fat calories.[9] Why won't McDonald's switch? Although McDonald's reduced trans fat in some menu items, switching to a zero-trans cooking oil may actually increase the "saturated" fat content of the fried foods. In addition, I suspect that the healthier oils may not produce that special "taste" and aroma that made McDonald's fries the gold standard.[8] But with the advent of new research on what makes food tasty, it would be relatively easy to make the switch and even *improve* the taste and flavor as Wendy's proved. You can have it both ways—no trans and plenty of taste!

References

1. Poundstone, W. 1983. *Big Secrets*. New York: Quill.

2. KFC. Wikipedia. http://en.wikipedia.org/wiki/Kentucky_Fried_ Chicken

3. Fast foods yummy secret. The economist. Aug. 25, 2005. http:www.economist.com/business/displayStory.cfm?story_id= 4316138

4. Paleodiet & paleolithic nutrition. Beyond vegetarianism. http:// www.beyondveg.com/cat/paleodiet/index.shtml

5. Schulkin, J. 1991. *Sodium Hunger*. Cambridge: Cambridge University Press.

6. Bertino, M. Beauchamp, G. K., and K. Engelman. Long-term reduction in dietary sodium alters the taste of salt. *Am. J. Clin. Nutr.*, 36:1134–44, 1982.

7.   Pangborn, R. M., and S. D. Pecore. Taste perception of sodium chloride in relation to dietary intake of salt. *Am. J. Clin. Nutr.*, 35:510–20, 1982.

8.   Editors of *Cook's Illustrated* Magazine. 2004. *The New Best Recipe*. 2nd ed. Brookline, MA: America's Test Kitchen.

9.   Jargon, J. KFC's trans-fat ban puts pressure on McDonald's. ChicagoBusiness, Oct. 30, 2006. http://www.chicagobusiness.com/cgi-bin/news.pl?id=22655

10. Adamy, J. How Jim Skinner flipped McDonald's. *Wall Street Journal*, Jan. 5, 2007.

CHAPTER 13

▼

WHY PEOPLE LIKE DIET VANILLA SODA

The brain has separate systems for behavioral reward; the picture of a well-known brand (Coke) completely biased the preference in a positive manner. [1]

"Papa, I love Diet Coke."
Clarissa, age 4 (my daughter)

Of all the myriad of soft drinks in the marketplace, this one is my favorite. I love the taste and flavor and the high carbonation of Diet Vanilla Coke. In fact, I like it so much I have to limit my intake some days. Apparently, I am not alone; there are numerous blogs touting the "Cult of Diet Coke," and a number of celebrities suffer this addiction as well, including Donald Trump, Mariah Carey, Elton John, and Shania Twain. I started thinking about why we like diet sodas so much. In particular, why does adding vanilla flavor to Diet Coke make the "real thing" more appealing? So we know it's pleasurable, perhaps uniquely so—but why? Why is Diet Coke (and all its variations) the third-best-selling soft drink worldwide?[2] Let's break down the physiology of Diet Vanilla Coke perception. We also need to explain that if real sugar is so pleasurable, why are more than half of all the Coke and Pepsi colas sugar free?

1. Diet Vanilla Coke Is Wet

Diet Coke's ingredient statement lists carbonated water, caramel color, aspartame, phosphoric acid, potassium benzoate, natural flavors citric acid, and caffeine. The high water content (about 99 percent) activates the oral receptors for water taste which in turn activate the hedonic cortical taste centers.[3] Hence, drinking water is pleasurable in its own right. Water taste in the mouth activates a unique place in the brain called the primary and secondary taste cortex. And after consuming salty food or after an intense workout, one can really feel the magnified hedonic properties of water ingestion (which makes sense). An ice-cold Bud Light after a long hike is almost a mystical taste/pleasure experience. Hence, Diet Coke's high water content contributes to both rapid hydration and oral water taste stimulation.

2. Diet Vanilla Coke Is *Really* Sweet

In addition to salt taste, sweet taste is the other huge generator of pleasure. Hardwired from birth, our liking of sweet taste almost knows no limits. In a study I completed on the level of sweetness liking in lemonade at UC Davis under Professor Pangborn, I was surprised to find that many people prefer really sweet lemonade, much higher than the standard 10 percent sucrose level. In fact, some panelist preferred 18 percent sugar—like drinking maple syrup! In the animal literature, scientists comment that the sweeter the stimuli the greater the animal will work to acquire it. And the perceived sweetness level of Diet Coke is *much* higher and more lingering than the sugary Classic counterpart (in my estimation). Although it is sensorially difficult to compare sugar and high-intensity sweeteners (aspartame) for sweetness equivalencies, I think Diet Coke and Diet Pepsi are very sweet indeed—perhaps equal to a sugar level much higher than 10 percent w/v. Sweetness level is directly proportional to pleasure perception.

3. Diet Vanilla Coke Is Carbonated

The importance of carbonation cannot be underestimated. Take your Diet Coke; shake the heck out of it, then see if it tastes just as good as before! In the same manner, take alcohol out of wine, and it tastes like watered down Kool-Aid. The importance of "feel" in the taste of food is underappreciated; that is why we (Hyde and Witherly) invented the dynamic contrast theory to account for all the extra pleasure derived from orosensation, first studied by physiologist H. P. Ziegler.[4] Carbonation creates intense sensation during the ingestion of soda; but it is the dynamic changing character that is the most important property—high to low intensity. The brain likes this contrast effect. Many years ago, I recall that Royal Crown Cola advertised its cola as "easy on the syrup and easy on the gas." Perhaps it was too *easy*. The company slowly lost market share and disappeared as a serious player in the soft drink marketplace.

Neuroscientists and sensory experts at UC Davis (including my good friend, Dr. Mike O'Mahony) studied carbon dioxide (CO_2) perception. His group discovered that carbonation was highly desirable, but the physiological underpinnings are not well understood.[5] They found that CO_2 (a small, lipophilic molecule) is a strong trigeminal stimulant affecting pain receptors when CO_2 converts to carbonic acid in the mouth. (The trigeminal nerve (V) is the cranial sensory nerve responsible for carrying the sensations of irritation, texture, and temperature to the brain.) The authors propose that CO_2 liking may involve the mere exposure effect (familiarity increases liking), thrill of sensation, reinforcing satiety effects (feeling fuller is rewarding), or a surge in brain endorphins due to a painful stimuli.[6] The authors may be correct on all points. I also believe that CO_2 provides dynamic contrast in the food, which increases *arousal* or the attention to the stimuli. In effect, carbonation enhances oral and mental attention to the ingested food, increasing overall sensation and pleasure. Hence, carbonation's wonderful activation of pain and arousal, similar to many spices, *enhances* overall food perception and pleasure.

4. Diet Vanilla Coke Contains CO_2, a Unique, 100 percent Trigeminal Aroma Stimulant

Aroma perception involves both an "aroma" component and a "feel" or "burning" component (called trigeminal). Almost all aromas are a combination of the two, but a few common odorants are considered pure aromas or pure trigeminal. Vanilla is considered a pure aroma without much feel to it in the nose. On the other end of the spectrum is carbon dioxide, which has no aroma whatsoever and is considered a *pure* trigeminal chemical aroma. In one study, aromas with a high trigeminal (TG) component (rosemary) activate more parts of the brain than aromas such as vanilla. In addition, high TG aromas tend to reduce the adaptation to an aroma—in other words; you become less bored with the flavor and can drink it every day. Now, this is a very important observation with huge ramifications in food preparation and design. The presence of CO_2, therefore, reduces or eliminates the sensory specific satiety to Diet Vanilla Coke flavor. People drink Diet Coke all day long and day after day, even though the aroma is very complex and distinctive. This trigeminal reduction of sensory specific satiety needs further investigation and clarification—the food pleasure implications are huge. For example, this "CO_2 Effect" might be used to increase arousal and decrease pleasure drop (during consumption) in many different food systems.

5. Diet Vanilla Coke Contributes to Ping-Pong Pleasure

Soda is low in sodium; in fact Diet Vanilla Coke contains only a few milligrams and qualifies for the very-low-sodium claim. Soda is frequently consumed with savory (salty) food items: French fries, hamburgers, sandwiches, and pizza. It is the perfect contrast to oral stimulation; that is, take a salty bite, swallow, wash the mouth out with low-sodium soda, and start the cycle of self-stimulation all over again, ping-pong pleasure.[7] Adults drink beer or wine with meals, and the same principle applies—both are very low in sodium. The sweet taste also has a ping-pong pleasure effect since food is savory and the soda is sweet. It's like eating dessert after each bite without getting too full!

Diet soda is also a major player in vanishing caloric density, foods are preferred because they contribute great oral hedonics but do not have enough calories to generate feedback satiation from the stomach. Popcorn is a prime example. Even Lay's potato chips qualify due to their thinness; lots of stimulation per gram of chip! Thus soda, being sweet, is the perfect complement to savory junk food. This is the answer to why Diet Vanilla Coke and diet sodas are so popular—sweet taste without satiety induction—more stimulation and at a higher level since calories dampen pleasure responses in the brain. Sipping sweet soda during bites of a savory lunch is the ultimate in taste contrast, both activities promote enhanced food pleasure, food stimulation, and perhaps, overeating.

6. Diet Coke Has Vanilla

The addition of a strong vanilla aroma adds a number of interesting effects to the basic Diet Coke flavor profile. We know that the aroma of vanilla does not seem to cause satiety or reduce unpleasantness in the brain; in contrast to a distinctive aroma like rosemary. This non-adaptation or habituation to vanilla is an intriguing and unsolved phenomenon and noted by many researchers in the sensory literature.

The ability of certain flavors to be eaten everyday may lie in the biology of aroma learning in utero and the flavors of breast or bottle milk. The fetus routinely samples the amniotic fluid after the twelfth week of gestation. Gary Beauchamp and the researchers at Monell Chemical Senses Center note that infants prefer the garlic and carrot flavors the mothers ate during pregnancy. Nursing women, given a vanilla flavor to ingest, prompted their infants to suck more vigorously and consume more milk.[8] Vanilla flavor readily transfers to breasts milk, and vanilla is one of the most common used spices in cooking.[9] Perhaps the universal liking for this aroma becomes conditioned in infancy, and whenever we smell (and taste) vanilla as adults, it brings forth associations of comfort, nutrition, and mom.

Vanilla flavor, not surprisingly, activates the pain-sensitive *vanilloid* receptors. Although much of the attention is on capsaicin (hot peppers) and black pepper (piperine) activating the heat-sensing pain neurons; vanilla can bind very tightly to this receptor, (along with heat and acids). The synthetic vanilla substitute, vanillin, and ethyl vanillin, if taken in higher amounts, has a unique burning and tingling effect, especially farther down the throat. I discovered this the hard way when I added too much artificial vanilla to a food product and noticed a strange but persistent burn in the back of my throat.

7. Diet Vanilla Cokes Uses Aspartame

Aspartame is a controversial sweetener, and numerous Web sites have been trashing this ingredient as cancer-causing, oozing methanol, and the cause of headaches and migraines.[10] I've even seen a paper indicating that aspartame is a painkiller at high doses. None of this bothers me. Aspartame, simply put, is a good, natural sweetener (made from amino acids). All high-intensity sweeteners have sensory and metabolic pros and cons—and Web sites that proclaim their toxicity. Although aspartame may be controversial, Diet Vanilla Coke is still number three in worldwide sales; you'd expect more complaints if the rumored harmful effects were true.

a. High-intensity sweeteners potentiate aroma. Researchers, using advanced sensory and physiological techniques (brain scans), find that sweetness can potentiate the perception of an aroma but not vice versa. Diet Vanilla Coke is very sweet, a lot sweeter than if it was sweetened with sucrose or high fructose corn syrup. This greatly increases the perception of aroma and helps form a very strong aroma-taste complex.[11]

b. High-intensity sweeteners may decrease appetite. Despite the negativity about the use of aspartame, researchers Peter Rogers et al. (1995) repeatedly demonstrate that aspartame may actually *increase* one's feeling of fullness and satiety—which is a positive effect.[12] The mechanism may be because the amino acids in aspartame increase the intestinal hormone (CCK), known to increase fullness during eating.

New Coke Blak

Just a few comments on the new product from Coca-Cola called Coke Blak. I purchased a bottle of Coke Blak from the local store—a bit higher in price than I expected—and tried it over ice. It tasted like mixing Coke with coffee and caramel. I haven't tasted anything this *confused* in a long time. My wife agreed with my sensory evaluation. Coffee and Coke don't mix unless you have had little exposure to each and are learning this flavor for the first time. Since Coke has a competent sensory evaluation staff, I'm guessing it passed the taste tests. Coke's president, Neville Isdell, says that Coke Blak is indulgent like the coffee at Starbucks.[13] The problem with his understanding of indulgence is that the true physiological definition carries a gastric-intestinal component of sensing calories—indulgence means high calories and high taste. Coke Blak is low in calories, at 45 kcals per bottle—with only twice the caffeine of regular Coke (80 mg, similar to Red Bull). Starbucks *is* indulgent, because you can pack 450 kcals into a high-caffeine milkshake with real sugar, salt, and fat. Blak, I believe, may evoke the principle of cognitive dissonance—separate and quite distinct sensory memories of flavors and tastes are suddenly combined, confusing the brain-gut-sensory memory and causing the evocation of *neophobia*—or food rejection. Cola is served cold, and coffee is served hot—as far as the brain goes; and each has its own distinct sensory signature. Coke Blak is likely to appeal to those who have limited sensory experience with either coffee or cola flavoring. But sales appear to be good (especially in France), so perhaps I'm *all wet* here.

References

1. McClure, S., Li, J., Tomlin, D., Lypert, K. S., and L. M. Montague. Neural correlates of behavioral preference for culturally familiar drinks. *Neuron*, 44:379–87, 2004.

2. Gillin, E. The cult of diet coke. The Black Table, March 17, 2004. http://www.blacktable.com/gillin040317.htm

3. de Araujo, I. E., Kringelback, M. L., Rolls, E. T., and F. McGlone. Human cortical response to water in the mouth and the effect on thirst. *J. Neurophysiol.*, 90:865–76, 2003.

4. Ziegler, H. P. Trigeminal orosensation and ingestive behavior in the rat. *Behav. Neurosci.*, 97:62–97, 1983.

5. Dessirier, J. M., Simons, C. T., Carstens, M. I., O'Mahony, M., and E. Carstens. Psychophysical and neurobiological evidence that the oral sensation elicited by carbonated water is of chemogenic origin. *Chem. Senses*, 25:277–84, 2000.

6. Carstens, E., Carstens, M. I., Dessirier, J. M., O'Mahony, M., Simons, C. T., Suda, M., and S. Sudo. It hurts so good: oral irritation by spices and carbonated drinks and the underlying neural mechanisms. *Food Qual. Prefer.*, 2002, 13:431–43, 2002.

7. Hyde, B. Ping pong pleasure principle. Personal communication, 1987.

8. Mennella, J., Griffin, C. E., and G. K. Beauchamp. Flavor programming during infancy. *Pediatrics*. 113:840-5, 2001.

9. Mennella, J., and G. K. Beauchamp. Human infants' response to vanilla flavor in mother's milk and formula. *Infant Behav. Dev.*, 19:13–19, 1996.

10. Soffritti, M., Belpoggi, F., Esposti, D. D., Lambertini, L., Tibaldi, E., and A. Rigano. First experimental demonstration of the multipoten-

tial carcinogenic effects of aspartame administered in the feed to Sprague-Dawley rats. *Environ. Health Perspect.*, 114:379–85, 2006.

11. King, B. M., Arents, P., Bouter, N., Duineveld, C. A., Meyners, D. M., Schroff, S. I., and S. T. Soekhai. Sweetener/sweetness-induced changes in flavor perception and flavor release of fruity and green character in beverages. *J. Agric. Food Chem.*, 54:2671–7, 2006.

12. Rogers, P. J., Burley, V. J., Alikhanizadeh, L. A., and J. E. Blundell. Postingestive inhibition of food intake by aspartame: importance of interval between aspartame administration and subsequent eating. *Physiol. Behav.*, 57:489–93, 1995.

13. Terhune, C. Recharging Coca-Cola. *Wall Street Journal*, April 17, 2006. http://online.wsj.com/public/article/SB114523376275027237 -apLj4CLqnqfmZ23_D1qdmI60t1s_20060425.html?mod=mktw

CHAPTER   14

▼

WHY WE LIKE FRENCH
FRIES

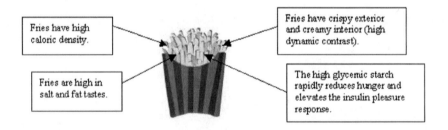

Fries have high
caloric density.

Fries have crispy exterior
and creamy interior (high
dynamic contrast).

Fries are high in
salt and fat tastes.

The high glycemic starch
rapidly reduces hunger and
elevates the insulin pleasure
response.

Evolution creates a physiological demand for fat-laden and salty French fries.[1]

Nothing is worse than a limp fry.[2]

Dr. Liz Sloan, a respected food writer and president of the consulting firm, Sloan
Trends (sloantrend@sbcglobal.net), cites a survey of the most preferred foods by
men, women, college kids, and children less than seven years old.[3] The results are
interesting, but not that surprising, based upon the pleasure principles we have
learned thus far. Highly preferred foods share the following qualities: high caloric
density; high amounts of salt, fat, or sugar; dynamic contrast (especially textural);
and rapid satiation or reduction of hunger. The results of the most preferred
foods were as follows:

Men	Women	Students	Kids <7
Hamburger	French Fries	French Fries	French Fries
French Fries	Hamburger	Hamburger	Pizza
Pizza	Pizza	Pizza	Chicken Nuggets

French fries are the food jewel in more than 31,000 McDonald's restaurants in 119 countries. In fact, McDonald's pioneered the modern French fry—cooked once (blanched in oil), then frozen and sent to restaurants for a second fry—a method first used by the French and Belgians in the early 1800's. Emily Sohn discusses the sensory and food science behind the perfect French fry.[4] In her article, she explains that the perfect French fry has "essential contrast"; crisp exterior and creamy interior. This, of course, is the theory of dynamic contrast—one of the major reasons we like fries or any other food with textural contrast.

In the fast-food arena, there are a number of ways to make good French fries; some are cooked twice, (McDonald's), some use a flavor-enhanced batter coating (Burger King), and some are just fried once, (In-N-Out Burger). The frying methods affect the caloric content and energy density (recall that humans like higher energy density). For example, McDonald's has a caloric density of 3.35 (570 kcals/170 g), and In-N-Out, only fried once, is still surprisingly high at 3.2 (400 kcals/125 g). Burger King (BK), an acknowledged leader in unhealthy fare, comes in at 3.1 (500 kcals/160 g). BK, however, hits the 50 percent fat calories level (McDonald's is 47 percent), *and* uses more hydrogenated fat than the other chains.[5] McDonald's fries, however contain 8 g trans fat versus 6 g for Burger King.

BK touts its fries as the "Taste that beat McDonald's." Burger King states that its taste test, (in 1998) revealed a 57 percent versus 35 percent preference for its fries.[6] The batter coating increases the crispness on the French fry exterior and keeps them hotter, longer. Currently, its Web site puts the sodium content of the large fries at 820 mg—significantly higher than at McDonald's. Thus, based on the physiology of pleasure, which is the better fry? The winner is Burger King for four reasons:

- Batter coating reduces the number of limp fries, thus more dynamic contrast.

- Batter coating enhances the amount of sodium and probably hidden MSG derivatives; the sodium content was almost 2–3 times the level of McDonald's.

- Batter coating allows a longer hold time in the fry itself before it becomes limp, a significant advantage in the fast-food industry.

- Batter coating acts as a "heat jacket" that significantly extends the heat-holding capacity. Hotter food is better food.

My favorite? I like the made-to-order fries at Jack in the Box; the potato skins are still on (visual contrast) and just an extraordinary potato flavor—it doesn't taste like the cooking oil.

The Perfect French Fry

Eric Schlosser, author of the popular and disturbing *Fast Food Nation* (a great read), goes into great detail about the French fry that made McDonald's famous.[7] In summary, he states it was the cooking oil that made the difference (93 percent beef tallow and 7 percent soybean oil); and this blend was used for decades. In 1990, the company switched to vegetable oil due to the health concerns vis-à-vis tallow, so the vegetable oil used was *flavored* like beef tallow to make up the difference.[7] To this day, the vented aroma of products cooking at McDonald's is so distinctive that I can pick out that restaurant miles before I see the yellow logo. Eli Sanders, writer for the *Boston Globe*, notes that the French fries at McDonald's are essentially cooked twice—central suppliers wash, steam-peel, cut, blanch, dry, par-fry, and add a bit of beef extract flavor before freezing.[8] However, just adding beef aroma does *not* automatically make it a preferred fry over another. Taste is not 90 percent aroma—I am always dismayed when I hear this statement. Each sense has a huge but *different* role to play in food pleasure. Food pleasure is mostly taste, not aroma, but aroma is the gatekeeper that allows the food to be eaten. The pleasure neurotransmitters (for example, opioids) are *best* activated by taste and orosensation.

But this is not the whole story.

McDonald's has recently disclosed that it also adds "wheat and dairy ingredients" to the fries; both are potential allergens and were probably "inadvertently" (their term) left off the ingredient list. Dave Carpenter, writes that McDonald's does not add wheat or dairy proteins to the potatoes, but the cooking oil has wheat and dairy derivatives as flavoring agents.[9] These flavoring agents are not protein based and therefore, cannot be allergenic.

So what exactly is going on here? A food scientist friend explained that McDonald's probably uses flavored cooking oil to make up for the loss of the nice beef flavor of tallow fat. The potato supplier uses his own flavoring blend before sending them off to McDonald's. I asked him this million-dollar question—what type of flavorings do they add to the cooking oil? His response? Well, the response was the same as I received when I asked a friend who worked as an engineer on a nuclear sub, "So really, how fast and deep does it really go?" His answer was, "I do know, and if I told you, I'd be sunk." The cooking oil flavors are probably a closely guarded flavor complex that management believes is part of McDonald's success. They are justifiably paranoid about changing anything that could possibly affect sales. Here is the latest update from the McDonald's Web site on the ingredients:

<u>French fry ingredients</u>
Potatoes, partially hydrogenated soybean oil, natural flavor (beef, wheat, and dairy sources), dextrose, sodium acid pyrophosphate (to preserve natural color). Cooked in partially hydrogenated vegetable oils (may contain partially hydrogenated soybean oil and/or partially hydrogenated corn oil and/or partially hydrogenated canola oil and/or cottonseed oil and/or sunflower oil and/or corn oil). Contains derivatives of wheat and dairy.

So let's speculate on what the flavorings could be. Whenever I see wheat extract I always think, a natural source of MSG. In fact, gliadin protein (one of the major wheat proteins) is the richest source of natural glutamates in the plant kingdom. The flavoring also contains beef flavoring compounds, which include tasty Maillard reaction products and a myriad of taste-active amino acids. In support of this, a company spokesperson says McDonald's adds a beef broth analogue to create a much tastier flavor complex.[8]

So both the potato supplier and the McDonald's oil have wheat and dairy derivatives (natural MSG) and flavors. There still is the problem of animal derivatives with vegetarians and certain religious groups. But the flavor derivatives undergo hydrolysis during manufacturing (protein is broken down by enzymes), which destroys the allergic epitopes on the gliaden molecule, so if you are gluten sensitive, there is little risk. Finally, the added dextrose in the spice blend (a reducing sugar) adds a little browning-reaction flavor to the French fry during deep frying. As for the cooking oil, the dairy extract listing *may be* dairy fat extractives (butter oil). Beef tallow and butter oil have common flavor elements (they come from the same animal).

Cooking Oil Secret: Trans Fat Oil (TF)

Humans prefer aromas that signal the presence of essential nutrients.[10]

In 2005, McDonald's lost a suit, brought by artery activist Stephen Joseph (bantransfat.com), over the high trans fat content in their foods. Although McDonald's laudably reduced trans fat in some chicken entrees, it still has not switched the fryer to the healthier oils. Just recently, Frito Lay has touted zero trans fat in most of its snacks, a significant nutritional achievement that has cost the company millions (in higher costs) for the high-stability oil (corn, cottonseed, or high-stability sunflower). MSNBC reports that a large order of McDonald's fries has 8 grams of trans fat per serving.[11] This is one of the highest levels found in any fast food. Scientists like Dr. Steen Stender (a cardiologist in Denmark) calls trans fat a *metabolic poison,*[12] similar to Dr. Randall Buddington's terminology "cellular sludge."

And the number three fast-food giant, Wendy's, has just announced the use of trans fat-free frying oil (Cargill combo of corn and soy oils) in the 560 million pounds of French fries it sells each year in the United States.[13] A spokesman for Wendy's said the switch was reportedly cost neutral, but the oil does have a shorter shelf life and must be treated with more respect. The new oil is also lower in saturated fat by 20 percent, yet another heart-healthy advantage. Frito Lay's switch to the healthy fats (Lay's and Ruffles use NuSun sunflower oil) proceeded smoothly with nary a sensory complaint.

Trans fat is made by hydrogenating oil using a metal catalyst and a little pressure. This forces hydrogen atoms onto the fatty acid molecule's double bonds, creating greater stability against rancidity. However, the fatty acid molecule changes from the natural cis (same side) to the trans (opposite side). The shape of the new fat molecule is not normally found in nature. This *trans* configuration and the removal of the double bond keep oxygen from attacking the oil during frying. So the oil stays fresher much longer and is more suitable for repeat deep frying. Old oil has soapy and greasy off-flavors that most people associate with linseed oil or bad food at diners. The trans fat, however, has another interesting physical property—it acts more like solid shortening than liquid cooking oils. This means that if it is used for frying, the food is crispier. Solid fat Crisco (new formula is trans fat free) makes better (crispier) fried chicken than, say, olive oil. I've done the experiment myself, and the effect is more noticeable the longer the food sits. So the use of trans fat gives the food extra crispness, and the oil can be reused, saving millions in oil costs. (Imagine changing frying oil frequently in thirty thousand restaurants.) Trans and saturated fat, therefore, make a crisper fry with a creamier interior, which, after all, is what a French fry is all about.[14]

In a hilarious example of how a Google Web inquiry and advertising operates, I searched for trans fat and found a great syndicated article by Linda A. Johnson titled "Fast Food Fries, Chicken Fattier in US."[12] The article describes the metabolic horrors of trans fat and the high content in some U.S. foods. For example, a McDonald's large fry and chicken nuggets combo contains almost 10.2 grams— compared to the *same* version in Denmark at 0.33 grams of trans fat. And just *five* grams per day increases ischemic heart disease risk by 25 percent! But as the link came up, so did an advertisement for those interested in owning a KFC franchise—which announced elimination of trans fat from all menu items by 2007.[15]

Cooking Oil Flavoring Faux Pas?

When one puts natural or artificial flavors in oil, the flavor will affect everything that it cooks. That distinctive McDonald's smell wafting out the vents is mostly fat-soluble aromatics that scream French fries, with a hint of chicken fat. Assume for the moment, that the flavors added are beef tallow-like—and then everything cooked becomes beef tallow flavored. According to the theory of sensory specific satiety, this constant and continuous aroma will actually dull the sensory pleasure over time by decreasing the rate of response of olfactory neurons (in the brain's orbitofrontal cortex) to foods ingested. In reality, how much of a problem is this? Difficult to say, but chefs know that if every dish they serve up smells like bacon, the customer will look elsewhere for sensory pleasure; the senses are satiated. Variety is the spice of food (and life), and we sense variety by texture, taste, and aroma. My son, after a trip to Taco Bell, remarked, "I really like tacos, but I can't eat them every day; the problem with the food here is that it all *smells* the same!"

French Fries Liking

> The French fry is almost sacred to me.
> Ray Kroc in his autobiography *Grinding It Out*

1. French Fries Are High in Salt, Fat, and Starch

With about 50 percent calories from fat (the ideal junk food level), high levels of salt, and high glycemic starch, this food ranks number one in preference with women and number two with men. Salt is a primary hedonic solute, and potatoes have a naturally high amount of synergistic MSG, a terrific "umami" combination.

2. French Fries Are High in Caloric Density (CD)

We now know that evolutionary pressures reduced jaw and stomach sizes and favored our dietary cuisine to be high in calories in a small volume of food. French fries are approximately 3.3 in CD versus the starting raw potato at less than 1!

3. French Fries Have a High Glycemic Starch

According to some scientists, people prefer those food carbohydrates that are digested quickly. The gut quickly senses that carbohydrates have been ingested; the resulting insulin surge is both pleasurable and addicting *and* helps the brain memorize that food as highly preferred. French fries also support the cookivore theory of human cuisine evolution. Raw potato starch isn't digested particularly well; double fry it in fat, and this changes very quickly—increasing the digestibility by a factor of four![16] A baked Russet potato has a glycemic index higher than glucose—111 versus 100![17]

Halton et al. (2006) found a relationship between French fry consumption and Type 2 diabetes.[18] In a sample size of 85,000 nurses, women who substituted fries for whole grains have an increased rate of adult onset diabetes. The authors believe it is the high glycemic nature of cooked potato starch that's behind the blood sugar dysregulation.

4. Fatty Acids in the French Fry Enhance Sugar and Salt Perception

Gary Beauchamp, director of the famous Monell Chemical Senses Center, speculates that fatty acids (in the fries) may also enhance the sweetness of sugar and the saltiness of sodium chloride.[1] We know that fat is sensed in the mouth via texture and fatty acid activation of taste cells (mostly the polyunsaturated type), and we also know that the mouth likes the taste of emulsions. Fatty acids actually boost the sensation of salt and sugar, which is an important sensory principle of food pleasure. Most foods, however, are composed of triglycerides and not large amounts of free fatty acids (many have a rancid, bitter, or acrid taste)—but it is possible that a small amount of free acids, generated by deep fat frying, boost hedonic solute pleasure.

5. French Fry Aromas Are Resistant to Satiation

Certain food aromas, like vanilla aroma, are resistant to adaptation or boredom and can be eaten every day—bread, popcorn, or vanilla ice cream. French fries are eaten by millions of consumers, not only with burgers, but with chicken dishes as well—to the tune of over 75 pounds annually. Brain scans of individuals smelling vanilla odorants demonstrate a resistance to aroma extinction. Perhaps potato aroma is acting physiologically like the prototypical "pure" aroma, vanilla, and does not extinguish hedonically. Potatoes, then, can be eaten everyday without any flavor burnout.

Some French Fry and Potato Trivia[2,4,19a,b]

- Potatoes are a tuber (botanically a modified stem) first discovered in Peru, cultivated by the Incas as far back as 200 B.C. Many colored varieties exist: black, blue, red, and yellow shades.

- The potato is a member of the deadly nightshade family (Solanacea), which includes tomatoes, peppers, tobacco, eggplant, and petunias.

- Potato is the fifth largest crop worldwide; wheat is number one.

- Though potatoes were originally thought in Europe to be poisonous, the French chemist, Antoine August Parmentier grew potatoes and developed many famous dishes that are still part of French cuisine today. (He supposedly lived just on potatoes for seven years while being imprisoned in Germany.)

- President Thomas Jefferson brought potatoes (French fries) to the White House in 1802.

- Japan is the largest importer of U.S. potatoes.

- More than 4.5 billion pounds of fries are sold domestically each year.

- French fries and soft drinks are the two most profitable items in food service today.

- Potatoes are surprisingly nutritious, and the protein content, although low, is higher in essential amino acids than many other plant foods.

- French fries account for 25 percent of all potatoes sold in the Unites States.

- The average American eats over 60 pounds of French fries per year, although the amount is declining.

- The relationship between the growth of the Irish population and the introduction of the potato (grows well in the cooler climate) gave the spud a reputation as being an aphrodisiac.

- In the 1830s the French fry became a taste sensation in France and Belgium.

- The McDonald brothers spent much time and effort to develop the perfect French fry. Curing freshly dug potatoes at least three weeks to reduce sugars into starches was one insight (sugars burn; starches do not).

Making Your Own Perfect French Fries

Making good French fries, known as *frites* in France, is a culinary skill worth mastering; they will taste even better than those at McDonald's, and your friends will think you're a culinary genius. And as a plus, you can eliminate all the trans fat by using common vegetable oils found in the supermarket—canola, peanut, safflower, corn, soy, and the new zero grams trans fat all-vegetable Crisco. I use peanut oil for the high smoke point and the slightly nutty taste.

The Key to Good Fries

- Use a high-density potato like the Russet; other potatoes with waxy starch structures don't fry as well—save them for potato salad. The exception is the Yukon gold, an acceptable frying potato.

- Cut the fries into 1/4-inch sticks, the length of the potato. The McDonald's size is the perfect template to follow for the best crisp surface-to-creamy-interior effect. French fry cutters are available, where you push the potato through a wire mesh, but cutting them yourself with your $100 Japanese-style santoku knife (with hollow edge) is a lot more fun. Try to get the potato strips about the same size for best frying results. Potatoes are slippery when wet, so be careful; curl your fingers in a bit when holding the potatoes to keep from injuring the finger tips.

- Throw the potatoes into cold or icy water bath immediately after cutting. Three important food-science reactions occur. First, this washes off the surface starch and sugars, reducing the browning to a minimum; second, it inhibits enzymatic browning that would quickly turn the potato brown and unappetizing (polyphenol oxidase need oxygen to turn the potato brown), and finally, the water reenergizes the potato with fluid to increase the turgor or firmness of the fry. Let the potatoes soak at least half an hour; you can actually leave them in the water bath for up to a day. I usually toss in a little lemon juice, 2 tablespoons per quart of water, to further retard browning and enhance the white color of the fry. The produce protector, Fruit Fresh, is made with Vitamin C, which works just as well; use one teaspoon per quart of water.

- Use the double-fry method. The classic French or Belgian method cooks them twice. Fry them first at a lower temperature of 320–340°F (some call it blanching), for 3–5 minutes, and then fry them again at a higher temperature of 350–360°F. (I use a Delonghi fryer; crank it up as high as it goes.) If you clean the oil with a strainer, you can fry many times, up to ten or twelve depending on the food. To help keep the oil fresh, use this culinary trick. Go in your backyard and cut a few stalks of rosemary (culinary, not ornamental), tie them together, and add them to the hot oil when you have finished frying. The essential oils in rosemary are potent antioxidants and will help keep the oil fresh. The slight rosemary flavor imparted to the oil boils off quickly when you reheat the oil. Don't forget to discard the rosemary before turning on the fryer the next time.

- Use a stable and flavorful oil (like peanut oil, the classic turkey-frying medium). A good second choice is canola oil; you can buy large quantities at a good price from Costco. Speaking of deep-frying, the flavor compounds produced in the finished bird are amazingly tasty, especially if you brine the turkey ahead of time. On one occasion I took the left-over oil and sealed it to keep oxygen out, then later used to it to make French fries. The turkey flavor did find its way into the fries, but they still tasted wonderful—perhaps similar to what McDonald's flavored fries and oil are meant to create.

There are many recipes on how to make the perfect French fry, here is a listing of good recipes:

- Melinda Lee (Los Angeles radio chef). http://www.melindalee. com/recipearchive.html?action=124&item_id=314

- http://www.foodnetwork.com/food/recipes/recipe/ 0,1977,FOOD_9936_22763,00.html Emeril Lagasse recipe.

- Anthony Bourdain: *Les Halles Cookbook*, page 236–239.

- Thomas Keller: *Bouchon*, page 249.

- http://chef2chef.net/features/cynthia/article/2005-05.htm A number of French Fry recipes.

Final Comment:

The uses of healthy oils in making French fries may actually translate into increased fat pleasure upon ingestion! The new no trans fat oils have higher levels of mono and unsaturated fats (oleic, linoleic, and linolenic acids). And by using these oils, Wendy's will create better-tasting fried food (I suspect the company didn't know this physiology). Since essential fatty acids are very necessary for proper health and mental development, it's logical (read that *evolutionary*) for the oral cavity to detect critically important nutritional factors and make them pleasurable.[10]

References

1.   Neighmond, P. Jonesing for fries? Blame the cave man. *Morning Edition*, National Public Radio, storyId=4618562, March 2, 2005. http://www.npr.org/templates/story/story.php?storyId=4618562

2. Oe, T. The perfect French fry—what is it? *NSDU Agriculture Communication*, Jan. 22, 2004. http://www.ext.nodak.edu/extnews/newsrelease/2004/012204/11theper.htm

3. Sloan, E. Top ten global food trends. *Food Technol.*, Jan., 2006.

4. Sohn, E. Want fries with that? *UC Davis Magazine online*, summer, 2001. http://ucdavismagazine.ucdavis.edu/issues/su01/feature_2.html

5. Liebman, B., and M. Wootan. Trans fat. *Nutrition Action Newsletter*, June, 1999. http://www.cspinet.org/nah/6_99/transfat3.html

6. Burger King proclaims America's favorite fries, based on taste new ad aims to set the record straight versus McDonald's claim. Burger King Corporation. http://www.prnewswire.com/cgi-bin/stories.pl?ACCT=104&STORY=/www/story/10-22-1998/0000778270&EDATE=

7. Schlosser, E. 1991. *Fast Food Nation*. New York: Houghton Mifflin.

8. Sanders, E. McDonald's confirms that its French fries are made with beef extract. *Boston Globe*, May 4, 2001.

9. Carpenter, D. McDonald's: fries have potential allergens. *Associated Press*, Feb. 14, 2006. http://abcnews.go.com/Health/wireStory?id=1616591

10. Goff, S. A., and H. Klee. Plant volatile compounds: sensory cues for health and nutritional value? *Science*, 311:815–19, 2006.

11. Hellmich, N. You *really* don't want fries with that. *USA Today*, Feb. 6, 2006. http://www.usatoday.com/news/health/2006-02-06-hospital-fries_x.htm

12. Johnson, L. A. Fast-food fries, chicken fattier in U.S. Associated Press, April 12, 2006. http://www.breitbart.com/news/2006/04/12/D8GUMLEO0.html

13. Horovitz, B. Wendy's will be first fast foodie with healthier oil. *USA Today*, June 8, 2006. http://www.usatoday.com/money/industries/food/2006-06-08-wendys-usat_x.htm

14. Kita, A., Linsinska, G., and M. Powolny. The influence of frying medium degradation on fat uptake and texture of French fries. *J. Sci. Food Ag.*, 85:1113–18, 2005.

15. Arnt, M. How KFC went trans-fat free. BusinessWeek.com, Jan. 3, 2007. http://www.businessweek.com/print/innovate/content/jan2007/id20070103_466580.htm

16. Kimura, S. Glycemic carbohydrate and health: background and synopsis of the symposium. *Nutr. Rev.*, 61:S1–4, 2003.

17. Home of the glycemic index. http://www.glycemicindex.com/

18. Halton, T., Willet, W. C., Liu, S., Manson, J. E., Stampfer, M. J., and F. B. Hu. French fry consumption and risk of type-2 diabetes in women. *Am. J. Clin. Nutr.*, 83:284–90, 2006.

19a. United States Potato Board. http://www.uspotatoes.com/

19b. Stoller, D. The secret history of French fries. http://www.stim.com/Stim-x/9.2/fries/fries-09.2.html

CHAPTER 15

▼

WHY WE LIKE SPICES

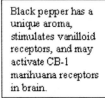

Black pepper has a unique aroma, stimulates vanilloid receptors, and may activate CB-1 marihuana receptors in brain.

Hot peppers bind to vanilloid receptors, increases endorphins and stimulate appetite.

Remy's ability to make steak au poivre is the only reason he is still employed.
Dan Brown in *The Da Vinci Code*

The culinary purpose of adding spices, herbs, smoking and salting food is to prevent bacteria from trying to kill us.[1]

In my lectures on food pleasure, I often ask the audience, "Why do we like black pepper on food?" and "Why is black pepper considered an essential part of almost any cuisine that has access to it?" Nearly every savory recipe ever made in Western cuisine says to add salt and pepper; the common phrase is to "correct the seasoning." This ubiquitous spice is used and found in just about every restaurant in the land with the exception of some Asian cuisines. So what is the response from the audience to my questions? Not a single hand goes up. Everyone knows black and hot peppers are great seasoning spices and make food taste better, but no one actually knows the physiological reasons.

Black Pepper

Black pepper, or *Piper nigrum*, is the fruit of a tropical vine that grows in a narrow climatological band—requiring lots of moisture, heat, and humidity. A native of the Indian region of the Western ghats of Kerala State, the fruits of the vine provide black, white, and green peppercorns.[2] The red type is actually another species entirely (*Schinus terebinthifolius*: pink pepper of the Brazilian type, or Peruvian type *Schinus molle*) but part of the same botanical family, *Anacardiaceae*. Black pepper is made by blanching the green berry in hot water, which ruptures the cell walls, allowing enzymes to blacken the pericarp during aging. White is a more mature black peppercorn with the outer pericarp washed off, exposing the inner seed. Green pepper is produced by freeze-drying the unripe fruit.

Piperine is the (mostly) fat-soluble alkaloid found almost exclusively in the black pepper vine *Piper nigrum*. *Piper longum* (Long pepper) is a well-known Ayurvedic ingredient. It was used in early commerce and prized by the Romans and early Eurocultures. *Piper longum* contains more piperine but lacks the wonderful aromatic terpenes of black pepper. Long pepper was used in many early dishes for its fire and sweet tastes.[3]

Hot Peppers

Few other spices caused such a commotion, influenced history, and spread so quickly as the black pepper berry from the East Indies; marijuana and hot peppers (*Capsicum annum*) are the notable exceptions. When Columbus accidentally stumbled on the New Word in search for black pepper, he found himself immersed in unfamiliar foods such as vanilla, potatoes, maize, beans, tomatoes, pumpkins, squash, and, of course, chocolate. Columbus called the hot chili plant "pepper," or pimiento, which is the Spanish word for black pepper.[4] Unlike the potato or tomato, hot peppers spread rapidly around the globe and are probably more popular than black pepper; and a whole lot cheaper. This South American plant was a favorite of the American Indians, and many cuisines would be less flavorful without it—Indian, Szechwan, Mexican, Korean (think Kimchi), and Thai are just a few examples. The taxonomy of peppers is quite confusing, but the most important varieties are covered by *Capsicum annuum*, var. *annum* (cayenne, jalapeno, and bell); *Capsicum frutescens* (Tabasco), and *Capsicum chinense* (Habanero).[4]

Capsaicin and its five analogues are the active compounds in hot peppers. They stimulate oral mouth burn and pain via the vanilloid receptor (VR-1—a trigeminal orosensory nociceptive neuron). Capsaicin also appears to stimulate taste buds in general, including the sense of bitter taste, similar to the effects of menthol.[5] For an excellent summary on capsaicin, see the link below from UC Berkeley.[6] Here are a few of the interesting capsaicin facts:

- Capsaicin is mostly fat soluble; hence, the mouth burn cannot easily be neutralized by rinsing with water.

- Most of the capsaicin surrounds the seeds and the ribs (called the placenta) of the pepper. Scrape this out, and the heat drops by 90 percent. I like the flavor of jalapenos (rose-like) but can't take the heat. Simply cut the pepper in half and spoon out the ribs and seeds.

- Capsaicin-sensitive neurons do *not* reside in the spinal column or brain.

- Capsaicin ingestion will deplete neurons of substance P, a neurotransmitter necessary for pain transmission. Thus, repeated tastings of a hot salsa will result in a lower perception of heat (pain) over time.

Spices Versus Herbs

There is much confusion as to what classifies as an herb or spice. In *my* classification, condiments and flavorings are based on whether they have a trigeminal or mouth burning property, a major reason to prefer a particular spice. Here are few examples with their major active flavor and orosensory compounds:

Spices (and Major Volatiles)

- Black, white, and green pepper (piperine)

- Hot peppers (capsaicin)

- Cinnamon (cinnamaldehyde and cinnamic acid)

- Peppermint, spearmint (menthol, menthone)

- Mustard (allylisothiocyanate)

- Ginger (gingerols)

- Turmeric (curcuminoids)

- Cloves (menthol, eugenol)

- Wasabi and horseradish (allylisothiocyanate)

- Allium species (propiin, isoalliin, methiin, [onion and garlic])

- Garlic (isoalliin, methiin, alliin)

- Cumin (cuminaldehyde)

- Rosemary and thyme, oregano, marjoram (ursolic acid, thymol, carvacrol, eugenol, camphor, 1,8-cineole)

- Nutmeg (essential oils, terpenes, and derivatives)

- Coriander seed (d-linalool, camphor, a TRPV3 receptor stimulator)

- Sage (thujone [major active in the banned Absinthe drink!], 1,8 cineole, limonene, borneol)

Pure Herbs: Parsley, cardamom, basil, tarragon, dill, and fenugreek (it can be argued that some of these have spicy characteristics as well).

The spices with the highest orosensation are: black pepper, hot peppers, mustard, ginger, and horseradish. Each one of these spices contains active principles that cause the mouth burn and sometimes "nose burn." And in each spice, the active principle possesses a unique and individual orosensory profile: heat level, time of onset, the part of the oral cavity affected, and sensitization properties. Black pepper burn tends to be on the front of the mouth, with a sharp onset and quick resolve. Hot peppers, on the other hand, affect more oral tissues (even internal ones), and the onset is more gradual and lingering. Hot peppers are unique in that the mouth burn becomes lessened with repeat exposure. Horseradish, mustard, and ginger tend to have very sharp and quick onsets of burn with a very quick or steep decline in sensation. Olfactory trigeminal activation is quite active in these three spices, and the pungent nose burn contributes to their arousing and pleasurable profiles.

In our food pleasure quest, spices can play a dominant, and sometimes unexplained, role in food preference. We know that trigeminal spices create orosensation (pain, temperature), and they activate vanilloid receptors (polymodal noiciceptors) that ultimately release pain-induced endorphins or similar feel-good neurotransmitters. Probably all the spices release reward neurotransmitters in one way or the other and, as a consequence, greatly influence cuisine design. Salsa now outsells ketchup as the condiment of choice, mainly due to the presence of capsaicin. Black pepper has such a unique aroma profile that it does not appear to interfere with any other savory food aromas. It is always an additive and is never smothering. This remarkable property is unique; few other spices or herbs are used so often without inducing sensory specific satiety. And as we will discuss, black pepper (piperine) is another strong activator of the vanilloid receptor. In fact, piperine binds to the receptor with more force than capsaicin—and with a much quicker onset of action.

Liking Spice

1. Spice usage helps preserve and maintain the sensory quality of a food, and reduce the levels of pathogenic bacteria and fungi.

Perhaps the most famous work on why we like spice is the paper by Sherman and Billing, who coined the term "Darwinian gastronomy."[1] An anthropologist teamed up with a neuroscientist, they reviewed the spices used in over 4,500 meat recipes. Here is a summary of some of the more interesting observations:

• Spice use is an evolutionary adaptation that adds color and flavor and makes the food taste better.

• Many of our favorite spices have antibacterial properties that helped prevent food-borne illness. Garlic, onions, oregano, allspice, and hot peppers are particularly good at pathogen reduction. In fact, at least half of all the spices Sherman and Billing tested had some antibacterial activity.

• The hotter the climate, the greater the use of spice and herbs because of the greater possibility of spoilage.

• Black pepper and lemon juice are a very popular flavoring combination, but they do not have high anti-bacterial activity. (Black pepper is actually a filthy spice with a high bacterial load.)

- Here is their listing of the most popular spices and flavorings in recipes in order: black pepper, onion, garlic, chilies, lemon and lime, parsley, ginger, and bay leaf.

The authors conclude that our taste buds and use of spice(s) coevolved under the constant pressure to preserve food and/or to keep it from killing us. Their theory states that humans developed a preference for spices because spices helped them survive and feel good—and humans spread the word.

A major problem with the "they felt better" argument is that capsaicin is an aversive stimulus—not really the type of ingredient that causes instant liking. Even today, humans with lots of taste buds, called supertasters, tend not to use hot peppers at all. In infants and young children, hot peppers can actually burn out or destroy the vanilloid receptors entirely—certainly not something that engenders preference. This argument is an extension of a similar theory that spices were used in history to help cover up bad or spoiled food, which was a very common problem in refrigeration-compromised times. The problem I have with this theory is that, even bad-smelling or tasting food is not improved much by adding spice or herbs. The olfactory system is especially adept at detecting foul-smelling foods that might kill the ingestor. Adding hot pepper or thyme or black pepper will simply not cover it up. Test it yourself. Go into your garage, add ground black pepper and Tabasco to your cat's canned food—and tell me if the mixture becomes more edible. You simply have spicy cat food. Oh, after the experiment please discard the food; cats are very sensitive to spicy food and will not appreciate the added seasoning!

Plants produce capsaicin to deter animal (especially rodent) ingestions; many animals feel the same pain (burn) as we do. Bird species, however, are free to eat peppers with impunity, since they lack the vanilloid receptor and have no pain response whatsoever. The pepper seeds, which are not destroyed during ingestion by birds, are then spread through the ecosystem and both species benefit. The capsaicin pain response also works to the advantage of the tarantula, whose venom activates the same vanilloid receptors creating a potent and lingering pain response.[7]

Although the Darwinian hypothesis by Sherman and Billing (spices make food safer) is interesting, *evolutionarily* speaking, I believe the use of spice is a more recent phenomenon. In European cuisine, the top five spices were in commerce only in the last thousand years or so and some of these less than five hundred years (chilies). The Bible, however, one of the earliest recorded works (over three thousand years old), mentions the *Allium* family—onions, garlic, and leeks—and a number of currently used spices—cinnamon, coriander, and mustard. In ancient Egypt, papyrus records indicate a rich tradition in herb and spice use as condiments and medicine. In Africa, the site of the human exodus (perhaps 50,000 to 75,000 years ago) Paleolithic excavations, have not found any of the current spices. However, there are records of very early food flavorings; for instance, the Masai tribe uses the bark of a local tree to flavor its combination of milk and blood. In the Americas, American Indians have used hot chilies for at least eight thousand years.[4] Although the Sherman and Billing hypothesis may still be correct, the spice blends available many hundreds of thousands of years ago are unlikely to be the ones we use today.

In the cookivore theory of human evolution, wherein fire played a direct role in our higher evolution, the Sherman and Billing hypothesis fits in nicely, since it is our nature to flavor food and appreciate the complex aromas formed during cooking. Hence, it is very likely that humans used locally available aromatic roots, flowers, leaves, and shoots to flavor food, keep it safe, and, perhaps, improve digestion.[8a-d]

Healthful Benefits of Spices and Herbs

All the spices and herbs we use contain phytochemicals, and many of them are potent antioxidants. The use of spices reduces or ameliorates many common diseases by down-regulating harmful cytokine(s) and reducing overall inflammation, helping improve both mood and movement.[9] We must wonder why the herbs and spices we use have so many health benefits. Did the spices and herbs first start as herbal medicines and then evolve into food flavorants? This reminds me of the famous maxim of Hippocrates, who said, "Let your medicine be your food."

In a fascinating article, scientists Aggarwal and Shishodia report that many common spices reduce the amount of the nasty biological cytokines (nuclear transcription factor kappaB), which may be behind many diseases: cancer, atherosclerosis, myocardial infarction, diabetes, allergy, asthma, arthritis, Crohn's disease, multiple sclerosis, Alzheimer's disease, osteoporosis, psoriasis, septic shock, and AIDS![10,11] In their paper, they suggest that the "reasoning for seasoning" is the health benefits associated with *all* of the spices we use in cooking. For another in-depth look at the chemistry of spices and the effects on health, see the article by Carolyn Fisher, "Spices of Life."[12]

There seems to be an interesting connection with spices, food pleasure, medicinal effects, food preservation, and even human embalming. Perhaps we are preserving ourselves with the ingestion of high antioxidant and antiseptic spices! Renowned German Egyptologist Georg Ebers, found papyrus records indicating extensive herb and spice usage as early as 1550 B.C., including anise, caraway, cinnamon, fennel, onions, garlic, thyme, fenugreek, and poppy seeds.[13] Egyptians used spices in medicine, cooking, fumigation of stored grains, and, most notably, in preserving the dead.

O'Mahony et al. (2005) tested many spices and herbs and their killing abilities against several strains of the ulcer-causing H. Pylori.[14] Here is a listing of the spices and herbs that had *no* effect: Bengal quince, nightshade, garlic, dill, black pepper, coriander, fenugreek, and black tea. The most effective were in this order: turmeric, cumin, ginger, chili, borage, black caraway, oregano, and liquorice. And the most potent spices that kept the bacteria from adhering to the stomach wall were turmeric, borage, and parsley.

2. The use of spices improves digestion and absorption of food.

Black pepper has a long history of use in Ayurvedic medicine—the 4,000-year-old traditional healing practice of India that is very similar to the TCM system of China. In fact, black pepper is used in over 25 percent of all the mixtures of herbs and spices that treat disease. Traditional healers believe that pepper improves digestion of nutrients and helps promote the actions of the other herbs in the Ayurvedic blends. As we will see, there is plenty of evidence that this is in fact quite true. In my nutraceutical work, I often add a small amount of Bioperine, a *Piper longum* extract from Sabinsa, to increase the absorption of important nutrients and phytochemicals. A few milligrams of Bioperine can actually increase such nutrients as beta carotene or CoQ10. I suspect that black pepper acts in a very similar way.

Since black pepper aids in the absorption of food, it is very possible this enhanced nutritional (caloric) load is sensed by the gut in a positive manner via hormones (or peptides) or direct vagal influence to the brain. This is speculation, of course, but the active principle piperine does increase intestinal water flow and subsequent digestion and absorption. Some scientists believe that enhanced nutritional absorption has a positive feedback loop that increases our preference for black pepper. The animal literature is rich in examples of enhanced preference to foods that enhance the absorption of nutrients. And humans will prefer foods if they sense satiety without even tasting the food. (This is known as *sham feeding*—the food bypasses the oral cavity). Thus, gastrointestinal sensing of increased satiety or fullness, *by itself,* will increase food hedonics and spice liking.[15]

3. Spices and herbs help prevent the oxidation of essential fatty acids.

The culinary herbs (rosemary, thyme, and oregano) are especially good at protecting the breakdown of essential fatty acids in food systems, such as meat, by inhibiting the oxidation of fatty acids, which create undesirable off-flavors and rancid notes. Thus, spicing suppresses off-flavors that reduce food pleasure. An example of an off-flavor is the phenomenon known as warmed-over flavors in meat products—a very undesirable feature, which is easily controlled by the use of antioxidant spice.

4. Herbs and spices provide aroma variety to food, which enhances appeal and increases intake.

Variety (the spice of life) opposes the satiety effects of food—the phenomenon known as sensory specific satiety. And variations in the sensory properties of food—texture, taste, and aroma—are best at enhancing the variety effect.

5. Herbs and spices are positively conditioned to food high in salt, fat, and sugar.

Herbs and spices are not intrinsically tasty in the sense that they are hedonically active like, say, sucrose. Rosemary aroma becomes preferred if it is paired with a food containing calories or macronutrients. This nutritional conditioning, if you are really hungry, only takes one pairing. Specific herbs that are constantly paired with certain foods (rosemary with chicken, tarragon with vinegar) form a strong memory engram (memory trace). Just smelling the aroma, especially if one is hungry, is enough to evoke the brain memory of roasted chicken.

6. Spices (not herbs) increase salivation and the pleasure of ingestion.

Salivation during food consumption is very important, since the major hedonic solutes must be dissolved in saliva or moisture in the mouth in order to be perceived. Amal Naj, in *Peppers: A Story of Hot Pursuits*, notes this in an astute discussion of saliva and food ingestion.[16] He says that the pepper-induced salivation makes the food on the tongue more delicious—"go for it," the brain says. The author said it's his theory (and doesn't want the experts to comment). Well, I will comment: his observations are concordant with my salivation theory of food ingestion. Mr. Naj's insight is a major part of hot peppers' allure—saliva stimulation and food ingestion share unique autonomic and hedonic properties.

7. Spices, especially capsaicin, activate the *trigeminal* (TG) receptor systems in the mouth more strongly than the receptors that carry taste.

Spices, then, create *sensation*; and this is paired with the act of eating food. The celebrated taste researcher Carl Pfaffman says that all food pleasure starts with sensation. And peppers, both black and hot, provide this in abundance. The oral cavity contains free nerve endings and receptors that carry the orosensations of heat, cold, and noxious stimuli. Capsaicin and piperine activate these neurons to release substance P and send a signal for pain; the mouth is saying, "I'm being burned." This pain signal reaches the brain and releases endogenous opioids for pain relief—hence, the addictiveness of hot pepper and black pepper (piperine and capsaicin are close relatives chemically). Paul Rozin, a noted food psychologist and pepper expert, first proposes that the brain, upon pepper ingestion, thinks the mouth is being burned, and in a protective response releases the feel-good neurotransmitter—endorphin(s). As mentioned by Amal Naj in his book, Dr. Rozin suggests that endorphin release increases pleasure. He also commented that humans are unique at reversing the natural aversion to these spices; he has tried to get rats (little success) and chimpanzees (a bit more) to like chilies![17, 18] Although hot peppers spread quickly around the world after their discovery, not all humans prefer them. Many Northern European and classic French cuisine ignore hot peppers entirely, unless they dabble in Asian fusion techniques.

Amal Naj also suggests that hot peppers heighten the mouth sensitivity in a generalized way. Amal suggests that other spices do this as well (garlic, coriander, ginger). Arousal or "attention to stimuli," is a very important component of learning and memory. So what happens when you put burning, stinging, tingling, and sweat-producing materials in your mouth? You get attention to food stimuli, as in—what's in my mouth is going to kill me. The brain then focuses on the oral sensations of tastes, textures, and aromas in an effort to memorize and/or reject the oral invader. But there is more insight by Amal Naj. Capsaicin not only actives the vanilloid receptor (suggested by Naj *before* the discovery of this receptor; he said hot peppers should be a taste of its own!), it may activate salty and sweet receptors as well.[19] Hot peppers, then, activate endorphins, increase food arousal, and excite the pleasurable sweet and salty sensations.

Capsaicin is mostly fat soluble (and odorless and colorless), so one must use a natural fat emulsifier, like casein in milk, to dislodge or flush it out of the mouth. Yogurt will also work, as will a little alcohol from wine or beer. A cold beer helps remove capsaicin and depresses the pain sensation; conversely, room temperature red wine with a much higher alcohol content, enhances the pain response. Capsaicin is also unique in that it causes its own desensitization by depleting substance P in the neuron. Hence, the more you eat, the less you feel the pain. Perhaps this explains why hot pepper eaters tend to escalate their pepper liking—they get used to the burn.

Most aromas, in order to be perceived, are under three hundred molecular weight. Since the capsaicin's molecule weight is 305, capsaicin *will* only volatilize upon heating, and you risk the inhalation of the pepper vapors. One summer, I grew habaneros just for the fun of it. During the preparation of a chili dish, I left a few halved habaneros in the sink. A few minutes later a friend decided to wash his hands, and turned the hot water on in the sink. The capsaicin volatilized and we had to evacuate the kitchen! Our sensitivity to capsaicin is quite strong; we can detect just a few molecules placed on the tongue. This sensitivity is used to good effect in the defensive police pepper sprays and in the garden, where capsaicin emulsions sprayed on plants will keep bugs off for almost a month (Bonide brand is a good one).

8. Spices may have antidepressant activity.

Spices, we have seen, activate noiciceptors (pain receptors) in the mouth; but they can be absorbed and act centrally, with interesting, pharmacological effects. Lee et al. (2005) suggests that piperine inhibits MAO activity and may be an antidepressant.[20] MAO A & B are enzymes responsible for breaking down certain neurotransmitters—dopamine, serotonin, and norepinephrine—involved with pleasure, movement, depression, and generalized mood. By inhibiting these break-down enzymes, the levels of these neurotransmitters increase in the brain (and periphery). Capsaicin, the active principle in hot pepper, releases anandamide, a possible feel-good neurotransmitter that attaches to cannabinoid (CB-1 & 2) receptors, supposedly the reason we like chocolate.[21] Hence, hot and black pepper ingestion may activate the pain-sensing trigeminal neurons in the mouth, releasing both the feel-good endorphins and the "blissful" anandamides in the brain.

Piperine has a number of additional effects in the body:

a. Piperine increases pancreatic production of digestive enzymes (an excellent effect when combined with a meal).[22]

b. Piperine may increase or prolong the action of Viagra by inhibiting the liver and intestinal CYP3A4 enzyme that degrades sildenafil. Grapefruit juice also is a potent inhibitor of intestinal CYP34A, the (first-pass) drug metabolism system for many drugs, including estrogens, diazepam, and erythromycin. Although I don't know of any direct studies on this, one should be careful about preparing *steak au poivre* after ingesting a sildenafil.[22]

c. Piperine may have anti-mutagenic activity and may prevent cancer via antioxidative and detoxifying enzyme induction.[23]

d. Piperine is very potent at activating the TRPV1 human vanilloid receptor—actually stronger than capsaicin—creating greater desensitization of the receptor itself. This means that piperine may have pain-killing effects superior to capsaicin, which is used in many creams and patches for pain relief.[24]

e. Piperine is a potent inhibitor of inflammatory cytokines, such as TNF-alpha, IL-1beta, IL-6, and GM-CSF.[25] A strong dose of black pepper may reduce aches and pains in such conditions as osteoarthritis.

f. Piperine may enhance the absorption of the healthy catechins in tea.[26] Tea catechins or polyphenols have many health benefits, such as lowering cholesterol, boosting the immune system, and lowering cancer risk. The popular hot beverage "chai," is Hindi for tea, and contains black tea and milk as the base with a variable combination of the following spices: ginger, cinnamon, cardamom, star anise, cloves, nutmeg, and black pepper. Black pepper is an ingredient in many Ayurvedic formulas and the practitioners must have sensed it helped with the absorption of the herbal actives. Chai, the Ayurvedic health beverage, is not easily made at home, but is as close as the nearest gourmet coffee house.

g. Piperine may help reduce the oxidative stress and elevated serum triglyceride levels induced by high-fat diets (junk food).[27] The authors gave rats a nasty diet of coconut oil, cholesterol, and bile salts and then, in the other two groups, the same diets but with added black pepper and piperine. The black pepper and piperine supplemented rats had (amazingly) near normal antioxidant status—despite the *Super Size Me* diet.

h. Spices may activate the bitter receptor. Green and Hayes (2004) report that about 50 percent of people find the big three spices to have bitter overtones.[19] Perhaps this explains why some individuals do not like highly spiced food. Supertasters, about 1/4 of the population, simply resist ingesting hot or spicy food.

i. The three hot spices (and their cousins) have a similar molecular structure—an aromatic ring with two ortho oxygens. Vanilla has the same ortho oxygen configuration as well. Vanilla in higher levels actually has a throat burn or tickle that feels like getting something stuck in your throat!

Flavor companies are actively investigating the aroma chemicals or spices that activate these cold or hot receptors. The reason is now obvious: the trigeminal orosensory system in the mouth has powerful effects on pleasure generation and food ingestion:

a. Spices may activate a new pain receptor. Activation of the TREK-1 (potassium gated, g-coupled receptor) increases sensitivity to heat and osmolality. This new receptor is colocalized with TRPV1 and may be another polymodal pain receptor activated by hot spices.[28]

b. Spicy food may promote weight loss. Studies indicate that combining tyrosine, capsaicin, catechins, and caffeine helps reduce fat mass (a bit) when added to a hypocaloric diet.[29]

c. Bay leaves contain 1,8-cineole, a terpene with anti-inflammatory activity.[30] Bay is used extensively in French (*bouquet garni*) and Middle Eastern cuisine (some curries). Thyme also contains this same terpene.

d.   The French frequently use *herbs de Provence* in their cooking. In a study
by Hoaxing et al. (2006),[31] the herbs oregano, savory, clove, and thyme
(containing carvacrol, eugenol, and thymol) activated the heat-sensing
TRPV3 receptor in the skin, nose, and mouth. These spices add more
sensation than just aroma when they are used in cooking. In addition,
oregano (carvacrol) desensitizes the TRPA1 receptor, which causes a
sharp stinging or burning sensation at high levels. (I have a pot of oregano growing on the patio, and the variety is called "spicy-type" oregano.
Now I know why!) Eugenol, in the bay leaf, is a very powerful binder to
the vanilloid receptor due to the fat-soluble nature of the molecule. Just
one leaf is enough to add a subtle, pungent character to a pot of stew or
stock. Thomas Keller, in his bistro book *Bouchon*, frequently combines
bay leaf with thyme. This spice combination, then, creates additional
oral sensation, providing both heightened interest and pleasure to the
dishes.

Spices and Calories

We have seen that spices are very *active* orally—they can activate heat, cold, pain,
tactile, and basic taste receptors.[32] And when we learn that eating hot peppers will
do no harm, we are free to self-indulge in this endorphin pain response. The
degree of spice liking, however, is largely based on your supertaster status. People
who are supertasters (have more taste buds) use less spicing in general. But the
main reason we use spices is found in the food pleasure equation: food pleasure
equals sensation plus calories. To keep the pleasure levels equal, when calories are
reduced in a food, we must increase the sensation—the snap, crackle, pop, spici-
ness, and the hedonic tastants of salt, sugar, and MSG.

When I was in India, on business, a professor told me why she thought Indians
liked heavily spiced food. She said the average Indian lacks fat in the diet because
it is very expensive. She postulated that a lack of calories induced a heightened
spice liking to increase the overall pleasure of eating. The more I study this phenomenon, the more I believe in the professor's hypothesis. Scandinavian cooking,
rich in meat, milk fat, and cheese, uses the least amount of spice. Those cuisines
which are calorically compromised tend to be the hottest and most elaborately
spiced. Indian cuisine, largely vegetarian, is justifiably famous for complex
orosensory spice blends. The most famous is curry (typically a mixture of black
pepper, fenugreek, mustard seed, coriander, cayenne, ginger, cinnamon, tur-

meric, and cloves). This spice mixture activates many receptor systems—hot, cold, pain, and probably tactile (touch) as well.

Foods That Burn Twice

A professor friend used to say that good Mexican food "burns *twice*." And anyone who has eaten very hot food will notice that capsaicin burns both the oral and, well, you know—the *other* end. There is a huge difference between the two areas in response to capsaicin. Orally, we can handle the fire (taste buds and the oral cavity are resistant to assault), and in time we adapt to the burn (substance P depletion) and increase our intake of fiery foods. The intestinal tract, however, has few pain receptors until the *end*, where chemoreceptor innervations are quite massive. Capsaicin is only absorbed in small amounts; the bulk of this fat-soluble substance is excreted in the stool. And that's where the problem lies. These distal pain receptors are very similar to those in the mouth, but they don't have the adaptation property that the oral cavity has. Hence, even hardened salsa warriors will feel the pain the next day, usually accompanied by diarrhea, since capsaicin accelerates and increases the secretion of water in the intestine. Why do we keep doing this to ourselves? (I am a repeat offender; my wife laughs at my folly.) The answer is that the pain in the butt is not associated with the pain in the mouth, because of a twenty-four-hour time lag before the second burning. People, therefore, do *not* form a conditioned response to the pain sensation and we are free to repeat the oral and internal endorphin response.

Bourdain writes about this phenomenon in his entertaining collection of essays in the book *The Nasty Bits*, which I highly recommend. After eating an especially hot Szechuan meal (with hot chilies *and* Szechuan peppercorns) his host guaranteed "diarrhea tomorrow." Bourdain suggested that his delicate Western metabolism was making him more susceptible to the adverse effects of the spice combination. The host replied that everyone pays the price the next day! But this never dampens the gustatory enthusiasm; heavily spiced food is simply addicting.

The Szechuan (or Sichuan) peppercorns come from two sources, the Japanese pepper tree (*Zanthoxylum piperitum* DC.) and the more common Sichuan pepper (*Zanthoxylum schinifolium*, Siebold & Zucc.), a type of thorny ash tree (evergreen) native to central China. The active numbing compounds are collectively called (alkyamides or sanshools) and are partly responsible for the prolonged lavatory sessions upon ingestion. The alkyamides bind not only to the vanilloid receptor, but to the heat and cooling receptors as well; and, very specifically, to "tactile" or "touch" receptors in the mouth and throat.[33] The highly water-soluble compounds actually numb oral tissues and provide the "pleasurable" sensation. The only other food with numbing and tingling properties is fugu, prepared from Tiger Blowfish and considered the greatest of all delicacies in Japan. The highly toxic compound (tetrodotoxin) shuts down the sodium channels present in the nervous system—causing progressive muscle paralysis. The gourmand, fully conscious, dies when the neurotoxin reaches the lungs and inhibits breathing. There is no antidote—I'll stick to sushi.

Cooks wishing to experiment with Sichuan peppers will not easily find this spice. No American supermarkets stock it, and I haven't been able to find an Asian store that carries it either. Sichuan pepper is a traditional member of the classic seasoning blend, Chinese five-spice, a reference to the traditional belief that this unique combination of spices excites all the five senses in the mouth: sour, bitter, sweet, salty, and mouth-burn. Typical spices used in the formulations include: cinnamon, ginger, cloves, star anise, fennel, and Sichuan peppercorns. Although five-spice mixtures are common in grocery stores, most contain black or white pepper as a substitute for Sichuan pepper; so be wary, you want the unique mouthfeel of real Sichuan pepper. Just a small amount of five-spice can liven up the most bland foods and makes a great general purpose seasoning for meat dishes.[34] I frequently mix five-spice with Emeril's Original Essence, a 50/50 blend, as a seasoning for coating roast chicken. Authentic Sichuan peppercorns may be found at igourmet.com and penzeys.com.

References

1. Sherman, P. W., and T. Billing. Darwinian gastronomy: why we use spices. *BioScience*, 49:453–63, 1999.

2. Black pepper—plant profile. Plant Cultures, exploring plants and people. http://www.plantcultures.org/plants/black_pepper_plant_profile.html

3. Long pepper (*Piper longum* L. and *Piper retrofractum* Vahl). Gernot Katzer's spice pages. http://www.uni-graz.at/~katzer/engl/Pipe_lon.html

4. Andrews, J. 1992. *Chilies to Chocolate: Food Americas Gave the World*. Tucson: Univ. of Arizona Press.

5.   Green, B. G., and M. T. Schullery. Stimulation of bitterness by capsaicin and menthol: differences between lingual areas innervated by the glossopharyngeal and chorda tympani nerves. *Chem. Senses*, 28:45–55, 2003.

6.   Capsaicin: an overview. Term paper code: 209. http://sulcus. berkeley.edu/mcb/165_001/papers/manuscripts/_209.html

7.   Owen, J. *Natl. Geogr. News*, Nov. 8, 2006. http://news.nationalgeographic.com/news/2006/11/061108-tarantula-venom.html

8a. Spices: time line. http://www.vigyanprasar.gov. in/comcom/spicetimeline.htm

8b. The spices of antiquity. American Spice Trade Association. http:// www.astaspice.org/history/history_01.htm

8c. Janick, J. Lectures 23-24. Herbals: The connection between horticulture and medicine. 2002. http://www.hort.purdue. edu/newcrop/history/lecture23/lec23.html

8d. Janick, J. Ancient Egyptian agriculture and the origins of horticulture. 2002. http://www.hort.purdue.edu/newcrop/history/lecture06/lec 6l.html

9.   Best, B. Phytochemicals as nutraceuticals. http://www.benbest.com/ nutrceut/phytochemicals.html

10. Aggarwal, B. B., and S. Shishodia. Suppression of nuclear factor-κB activation by spice-derived phytochemicals: Reasoning for seasoning. *Ann. N. Y. Acad. Sci.*, 1030:434–41, 2004.

11. ———. Molecular targets of dietary agents for prevention and therapy for cancer. *Biochem. Pharmacol.*, 71:1397–421, 2006.

12. Fisher, C. Spices of life. Chembytes e-zine. http://www.chemsoc.org/ chembytes/ezine/2002/fisher_jan02.htm

13. Rosengarten, Jr., F. 1973. *The Book of Spices*. New York: Pyramid Books.

14. O'Mahony, R., Al-Khtheeri, H., Weerasekera, D., Fernando, N., Vaira, D., Holton, J., and C. Baset. Bacterial and anti-adhesive properties of culinary and medicinal plants against helicobacter pylori. *World J. Gastroenterol.*, 11:7499–507, 2005.

15. Provensa, F. D. Postingestive feedback as an elementary determinant of food preference and intake in ruminants. *J. Range Manage.*, 48:2–17, 1995. http://www.cnr.uidaho.edu/range556/Notes/Provenza-JRM-95.pdf

16. Naj, A. 1993. *Peppers: A Story of Hot Pursuits.* New York: Vintage Books.

17. Rozin, P., Gruss, L., and G. Berk. Reversal of innate aversion: attempts to induce a preference for chili pepper in rats. *J. Comp. Physiol. Psychol.*, 93:1001–14, 1979.

18. Rozin, P., and K. Kennel. Acquired preference for piquant foods by chimpanzees. *Appetite*, 4:69–77, 1983.

19. Green, B. G., and J. E. Hayes. Individual differences in perception of bitterness from capsaicin, piperine and zingerone. *Chem. Senses*, 29:53–60, 2004. http://chemse.oxfordjournals.org/cgi/content/abstract/29/1/53

20. Lee, S. A, Hong, S. S., Han, X. H., Hwang, J. S., Oh, G. J., Lee, K. S., Lee, M. K., Hwang, B. Y., and J. S. Ro. Piperine from the fruits of Piper longum with inhibitory effect on monoamine oxidase and antidepressant-like activity. *Chem. Pharm. Bull. (Tokyo)*, 53:832–5, 2005.

21. Akerman, S., Kaube, H., and P. J. Goadsby. Anandamide acts as a vasodilator of dural blood vessels in vivo by activating TRPV1 receptors. *Br. J. Pharmacol.*, 142:1354–60, 2004.

22. Mills, R. Piperine multiplies the strength of many supplements and drugs. The Delano Report. http://www.delano.com/Articles/piperine-multiplies.html

23. Selvendiran, K., Thirunavukkarasu, C., Singh, J. P., Padmavathi, R., and D. Sakthisekaran. Chemopreventive effect of piperine on mito-

chondrial TCA cycle and phase-I and glutathione-metabolizing enzymes in benzo(a)pyrene induced lung carcinogenesis in Swiss albino mice. *Mol. Cell. Biochem.*, 271:101–6, 2005.

24. McNamara, F. N., Randall, A., and M. J. Gunthorpe. Effects of piperine, the pungent component of black pepper, at the human vanilloid receptor (TRPV1). *Br. J. Pharmacol.*, 144:781–90, 2005.

25. Pradeep, C. R., and G. Kuttan. Piperine is a potent inhibitor of nuclear factor-kappaB (NF-kappaB), c-Fos, CREB, ATF-2 and proinflammatory cytokine gene expression in B16F-10 melanoma cells. *Int. Immunopharmacol.*, 4:1795–803, 2004.

26. Lambert, J. D., Hong, J., Kim, D. K., Mishin, V. M., and C. S. Yang. Piperine enhances the bioavailability of the tea polyphenol (–)-epigallocatechin-3-gallate in mice. *J. Nutr.*, 134:1948–52, 2004.

27. Vijayakumar, R. S., Surya, D., and N. Nalini. Antioxidant efficacy of black pepper (Piper nigrum L.) and piperine in rats with high fat diet induced oxidative stress. *Redox Rep.*, 9:105–10, 2004.

28. Alloui, A., Zimmermann, K., Mamet, J., Duprat, F., Noël, J., Chemin, J., Guy, N., et al. TREK-1, a K⁺ channel involved in polymodal pain perception. *The EMBO J.*, 25:2368–76, 2006.

29. Belza, A., and B. A. Jessen. Bioactive food stimulants of sympathetic activity: effect on 24-h energy expenditure and fat oxidation. *Eur. J. Clin. Nutr.*, 59:733–41, 2005.

30. Yuan, G., Wahlqvist, M. L., He, G., Yang, M., and D. Li., Natural products and anti-inflammatory activity. *Asia Pac. J. Clin. Nutr.*, 15:143–52, 2006.

31. Hoaxing, X., Delling, M., Jun, J., and D. E. Clapham. Oregano, thyme and clove-derived flavors and skin sensitizers activate specific TRP channels. *Nat. Neurosci.*, 9:628–35, 2006.

32. Szallasi, A. Piperine: researchers discover new flavor in an ancient spice. *Trends Pharmacol. Sci.*, 26:437–9, 2005.

33. Szechuan peppercorns—burn and numb your senses. bbc.co.uk, May 21, 2003. http://www.bbc.co.uk/dna/h2g2/A1038773

34. Parkinson, R. Five-spice powder and the five elements theory. Was five-spice powder the first "feel-good" drug? http://chinesefood.about. com/library/weekly/aa041900b.htm

CHAPTER 16

▼

WHY WE LIKE CHOCOLATE

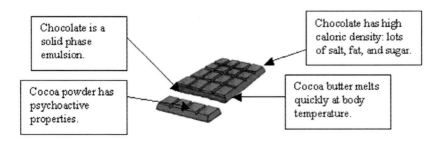

Chocolate is a solid phase emulsion.

Chocolate has high caloric density: lots of salt, fat, and sugar.

Cocoa powder has psychoactive properties.

Cocoa butter melts quickly at body temperature.

Chocolate is cheaper than therapy, and you don't need an appointment.
Author unknown

The combination of sugar and fat is pure cerebral ecstasy.[1]

Much has been written on chocolate perception, cooking, and physiology. On the question of "why we like the taste of chocolate," the majority of theories fall into three camps:

- Chocolate is a comfort food.

- Chocolate is loaded with salt, fat, and sugar (junk food).

- Chocolate contains pharmacological substances that:

- Are similar to "love" hormones
- Are similar to marijuana
- Are nonspecific psychoactives.

Some of the most romantic theories rely on the "falling in love" chemistry of biogenic amines found in chocolate; the major one is the brain neurochemical phenylethylamine (similar in structure to amphetamine). This theory is, in fact, often mentioned as the reason behind chocolate liking. I think we rely too much on such sublime, chemistry-inspired theories when the real reason behind chocolate craving is likely a *combination* of sensory factors (taste), nutritional activation of satiety factors (calories), and cocoa psychoactive compounds (theobromine).

Chocolate is a highly preferred food, both as a flavoring and as a confection. A *Bon Appetit* survey in 2003, respondents were asked to list their favorite foods. The order was: ice cream, chocolate, cake, cheesecake, and potato chips.[2] Marketing professor, Brian Wansink et al. (2003), surveyed 1,005 people, asking the respondents about their favorite "comfort" foods. The women preferred snack-like comfort foods (such as chocolate and ice cream) and men preferred meal-related comfort foods (steak, casseroles, and soup).[3] But when Wansink's team asked, "What foods make you feel guilty?" males responded with potato chips and females said candy or chocolate. Similarly, Parker et al. (2006) notes that women in the United States said chocolate was the number one craving, while men listed pizza and beer.[4]

The Pleasures of Chocolate

1. Chocolate Is High in Salt, Fat, and Sugar

Joel Glenn Brenner, in *The Emperors of Chocolate*, asked MIT researchers about the genesis of chocolate pleasure. The scientists remarked that when animals are given access to sweet and fatty foods, they go "mad" with ecstacy.[1] Dr. Adam Drewnowski, who directs the Human Nutrition Program at the University of Michigan in Ann Arbor, says that his research indicates that craving for high-sugar and high-fat foods is brain-opioid based, and chocolate is probably the greatest pleasure food.[5]

Chocolate Is High in Sucrose

Milk chocolate typically contains about 50 percent sugar (sucrose) by weight that is solubilized into a solid emulsion. The hedonic properties of sucrose are special. Professor Rose Marie Pangborn once told me that of all the sweeteners she has tested for palatability, sucrose (table sugar) is always preferred by taste panelists. And when I asked why, her response was, "You can feel it!" In other words, sucrose has a special mouthfeel that is not present in any other sweeteners, including glucose, fructose, or maltose. And when sucrose is sensory tested against the artificial sweeteners (aspartame, acesulfame K, and sucralose), it still receives top hedonic ratings. Physiologically, it is probably no coincidence that we have lots of the enzyme, *sucrase,* in our small intestine to digest all the sugar in the chocolate. Many people are surprised to learn that some infant formulas use sucrose as the main carbohydrate. Sucrose, then, has the highest hedonic appeal of any sugar, and it generates equally desirable flavor compounds upon heating.

The brain prefers the sucrose in chocolate, and the taste of this sugar releases mu-opioids; the sucrase breaks down sucrose into glucose and fructose for immediate absorption. Glucoreceptors exist throughout the gut and the brain, and their activation is a signal that feeding has begun. Parker et al. (2002) state that carbohydrates stimulate "feel-good" sensation via stimulation of gut receptors and brain peptides.[6] The sugar-induced insulin rush helps store the sugar as glycogen or convert it into fat. Insulin itself is rewarding in the brain and helps form memories of the food just eaten. In addition, the high sugar content and the rise in insulin may increase the amount of *serotonin* in the brain by selectively increasing the transport of the amino acid tryptophan from the bloodstream. Serotonin is a calming neurotransmitter that helps reduce pain sensation. This effect is reduced if the food has too much protein, because the amino acids in protein compete with the uptake of tryptophan across the blood brain barrier. Dark chocolate is fairly low in protein (and the protein is not of good quality), so this effect is more likely to occur in dark than milk chocolate. However, Parker et al. (2006) voice skepticism over the purported "carbohydrate craving" mechanism behind chocolate liking.[4] The authors believe that chocolate preference may be due to some other constituent or through the action of tasting the sugar itself. The robust effect of opioid release by sweet taste should not be underappreciated. Just the *taste* of sweetness by newborns reduces pain and crying—presumably from the release of mu-opioids in the brain (hypothalamus).[7]

Chocolate Is High in Fat

Chocolate is approximately 50 percent fat by weight. Adam Drewnowski points out that liking fat appears to be a universal human trait.[8] Unfortunately, the intestinal tract is not very efficient at sensing fat intake and inducing satiety, thus we tend to overeat high fat foods. In addition, fat digestion can act as an antidepressant; human beings are much calmer and nicer after chocolate ingestion. One scientist speculated that fat ingestion activates CCK (a gut hormone) in the intestine, which simultaneously activates brains regions for "satisfaction." Scientists are now looking at CCK analogues as antidepressants.[9] Dallman et al. (2005) even state that "comfort foods" (high in fat), activate the brain's pleasure circuits (anterior part of the nucleus accumbens.[10] Trottier et al. (1998) also found that in rat pups (newborns), fat ingestion possesses opioid-like pain-reduction, and calming properties; the hormone leptin may be behind this fat-induced reduction of stress.[11] When you couple the antidepressant actions of fat with the opioid boosting actions of sucrose; you have a powerful mood elevating food. It's little wonder that a piece of chocolate is often ingested in stressful or painful times. Thus, from an evolutionary standpoint, an energy-dense, highly palatable food containing salt, fat, and sugar, proves very irresistible.

2. Chocolate Melts

Chocolate has a very unusual lipid composition that lends itself to rapid melting in the mouth at body temperature. Chocolate is composed of stearic, oleic, and palmitic acid, these fatty acids are fairly saturated and are solid at room temperature but melt completely at 95–100°F—the oral cavity temperature. Hence, chocolate fat or cocoa butter has high dynamic contrast, a major reason for the pleasure it induces. Rapid meltdown is arousing by itself and helps induce saliva, which dissolves the 50 percent sucrose concentration of this solid emulsion. Chocolate perception is a crescendo or rush of sensory flavors and tastes as the chocolate changes from solid to liquid.

3. Chocolate Is High in Caloric Density

We have said many times that the brain and the stomach like food with high caloric density. Most snack and junk foods qualify, but none of them compares to chocolate. Dark chocolate (70 percent cocoa fat and solids), is near 5.6 on the caloric density scale, along with such snack food classics as potato chips (5.3) and Doritos (5.0).

4. Chocolate May Have Psychoactive Properties

It was very fashionable a few years ago, to explain the popularity of chocolate by what is *in it*. For example, here is a current list of the possible psychoactive compounds:

a. Phenylethylamine(s)

b. Anandamide precursors

c. Anandamide breakdown inhibitors (N-acylethanolamines)

d. Serotonin, tyramine, tryptamine, and related compounds

e. Methylxanthines (theobromine and caffeine)

f. Tetrahydro-beta-carbolines

g. Casomorphins

First, there were the theories that chocolate contains the "fall-in-love" neuro-chemical phenylethylamine—and it does, but not in large amounts, and it is probably broken down by the enzyme, MAO-B in the gut. Then Daniele Piomelli and coworkers at the Neurosciences Institute in San Diego, made quite a stir when they isolated a fatty acid in chocolate (actually a few other mimetics exist) that is similar to a compound in the brain called anandamide, a neuro-chemical that binds to marijuana CB1 receptors (yes, we do have them in abundance).[12] These receptors help regulate the sleep cycle, increase food intake, and modulate the pleasure center. They also found a compound that may reduce the breakdown of one's own natural anandamides in the brain. Although the paper created quite a sensation in the popular press (20,000 Google hits), the amount in chocolate is quite small and is unlikely to survive digestion. Sparling et al. (2003) suggests that exercise also activates the endocannabinoid system; this is why we may feel good and have lessened pain after a workout.[13] Before this, researchers thought that beta endorphins were the only neurotransmitters involved.

Chocolate also contains interesting psychoactive indoles, called beta-carbolines; the darker the chocolate, the higher the beta-carboline content.[14] These compounds may have the following actions:

a. Inhibit monoamine oxidase (MAO A and B). This action would increase the amount of the "feel good" neurotransmitters in the brain (dopamine, norepinephrine, and serotonin).

b. Inhibit the reuptake of serotonin, similar to the newer antidepressants like Paxil.

c. Act as potent antioxidants.

The combination of the major classes of psychotropic compounds (methylxanthines [theobromine], phenylethylamine, and anandamide compounds) enhance liking for chocolate, but it is difficult to tease these effects apart from sensory stimulation, caloric density, and post-metabolic effects. In a 2006 paper, Parker et al. reviewed all the possible theories on why we like chocolate (craving) and whether it is a food "drug" or "antidepressant."[4] Their conclusion is simply that chocolate has a unique sensory profile (texture, taste, and aroma) and that the fat and sugar activate both dopamine and opioids in a strong (but dysfunctional) manner. Yet, in a report by Larry Reid et al. (2004) cocoa powder (and not solid chocolate) ingestion in rats had an addiction-like activity, when it was withdrawn from the diet (i.e., cocoa acted like morphine).[15] The researchers ponder if there is a meaningful difference between *delicious* and *addictive* perceptions. We are left, then, with the conclusion that chocolate is pleasurable via three mechanisms: 1. It has dynamic contrast (it melts at mouth temperature quickly); 2. It contains fat and sugar, both rewarding (opioids); and 3. Cocoa powder may contain bioactives that affect pleasure generation or perception (phenylethylamines, anandamide mimics, or beta-carbolines).

Milk chocolate is made by adding whole cow's milk, condensed milk, or milk powder to the dark chocolate base. The main protein in milk is casein, and upon digestion, breaks down to produce a number of peptides that mimic the opioids, called the casomorphins. Some scientists believe these peptides have real opioid activity in the body and can make food more attractive. Casomorphins may also bind to serotonin receptors in the body, acting as a mild calming agent similar to the serotonin-reuptake inhibitors (Prozac).[16] Hence, psychoactive combination of fat, sugar, and casein (unique to chocolate and ice cream) may underlie chocolate devotion and subsequent "craving."

5. Chocolate Is an Emulsion

Chocolate is a solid phase emulsion composed of 30–70 percent cocoa butter, 20–30 percent cocoa solids (powder), and up to 50 percent sucrose (with added vanilla, salt, and lecithin). The making of chocolate is a difficult task that requires many hours of roasting, grinding, conching (a refining process with heavy rollers that breaks down the particle size and heightens flavor development), blending, and tempering—the art of getting the naturally unstable crystal structure of the cocoa butter just right for proper melting properties in the mouth (beta crystal V & VI formation). Most high-quality dark chocolate is 50–70 percent cocoa fat.

We have seen that animals and humans like emulsions. For example, Drewnowski and Greenwood note that combining sugar with milk in an emulsion is highly preferred.[17] Whether it is mayonnaise, butter, or solid chocolate, the high concentration of solutes in the aqueous phase (saliva in the case of chocolate) is highly pleasurable when put into an emulsified form. Skilled chefs and home cooks who know how to make proper emulsions will always make better-tasting food. In chocolate, the conching and refining process makes the sucrose crystals very small (measured in microns!), and these melt very quickly in the mouth with the application of saliva. This oral flavor explosion (upon melting) is actually the primary driver of chocolate liking—no other.

6. Chocolate Is a Potent "Intestinal Nutrient Rush"

In a 1991 paper on chocolate liking, Rozin et al. suggest that chocolate cravings in men and women are based on the sensory properties of chocolate, combined with the post-ingestional effects of the nutrients. This is, of course, similar to my food pleasure equation. Since this early paper, we have learned that calories in the form of fat and sugar have profound actions on the gut receptors and the many hormones that react in their presence. The stomach and intestine sense this incoming nutritional rush and help ensure that the person eats this food again. Foods high in caloric density, sugar, and fat form the strongest and boldest dopamine-opioid rush when they are consumed.

Final Thoughts

In an excellent summary of chocolate cravings, Bruinsma and Taren (1999) concluded that the allure of chocolate is based on the sensory pleasure, psychoactive ingredients, and relief from the mood swings of the monthly cycle in women.[19] And I think with the evidence presented above, their conclusions are sound.

Numbered References

1. Brenner, J. 1999. *The Emperors of Chocolate: Inside the Secret World of Hershey and Mars.* New York: Random House.

2. How America eats. *Bon Appétit.* http://www.epicurious. com/bonappetit/features/survey2003

3. Wansink, B., Cheney, M. M., and N. Chan. Exploring comfort food preferences across age and gender. *Physiol. Behav.*, 79:739–47, 2003. http://foodpsychology.cornell.edu/pdf/comfortfoods.pdf

4. Parker, G., Parker, I., and H. Brotchie. Mood state effects of chocolate. *J. Affect. Disorders*, 92:149–59, 2006.

5. Drewnowski, A. Taste and preferences and food intake. *Annu. Rev. Nutr.*, 17:237–53, 1997. (This paper is a classic.)

6. Parker, G., Roy, K., Mitchell, P., Wilhelm, K., Malhi, G., and D. Hadzi-Pavlovic. Atypical depression: a reappraisal. *Am. J. Psychiatr.*, 159:1470–79, 2002.

7. Blass, E. M., and L. B. Hoffmeyer. Sucrose as an analgesic for newborn infants. *Pediatrics*, 81:215–18, 1991.

8. Drewnowski, A. Why do we like fat? *J. Am. Diet. Assoc.*, 97(Suppl.):S58–62, 1997.

9. Smadja, C., Ruiz, F., Coric, P., Fournié-Zaluski, M. C., Roques, B. P., and R. Maldonado. CCK-B receptors in the limbic system modulate the antidepressant-like effects induced by endogenous enkephalins. *Psychopharmacology*, 132:227–36, 2004.

10. Dallman, M., Pecoraro, N. C., and H. Brotchie. Chronic stress and comfort foods: self-medication and abdominal obesity. *Brain Behav. Immun.*, 19:275–80, 2005.

11. Trottier, G., Koski, K. G., Brun, T., Toufexis, D. J., Richard, D., and C. D. Walker. Increased fat intake during lactation modifies hypothalamic-pituitary-adrenal responsiveness in developing rat pups: a possible role for leptin. *Endocrinology*, 139:3704–11, 1998.

12. di Tomaso, E., Beltramo, M., and D. Piomelli. Brain cannabinoids in chocolate. *Nature*, 382:677–78, 1996.

13. Sparling, P. B., Giuffrida, A., Piomelli, D., Rosskopf, A., and A. Dietrich. Exercise activates the endocannabinoid system. *NeuroReport*, 14:2209–11, 2003.

14. Herraiz, J. Tetrahydro-beta-carbolines: potential neuroactive alkaloids, in chocolate and cocoa. *J. Agric. Food Chem.*, 48:4900–4, 2000.

15. Reid, L., Boswell, K. J., Lacroix, A. M., Caffalette, A., and M. L. Reid. Withdrawal from extensive intake of chocolate cake mix batter by female rats induces more weight loss than observed after withdrawal from white cake mix batter. Poster presented at the *Society for the Study of Ingestive Behavior*, Annual meeting, June, 2004.

16. Sokolov, O. Y, Pryanikova, N. A., Kost, N. V., Zolotarev, Y. A., Ryukert, E. N., and A. A. Zozulya. Reactions between beta-casomorphins-7 and 5-HT2-serotonin receptors. *Bull. Exp. Biol. Med.*, 140:582–4, 2005.

17. Drewnowski, A., and M. R. C. Greenwood. Cream and sugar: human preferences for high fat foods. *Physiol. Behav.*, 30:629–33, 1983.

18. Rozin, P., Levine, E., and C. Stoess. Chocolate craving and liking. *Appetite*, 17:199–212, 1991.

19. Bruinsma, K., and D. Taren. Chocolate: food or drug? *J. Am. Diet. Assoc.*, 99:1249–56, 1999.

References, General

Working with chocolate is therapeutic

* http://www.feminaindia.com/articleshow/253746.cms

New romances and the chocolate sugar high

* http://www.womentodaymagazine.com/relationships/chocolate.html

Chocolate neurochemistry

- http://sulcus.berkeley.edu/mcb/165_001/papers/manuscripts/
  _303.html

Similarity of drugs and chocolate

- Grigson, P. S. Like drugs for chocolate: separate rewards modulated by common mechanisms. *Physiol. Behav.*, 76:345–6, 2002.

- http://www.rps.psu.edu/probing/sugar.html

Salt, fat, sugar, and reward

- Kelley, A., and K. Berridge. The neuroscience of natural rewards: relevance to addictive drugs. *J. Neurosci.*, 22:3306–11, 2002.

Chocolate can be very healthy

- http://www.sciencenews.org/articles/20050813/food.asp

- Steinberg, M, Bearden, M. M., and C. L. Keen. Cocoa and chocolate flavonoids: implications for cardiovascular health. *J. Am. Diet. Assoc.*, 103:215–23, 2003.

- Baumann, L. Chocolate and cocoa: antioxidant content and skin care. *Skin & Allergy News*, 36:20, 2005.

- CocoaVia is a brand of chocolate by Mars Inc. that is tasty and heart healthy—it even lowers cholesterol (added phytosterols). See: http://www.cocoavia.com/story/

CHAPTER 17

▼

WHY PEOPLE LIKE
ARTICHOKES

Chlorogenic acid (in artichokes) may have anti-inflammatory and pain reducing
activity.[1]

Eating an artichoke (*Cynara scolymus* L.) seems, to the uninitiated, like a complete waste of time; a lot of effort is required for just a few tablespoons of the
"meat." I learned to like chokes at an early age and relished the spring season,
since it meant one of my favorite foods would soon appear in the stores. An artichoke is surprisingly nutritiously dense, containing 16 essential nutrients, 7
grams dietary fiber, and only 25 calories. The soluble fiber is called inulin. It acts
as *prebiotic* that encourages the growth of good bacteria in the gut. Artichoke
leaves also contain the powerful antioxidants and detoxicants, chlorogenic acid,
cynarin, and silymarin.[2]

Artichoke Liking

Artichoke liking could be as simple as an excuse to eat butter or mayonnaise, two emulsions that humans crave. To ease this guilt, I like to make mayonnaise out of the new "designer" oil called Enova, which entered the U.S. marketplace in January, 2005. Enova is the special cooking oil that contains higher amounts of natural diacyglycerols (DAG), two fatty acids attached to a glycerol backbone, versus triacylglycerols (TAG)—the normal configuration of a vegetable or animal fat. This unique fat is digested in the intestine and instead of being reassembled and sent to your body fat stores, it goes to the liver and is burned for energy. This means that Enova is much less likely to be stored as body fat.[3] Available in most supermarkets, Enova is *almost* a "guilt-free" cooking oil. Making your own mayonnaise with Enova is pretty easy; it produces a nice, thick emulsion that can be used as a base for endless flavor variations (garlic mayo is tasty). DAG oil, first introduced in Japan under the brand name Healthy Econa Cooking Oil in 1999, quickly became a national sensation, with sales now approaching $300 million a year.

Another reason we like artichokes is its taste modifying effects on food perception, first described by Linda Bartoshuk et al. (1972).[4] Boil some artichokes in a big pot of salted water. When the leaves are tender, take out some of the "soup" and let cool. Rinse your mouth with plain water first, then take a sip of the artichoke water soup and swish thoroughly in the mouth and expectorate. Then take a glass of room temperature water, take a sip, and notice the sensation. The artichoke solution made the water taste *sweet*! The modifying compounds (chlorogenic acid and cynarin, which are primarily in the leaves) fool the taste bud into thinking you just tasted a sweet solution. Because sweetness is a hardwired opioid pleasure, foods eaten with the artichokes taste just a little bit better. Eating artichokes increases overall food hedonics, but may also modify some foods and make them distasteful. A glass of a very dry Chardonnay tastes quite strange and out of character after artichoke consumption. Pairing foods with artichokes can be a tricky sensory endeavor. Chlorogenic acid and cynarin also suppress bitter and sour tastes.[5]

Chlorogenic Acid (CA) and Cynarin

CA is the most abundant polyphenolic compound (specifically a hydroxycinnamic acid) and found in a wide variety of vegetables and fruits, including blueberries, grapes, apples, tomatoes, broccoli, and spinach.[6] The richest source, aside from artichoke, is green coffee, almost 10 percent CA by weight. Chlorogenic acid has a number of interesting effects; one coffee researcher, Dr. Darcy Lima, thinks this antioxidant is *psychoactive*.[7] Here is a summary of the published effects:

- CA reduces blood pressure in hypertensive rats.[8]

- CA may have anticancer activity.[9]

- CA may have antioxidant, antibiotic, antihypertension, and anti-inflammatory effects.[1]

- CA is broken down during roasting, producing feruloilquinic acid, a powerful opioid antagonist like naloxone (which, when administered to people, reduces the craving for junk food and alcohol).[10]

Artichokes are one of the world's oldest medicinal plants—used by the Romans and Greeks as a diuretic and to aid digestion. The phytoactive compounds (chlorogenic acid, cyanarin, luteolin, anthocyanins) may also help reduce cardiovascular disease by protecting LDL cholesterol from oxidation. Standardized extracts are used in Europe (especially Germany) to treat high cholesterol and blood lipids and are subject to many clinical trials.

I *now* know why we cook them and don't eat them raw. Just recently I chopped up a few chokes for dinner and accidentally licked my finger when a needle on top of the choke punctured my ring finger. A most unpleasant bitter sensation developed that lasted for a few minutes—not a bitterness like caffeine, but a pharmaceutical-like bitterness. Cynarin may be the bitter-tasting compound, which, coincidentally, helps the body to secrete bile acids and digestive enzymes—the perfect physiological *aperitif*.[11]

Cooking Artichokes

Artichokes are best cooked in a large pot that is seasoned with kosher salt, bay leaves, peppercorns, and a few smashed cloves of garlic. Herbs may be added if desired—*herbs de Provence* contributes a nice aroma complexity to the mostly musty green artichoke flavor complex. A note of caution on the addition of salt, I have found that artichokes will soak up excess salt if they are left in the water too long. Another cooking tip is to keep the artichokes *under* the boiling water; Chef Emeril adds a plate that fits on top of the cut chokes that is heavy enough to keep them from bobbing up. The boiled peppercorns are not only tasty but improve digestion.

Numbered References

1. dos Santos, M. D., Almeida, M. C., Lopes, N. P., and G. E. de Souza. Evaluation of the anti-inflammatory, analgesic and anti-pyretic activities of the natural polyphenol chlorogenic acid. *Biol. Pharm. Bull.*, 29:2236–40, 2006.

2. Nutrition facts, artichokes. OceanMist.com. http://oceanmist.com/artnutrition.htm

3. Enova oil Web site. http://www.enovaoil.com/

4. Bartoshuk, L. A., Chi-Hang, L., and R. Scarpellino. Sweet taste of water induced by artichoke (*Cynara scolymus*). *Science*, 178:988–90, 1972.

5. Jacobs, T. The physiology of taste. http://www.cf.ac.uk/biosi/staff/jacob/teaching/sensory/taste.html

6. Gonthier, M., P., Verny, M. A., Besson, C., Rémésy, C., and A. Scalbert. Chlorogenic acid bioavailability largely depends on its metabolism by the gut microflora in rats. *J. Nutr.*, 133:1853–59, 2003.

7. Lima, D., R., A. Project coffee and health. http://www.ico.org/event_pdfs/lima.pdf

8. Suzuki, A., Yamamoto, N., Jokura, H., Yamammoto, M., Fujii, A., Tokimitsu, I., and I. Saito. Chlorogenic acid attenuates hypertension and improves endothelial function in spontaneously hypertensive rats. *J. Hypertens.*, 24:1065–73, 2006.

9. Belkaid, A., Currie, J. C., Desgagnes, J., and B. Annabi. The chemopreventive properties of chlorogenic acid reveal a potential new role for the microsomal glucose-6-phosphate translocase in brain tumor progression. *Cancer Cell Int.*, March 27;6:7, 2006.

10. ProCOR conference on cardiovascular health. ProCOR.org. http://www.procor.org/discussion/displaymsg.asp?ref=880&cate=Pro COR+Dialogue

11. Artichoke. Raintree Nutrition. http://www.rain-tree.com/arti choke.htm

Artichoke recipes

- http://www.foodnetwork.com/food/recipes/recipe/0,FOOD_ 9936_14974,00.html

- http://www.cheftalk.com/content/display.cfm?articleid=121 &type=article

For botanical and medicinal information
http://www.rain-tree.com/artichoke.htm

CHAPTER 18

WHY WE LIKE PIZZA

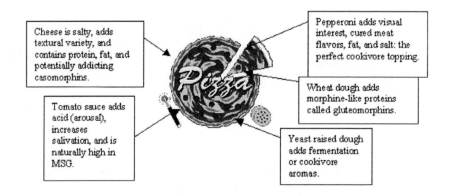

Cheese is salty, adds textural variety, and contains protein, fat, and potentially addicting casomorphins.

Tomato sauce adds acid (arousal), increases salivation, and is naturally high in MSG.

Pepperoni adds visual interest, cured meat flavors, fat, and salt: the perfect cookivore topping.

Wheat dough adds morphine-like proteins called gluteomorphins.

Yeast raised dough adds fermentation or cookivore aromas.

Why do we have so many pizzas? They are as distinctive as the mouth that eats them.
Pizza Hut Web site, 2006

Studies reveal that three-quarters of all Amercians live within three miles of a Pizza Hut, a Taco Bell, and a KFC.[1]

If you have made it this far, *you* could probably answer the question as to why we like pizza. This popular food ranks third in preference for men and women and is number two for young kids—French fries and hamburgers still win the top spots.[2] Yet culinologists and food surveyors note that pizza is starting to drop in appeal, as a number of other foods are chipping away at its dominance—Chinese food is one such example. Since pizza is a $30 billion industry, let's explore why people eat almost fifty slices each year.[3]

1. The Tostada Effect (Dynamic Contrast Variant)

Certain popular and palatable foods appear to have similar fundamental constructions. The hamburger, the number one preferred food by men, contains meat and condiments encased (toasted) by two bread buns. Tacos are also very popular in the United States and Latin countries and probably descended from the tostada, a flat and circular, deep fried piece of corn tortilla. Tacos are traditionally filled with grilled spiced meat—as in *taco el pastor*, popular in Mexico—with added condiments of salsa, cilantro (leaf), cheese, and/or sour cream. The taco is as ubiquitous as the hamburger, and the shape, crunch, and contrast from the hard, dry exterior to an immediate explosion of taste and flavor in the interior is very pleasurable—similar in design to the hamburger. My roommates in college most preferred food was the tostada—fried corn tortilla topped with as many tasty toppings as they could pile on, until the toppings either fall off or the shell cracks under its own weight. Eating a tostada was strangely exciting but dangerous, as one bite could crack the shell—and dump the carefully arranged toppings onto one's lap!

Pizza and the tostada share similar structural elements—moist and taste-active toppings placed on a crunchy or chewy bottom crust. Bread dough replaces the corn tortilla, and toppings are replaced by cheese and tomato sauce in the most basic type. Toppings are the focus in American pizza (see below), but the type most often found in Italian (Neapolitan) pizzerias is the Margherita-style—a thin crust (non-bready) that is light and crispy topped by tomato sauce, mozzarella, fresh basil, and quickly fired up in a wood oven. Hence, Italian-style is pizza all about the dynamic contract of the much thinner crust. Italians take their pizza seriously, and the Italian Ministry of Agriculture has strict guidelines on how to make true *Napoletana* (from Naples) pizza:

a.   Only three varieties are allowed:

   1.   Marinara (tomato, garlic, and oregano)

   2.   Margherita (tomato, basil, and mozzarella)

   3.   Margherita Extra (*extra* tomatoes, basil, and mozzarella).

b.   Pizzas are no more than 14 inches in diameter and must be round.

c. Pizza dough must be kneaded by hand.

d. Oven must be wood fired.

e. All ingredients must be from Italy.

f. Mozzarella must be from South Apennines.

In many Italian pizzerias, this national dish (the Ministry wants to patent it, much to the chagrin of Dominos), is made in front of you by a *pizzailo* (pizza-maker) who hand-rolls the crust and adds the simple combinations of tomato sauce, basil, mozzarella, and olive oil—all delivered from a wood-fired oven in three minutes.

If you can't visit Naples, you can make your own Margherita at home, though crafting the true Neapolitan crust is tricky—think light and crispy; it should shatter like a saltine cracker. Erika Bruce, writing in *Cook's Illustrated*, developed a streamlined version using two types of bread flour, canned tomatoes (with added basil and garlic), and the addition of mozzarella *halfway* through the 10-minute cooking time, at 500°F.[4]

For those who hate to cook and still want their Margherita pizza, there still is hope! I just received a menu flyer in the mail from Red Brick Pizza, advertising its Fire-Roasted Gourmet Pizza. This new chain sears the pizza in a 1,000 °F oven for just three minutes. The crust is thin and golden, and the chain uses only the best Italian cheeses.

My family and I tried the pizza, and we loved the thinner and crispier crust; it has more of the tostada effect. Now, chewy and thick crust has its place, but I don't like all that bread (deep dish) in a pizza. Margherita-style of pizza is more for sensory-sensation than for the gut-fill lovers, although I guess you could eat four of them if one is in the latter category!

Thus, the simple contrast of a harder exterior and a softer interior loaded with taste-active solutes and ingredients is one of the most fundamental aspects of good food construction. Whether it is a chocolate coating around ice cream (like a Klondike Bar); a *crème brûlée* with a crunchy, sugary top and creamy, custard-like interior; a simple taco with external crunch and tasty innards; a pizza with textural contrasts; or an Oreo cookie—all use dynamic contrast to add food surprise and pleasure. This variation of DC, called the tostada effect, is simple in presentation but seriously exciting to the palate. Researchers are only now beginning to work out the underlying pleasure response and neurochemistry. But it appears that noradrenaline (arousal or surprise) may be activated by this form of texture contrast, and this has an influence on the reward or reinforcement neurotransmitters (opioids, GABA, benzodiazepines, and dopamine).

2. Pizza Can Be High in Fat and Salt

Pizza Hut's huge selection of basic pizza types and toppings generates a dizzying array of nutritional options. A Fit-N-Delicious 14" veggie is only 24 percent fat calories with a caloric density of 2.3; whereas a Full House Pepperoni pizza is 2.7 in caloric density and close to 45 percent fat calories (which is a bit lower than many fast foods). The sodium content of the 14-inch pizza can vary greatly, however, from a low of 490 mg in the Veggie Lover's to a high of 1700 mg for just one slice of the Meat Lover's Stuffed Crust pizza. As we have discussed, salt taste is pleasurable, and pizza can be quite high in sodium; it appears that the cured-meat ingredients are mostly to blame—in other words, pepperoni and sausage. Health experts debate the issue of salt and high blood pressure—some think it's one of the worst features of fast food, while others suggest that sodium is easily excreted by our kidneys—and only 15 percent of Americans are salt sensitive.[5] Beyond the salt issues, pizza can be quite nutritious, especially if it is made with whole wheat and plenty of veggies (mozzarella is one of the lower fat cheeses). Even the American Dietetic Association recommends cheese pizza (skip the fatty toppings) as a healthy food option.

3. Pizza Variety Allows for Hedonic Optimization (Especially Pizza Hut)

Pizza pie (bread) variations can be bewildering. At the local Pizza Hut (my favorite pizza chain) I have numerous choices on just the crust: Pan Pizza thick crust (crispy on the outside, soft and chewy on the inside for dynamic contrast); Hand-Tossed Pizzeria-style; Thin and Crispy; Stuffed Crust Pizza; 4forALL Pizza (clever concept of having four topping versions; this reduces sensory specific satiety); the Full House XL Pizza; Fit N Delicious Pizza; Hand-Tossed Pizza; and the P'Zone Pizza (actually a calzone). I remember the days when all I had to remember was what topping(s) I desired!

Lots of Choices

Like Starbucks and Cold Stone Creamery, one aspect of Pizza Hut's success is the almost unlimited choices of pizza and topping combinations. Here is an example. Let's start with the fundamentals:

- Seven pizza styles (I am excluding P'Zone)

- Fourteen types of toppings

- Toppings can be a normal portion or the larger "Extra" option

Each of the seven types of pizza can have an amazing fourteen types of meat, fruit, and vegetable toppings. Using combination theory (probability statistics), the result is many thousands of possible flavor variations or combinations for *each* pizza. If you wish to calculate this for yourself, the number of possible flavor options for "one" pizza with 14 topping options, is 2^{14} (2 times 2 fourteen times) or over 16,000 topping combination possibilities.[6] You still have the option of regular or extra amounts of each topping! Pizza Hut, therefore, offers a total fulfillment of Cabanac's maximization of hedonic pleasure theory. Pizza Hut, along with Starbucks and, gives consumers exactly what they want: a personalized eating experience in which you can "have it your way!" Burger King, the number two fast-food chain with over 11,000 stores, invented this slogan in 1974 to differentiate itself from McDonald's. And from what we have learned about the hedonic advantages of personalization—it was a great idea. For a highly entertaining way to build a burger "your way," see the Burger King Whopperettes' Web site.[7]

Pizza Hut is also the number one pizza chain in China, as the Chinese have taken a liking to pizza (along with KFC's chicken), although the toppings reflect a more localized taste. For example, China's Hello Pizza chain developed by French émigré Anthony Le Corre has twenty different pizzas, with such toppings as curried chicken, cherries, and thousand island salad dressing. He says that people want low price *and* choice.

Pepperoni (a Classic Cookivore Food)

Thirty-six percent of all pizzas carry this number one favorite topping. Sausage is also another highly favored addition. (Pizzas Hut's tasty Meat Lover's pizza contains six kinds of meat—pepperoni, Italian sausage, ham, bacon, beef, and pork!)

The name pepperoni is actually a lingual corruption of the Italian word for bell pepper (*peperone*). When in Italy, you should order *salame piccante*, or your pizza will have a vegetarian look (bell peppers instead of pepperoni)! Usually made from beef and pork, pepperoni (a dry sausage) has some interesting physical and nutritional characteristics that make it *the* favorite pizza topping:

a.   High in Salt. Many pleasurable foods are high in salt—bacon and soy sauce, to name just a few. Pepperoni is loaded with salt, almost 5 percent by weight, to partially cure and preserve the protein ingredients. Salt and sugar are the two most important hedonic tastants in foods, and it is no surprise that pepperoni popularity rests partially on the sodium content.

b.   High in Fat. With a fat-calorie percentage of nearly 78 percent, eating pepperoni is almost like eating a stick of butter. Fats and fatty acids do activate taste buds in a pleasurable way, and fat has been shown to have a secondary metabolic action in the gut—fat increases CCK more than protein or carbohydrates do and creates a calming effect—and may increase central serotonergic receptors as well. The animal fat most often used in pepperoni and salami in general? You guessed—it's pork fat!

c.   High in Taste-Active Solutes. Pork has naturally high glutamic acid levels, and when it's cured properly, the salami releases free glutamates. In addition, many recipes add garlic, and we know that garlic is particularly good at boosting "umami" flavors. Some pepperonis may go through a fermentation stage, in which a starter culture is added to the meat; this creates additional fermentation flavors—and lowers the pH (adding acidic elements).

d.   High Caloric Density (HCD). Pepperoni's caloric density is 4.6, which is very close to many junk foods (snacks). We have seen that humans like HCD foods, and we have evolved to seek them out. Pepperoni is aged and air-dried, both of which extract moisture and increase the caloric density.

e.   Cured Cookivore Aroma and Taste. As discussed in chapter one, Wrangham first coined this phenomenon in his *Harvard Review* article. He believes that man coevolved with fire, and cooking food is part of what makes us human. Pepperoni develops cooked-meat flavor notes during the curing process (2–3 month aging), and the starter culture creates tasty fermentation flavors.

4. Pizza Contains Gluteomorphins *and* Casomorphins

Digestion of wheat and dairy products (cheese) produces gluteomorphins and casomorphins, collectively called food exorphins. The compounds *may* act like morphine and add addictive properties to foods. Although scientifically controversial, it is possible that these protein fragments add to the enjoyment of ingested food. One may wonder if unscrupulous food companies could enrich their products with these protein peptides for commercial profit. In a comprehensive review on the production of physiologically actives peptides derived from milk proteins, Korhonen and Pihlanto (2006) disclose that bioactive products are not only generated during digestion of cheese, but by bacteria and fungi during the cheese ripening process as well.[8] Curiously, *Emmental* cheese (a fancier Swiss cheese) is a richer source of mineral-enhancing, antimicrobial, antihypertensive, and immune-stimulating food peptides than most all other cheese types. The list of possible effects of casomorphins is amazing: reduction of blood pressure, and anxiety, increased absorption of calcium, reduction of dental caries, increased energy and athletic performance, and enhanced REM sleep.[8]

Some Fun Pizza Facts[3]

- Americans consume a hundred acres of pizza a year.

- Over three billion pizzas were made last year in the United States.

- 93 percent of Americans eat at least one pizza per month.

- Americans eat twenty-three pounds of pizza per year.

- Italian food is number one in the United States. (Chinese is closing in fast.)

- 94 percent of Americans like pizza.

Favorite U.S. Toppings

- Pepperoni (36 percent of all pizzas; cookivore theory)

- Mushrooms (5'-nucleotides)

- Extra cheese (extra casomorphins)

- Sausage (cookivore theory)

- Green pepper and onions (pyrazines and orosensation)

- Least favorite topping in America: anchovies

<u>Favorite World Wide Toppings:</u>

- India: pickled ginger, minced mutton, Tandoori chicken

- Japan: mayonnaise+potato+bacon, eel, and squid

- Brazil: green peas

- Russia: "*mockba*," or sardines+tuna+mackerel+salmon+onions

- France: "*flambé*," or bacon+onions+fresh cream

- Australia: shrimp and pineapple

- Netherlands: "Double Dutch," or double cheese, onions, and beef

Numbered References

1. Yum! Brands. Fast food's yummy secret. *The Economist*, Aug. 25, 2005. http://economist.com/business/displaystory.cfm?story_id= 4316138

2. Sloan, E. A. What, when, and where America eats. *Food Technol.*, Jan., 2006. http://members.ift.org/NR/rdonlyres/65A7B82E-0AFF-4639-95B2-733B8225D93A/0/0106americaeats.pdf

3. Pizza industry facts. Pizzaware.com. http://www.pizzaware.com/ facts.htm

4. Bruce, E. Pizza Margherita at home. *Cook's Illustrated*, July & Aug., 2006. http://www.cooksillustrated.com/login.asp?did=3516&Login Form=recipe&iseason=

5. Schulkin, J. 1991 *Sodium Hunger*. Cambridge: Cambridge University Press.

6. Dr. Math. Fast food combinations. http://mathforum.org/dr.math/faq/faq.mcdonalds.html

7. The original Whopperettes—have it your way. http://www.whopper ettes.com/index.html

8. Korhonen, H., and A. Pihlanto. Bioactive peptides: production and functionality. *Int. Dairy J.*, 16:945–60, 2006. http://www.aseanbio technology.info/Abstract/21020011.pdf

References, General

• http://www.chicagostylepizzainc.com/ownership/pizzafacts.shtml

• http://library.thinkquest.org/J0112790/facts.html

• http://www.absoluteastronomy.com/enc1/taco

• http://www.foodproductdesign.com/archive/1996/0396PR.html

• http://www.pizzamarketplace.com/article.php?id=3019

• http://en.wikipedia.org/wiki/Pepperoni

CHAPTER 19

▼

WHY WE LIKE TO EAT DESSERT LAST

We eat the pie at the end of a Thanksgiving meal because the pleasure overrides the satiety.[1]

Dessert, derived from the Old French, *desservir*, or to clear the table, is the term used for the final or ending course of a meal. Almost every culture and/or cuisine prepares the savory meal first, followed by the sweetness-dominant dessert. Even our moms have been known to admonish us not to spoil our appetites by eating candy or sweet snacks before dinner. But the question remains, is there some fundamental physiological reason why we save the sweetest dishes for last? In other words, what explains the phenomenon of *dessert*?

Each culture varies on whether they eat dessert last or eat any at all. Americans and European are dessert-at-the-end traditionalists. Elaine Carley, in *Classics from a French Kitchen,* quoted French gastronome, Grimod de la Reyiere, as saying that true gourmands always eat dessert after dinner. Louis Outhier, of nouvelle cuisine fame, exclaims that the dinner exit must be in "grand style."[2] But many French restaurants, desserts do not have to be sweet. A strongly flavored cheese plate with fruit along with fortified wine (port) is common after dinner. French gastronome, Anthelme Brillat-Savarin observed that, a dessert without cheese is like a beautiful woman with only one eye.

In contrast to the West and Northern Europeans, Asian cultures rarely eat dessert. Sweet dishes are reserved for special occasions; for example, the Moon Festival or a quick snack. [3,4] When dessert is served, it may be the lightly sweetened egg custard, sweet red bean (*dousha*) pastries, deep-fried sesame red bean balls, deep-fried sweet potatoes, tapioca pudding or just fruit. Even today, modern Chinese bakeries serve much lighter and less sweet versions of cookies, cakes, and pastries. This lightness in the dessert palate may reflect the relative lack of butter, cream, and sugar as dietary staples in the Asian countries. In addition, the high Asian prevalence of lactase deficiency—the inability to digest the milk sugar lactose discourages milk consumption.

1. High Osmotic Load

Most desserts are high in sugar, fat, and solutes. As we have discussed, when you are very hungry, high amounts of concentrated sugar, rapidly digested starches, or fatty acids can be tough to stomach. Fat is a very potent inhibitor of gastric emptying, allowing the sugar(s) in the dessert to pull water from the stomach in an effort to dilute the contents. A Kristy Kreme donut—or worse, an apple fritter (*really* osmotically loaded)—can actually cause gastric distress in some people— but not *after* a full meal. Any generation of gastric distress lowers food pleasure and is not a desirable state to be in; people can develop food aversions with just one exposure! Thus, after a meal, the stomach is full, and the additional solute load from dessert does not add further irritation. Savory first, dessert later is probably more physiologically correct than the opposite situation.

2. Inhibition of Sensory Specific Satiety

Eating dessert first could theoretically reduce the total amount of food to be eaten, which is not the primary goal of the brain—it is to maximize caloric intake. The theory is the rapid rise in serum glucose, and hence insulin, would put a break on the eating process. However, a 1991 study by Rolls et al. found little change in food intake when subjects ate a candy bar before cheese and crackers.[5] In high school, I used to eat the dessert first, probably due to its higher palatability (Ding Dongs and Twinkies). Nevertheless, almost all cultures eat the savory course first.

Speaking of snack foods, why do we still eat Ding Dongs and Twinkies? These snack foods have two important dynamic contrast properties—rapid meltdown and a creamy filling with moist cake on the outside. Rapid meltdown generates hedonic solutes very quickly (which is good), and the creamy core is not only visually different from the surrounding cake, but it is flavored differently to increase aroma and taste contrast. (The creamy Twinkie filling is banana flavored.) Although Ding Dong may have a waxy chocolate coating and ingredients not found in nature, I still would eat one today if offered; it has multiple sensory contrasts and brings back *mémoires heureuses* (mostly happy) of my Loyola High School days. The flavor signatures of both snacks remain unchanged for over thirty years!

Another reason why we structure meals with savory followed by dessert courses may be related to Cabanac's theory of the maximization of sensory pleasure. Some studies suggest that the two major classes of food, the savory and the sweet, help reduce the sensory specific satiety of the whole eating experience. In other words, as we eat the savory course we rapidly reduce our hunger pangs and become full—the pleasure of the first course has passed (savory and *hot*). But as we indulge again with a new set of foods (sweet and *cold*), our appetite reenergizes—and we indulge in the pleasures of eating once again. Hence, savory and sweet ingestion maximizes overall food pleasure via the reduction of sensory satiety mechanisms—the gastric breaking mechanism of the sweet-course ingestion is no longer an issue. All subjects in the Rolls et al. (1991) study *preferred* to eat dessert last!

References

1. Manier, J., Callahan, P., and D. Alexander. OREO. Craving the cookie. *Chicago Tribune*, Aug. 21, 2005. http://www.chicagotribune.com/news/specials/chi-oreo-1,1,7603329.

2. Carley, E A. 1983. *Classics from a French Kitchen*. New York: Crown Publishers.

3. Miller, G. B. 1984. *The Thousand Recipe Chinese Cookbook*. New York: Simon & Schuster.

4. Wertz, R. R. Food and Drink: Cuisine. *Cultural Heritage of China*. http://www.ibiblio.org/chineseculture/contents/food/p-food-c01s 01.html

5. Rolls, B. J., Laster, L. J., and A. Summerfelt. Meal order reversal: effects of eating a sweet course first or last. *Appetite*, 16:141–48, 1991.

CHAPTER 20

▼

SECRET-WEAPON PLEASURE FOODS

"You must like cooking for other people, even if you neither know nor like them.
You must enjoy the fact that you are nourishing them, pleasing them, giving
them the best you've got."
Anthony Bourdain[1]

Introduction

Professional chefs know that *specific* food ingredients added to almost any recipe increase flavor and complexity, both of which contribute to food pleasure. In this chapter, we will explore these pleasure ingredients and how to use them in everyday cooking; they are applicable to many different recipes, regardless of the type of cuisine. I've used these food-pleasure tricks in a variety of foods cooked for friends and always get a kick out of their reactions, such as "these are the best hamburgers I've ever tasted," which happened, by the way, at a recent family gathering. I had modified the hamburgers by a centuries-old, Chinese super-food addition we will discuss below.

The only tricky part in using these Super Pleasure Foods (SPF) is to know where to use them and in what amount. In fact, the ingredient level is the key. Too much and you may activate food neophobias (food fright), and the food could be rejected. It is also possible that the exuberant use of SPF could actually make the food taste like another cuisine entirely, which would add food confusion and not fusion (think sweet and sour tacos). Speaking of flavor fusion, in 1983, Wolfgang Puck (an Austrian trained in three star French cuisine kitchens), started this trend when he opened "Chinois on Main" in Santa Monica, where Californian/French cuisine was melded with Asian ingredients and techniques. Although quite *avant-garde* at the time and widely copied now, the use of Asian SPF with French technique may be the most pleasurable fusion cuisine ever invented.

Each of the SPF discussed below is used extensively within a variety of cuisines—always adding flavor, texture, and unique taste elements that are often based on boosting "umami" perception. You will recall that umami is the fifth sense of taste and is largely activated by MSG, 5'-nucleotides, and certain amino acids. Many taste-active compounds also excite this pleasure-oriented sense of taste: the brown bits called *fond* in the bottom of a pan (from cooked meat), the roasted skin of a turkey or duck, or the rich glaze of veal stock. A spectacular example of the generation of flavor-active compounds that I've witnessed was a fortuitous (just for the fun of it) deep frying of a precooked ham in a turkey fryer. The flavor of the ham in contact with the hot oil is a taste experience like no other, crisp on the outside, moist on the inside, with a ham flavor I've never tasted before! Although we can't cook ham like this routinely, we can use a version of this—bacon—to greatly liven up many dishes. Pork belly and pork fat are examples of power-food ingredients that are transformed when subjected to brining and flavor additives.

Luckily for the home cook, many of these SPF are as close as your kitchen cupboard! Let's take a look at the flavor principles of some popular cuisines for key (signature) ingredients that may qualify as pleasure foods:

1. Italian

   • Parmigiano-Reggiano cheese (and many others)

   • Prosciutto and other aged meats

   • Garlic

2. French
   - Shallots
   - Veal stock
   - Cheese (many types)
   - Butter and cream
   - White pepper
   - Black pepper
   - Nutmeg

3. Asian
   - Soy sauce (regular and dark)
   - Fish sauce
   - Oyster sauce (many types)
   - Mushrooms (shitake et al.)
   - Egg yolk
   - Crab, shrimp, lobster
   - Five spice powder
   - Black vinegar

4. Mexican/Spanish
   - Hot peppers
   - Chocolate
   - Cinnamon
   - Cumin
   - Coriander

5. Fundamental ingredients in many other cuisines
   - Brown sugar/molasses
   - Vinegar(s)

- Balsamic
  - Red/White wine-based
- Mayonnaise
- Vanilla extract
- Worcestershire sauce

Super pleasure foods (SPF) can be added to almost any dish (except, perhaps, ice cream or chocolate) and will increase the flavor, taste, and, ultimately, the food pleasure. Just sneaking some of these ingredients into your standard recipes will certainly improve the food's flavor. For example, recently I visited a relative who made spaghetti for dinner with a good-quality bottled sauce. By using some of these super pleasure foods (discussed below) we easily improved the taste and richness of flavor. The kids ate all of their dinner without much prompting!

Based on my experience and the action of these foods on the physiology of taste and smell, here are the most important super pleasure foods.

The Big 10:

1. Soy sauce

2. Cheese (Cheddar, Parmesan, Romano)

3. Garlic (fresh and roasted)

4. Butter/cream

5. Shallots

6. Sugar and reaction-flavor additions

7. Worcestershire sauce

8. Bacon

9. Egg yolk

10. Superstar salts and spices

Honorable Mentions:

1.   Mushrooms (especially shitake, chanterelles, morels)

2.   Black and white pepper

3.   French-style veal stock

4.   Mayonnaise

5.   Mustard (Grey Poupon or the good French types)

1. Soy Sauce—Liquid Pleasure Condiment

This ubiquitous Asian seasoning tops the list as a universal flavor booster. Many people are surprised when I explain in my food pleasure lectures the actual composition of soy sauce and how it is used in Asian cuisines. There are many types of soy sauce, and we will delve into them in some detail, but what is the universal appeal of this ubiquitous seasoning? It's simple: salt, and MSG, and plenty of taste and aroma-active flavorants. Before we go much further, I want to assure you that MSG in food is quite harmless, despite all the nonsense you've heard over the years in the popular press and on the Web. And I know that many food establishments advertise that they don't use it—emphasizing the point with a line through a circle MSG!

MSG is a natural part of many foods, and our bodies make it naturally (glutamic acid is an amino acid) to support our body's protein requirements. In one day, close to 20 grams recycle through our systems. It is also the most abundant neurotransmitter in the brain and is used extensively by the gut as an energy source. The protein you eat from steak, chicken, and even potatoes is about 20 percent glutamic acid. Breast milk has it, Parmesan cheese is loaded with it, and yeast is a rich source. Wheat protein is a particularly rich source of MSG. So don't worry about ingesting this fundamental flavor booster. Even health professionals can be confused, however. Once, after an hour-long lecture on food perception to California dietitians, the only statement that made the press was "top physiologist says MSG is okay!" The thirty years of MSG fear (inspired by John Olney, neuroscientist) appears to be waning, and this ingredient is now found in many common kitchen staples, like chicken and beef broth. For a complete discussion on MSG safety see references two through four.

Kikkoman soy sauce contains over 200 taste and aroma-active compounds. The major hedonic tastant of soy is sodium chloride, of course, as much as 18 percent salt by weight! There is a *reason* you don't see salt shakers in Chinese restaurants. (Note that lite soy sauce is an acceptable substitute, and I highly recommend it; it is 40 percent lower in sodium.) In addition to salt, soy sauce is also very high in naturally brewed MSG. I've seen some analyses that indicate MSG as high as 2 percent w/v! Where does the MSG come from? Simple: soy is a brewed concoction of roasted wheat and soybeans, sea salt, and koji (*Aspergillus oryzae*). The complex fermentation creates MSG and many interesting compounds; we also find the 5'-nucleotides or "umami boosters." Fermentation also creates lactic acid, which helps to maintain a pH of 4.8. Schultz (2005) reports the presence of other acids (acetic and succinic) and many sugar derivatives from wheat.[5]

There is yet another compound in soy sauce that may add extra pleasure to food from a pharmacological perspective (similar to the butyrolactones found in red wine). Upon digestion, wheat protein (gluten, the ingredient that makes bread structure) breaks down into amino acids and small peptides called gluteomorphins and gliadinomorphins. You'll notice that both words end in-morphin—as in morphine—and have morphine-like effects! Similar to milk-derived casomorphins in structure, these compounds have interesting effects in the body:[6]

a.   Stimulate T-cells (immune response)

b.   Have pleasure-like effects in the brain (similar to casomorphins)

c.   Slow digestion

d.   Reduce pain sensitivity

e.   Enhance learning performance

The Addition of Wheat

Wheat is the most popular grain grown on the planet. Wheat's flavor, its wide-spread use in bread making, and its high yield per acre no doubt account for the wide popularity of this grain. Despite its relatively poor amino acid profile (as compared to egg or whey protein), wheat, when combined with soy protein, can make the blend fairly nutritious and complete food.[7] Hence, soy sauce is not only tasty but adds an element of complementary (more nutritious) proteins as well.

Chinese Restaurant Syndrome, a supposed allergy to MSG does not exist; many studies have failed to find a connection between MSG consumption and adverse reactions.[8,9] Perhaps this syndrome is due to a reaction to the gluten derivatives in soy and/or wheat proteins. Gluten sensitivity, or celiac disease, is surprisingly common (up to 1 percent of the population); it occurs when the ingestion of wheat causes intestinal problems and possibly rashes. However, Kataoka (2005) states that the fermentation process in soy sauce effectively destroys the epitopes on the wheat proteins and eliminates allergic potential.[8] For a detailed discussion on Chinese Restaurant Syndrome, MSG, and food allergy see Walker and Lupien (2000).[9]

Far from being a villain, soy sauce may be a modern *health* food (if you discount the high salt content)! Kataoka lists the following interesting physiological aspects of soy sauce:[10]

a.   Promotes digestion—increases gastric acid secretion

b.   Increases antimicrobial activity against gram negative bacteria (the bad bugs)

c.   Contains antihypertensive compounds (ACE inhibitor)

d.   Contains anticarcinogenic and antioxidant compounds

e.   Contains shoyuflavones that may reduce allergy and inflammations

f.   Enhances antiplatelet activity (blood thinning)

Hence, the health-promoting soy sauce (SS) adds flavor complexity, masks bitter notes, adds umami flavoring, and works well in both sweet and savory systems. SS also contains a number of flavor-active amino acids, dipeptides, and various sugar derivatives. Add a little SS (1 tablespoon) to a standard batch of chocolate chip cookies, and you'll see what I mean. You won't detect the soy sauce, but the cookies will taste better.

As the story goes, soy sauce was invented in China 2,500 years ago when Buddhist monk noticed that salted soybean paste fermented on its own. Much later, a Zen priest took the 100 percent soybean formula to Japan, where wheat was added to the mix (around the 1600s) and now called *shoyu*. Today, most modern soy sauce is made by combining wheat with soybeans in a fermentation vessel along with salt and the fungus culture *Aspergillus oryza*–creating a *Koji* mash. Schultz (2005) notes that wheat adds flavor, body, complexity, and preservative properties.[5] The resulting fermentation creates lactic acid and ethanol, both of which act as preservatives and keep certain nasty bacterias and yeast from forming. Lactic acid is antifungal and promotes a bacterial flora in the large intestine that is human friendly (the milk sugar called lactose does the same thing). Ethanol is fairly toxic to all microbial life and adds extended shelf life at concentrations around 3 percent and above (think beer).

Today, Chinese soy sauce is typically available in three varieties, the normal light table and cooking sauce, a stronger flavored and more viscous "dark" soy sauce with added sugar, and a hot chili soy paste. The Japanese have many types of soy sauce, from the lighter *usuikuchi*, to the robust and twice fermented *saishikomi*. However, a more popular version is called *tamari*, considered the foundation of Japanese cuisine, fermented with higher soy protein content and just a touch of wheat. Kikkoman's Tamari soy sauce is widely available in Chinese, Japanese, and Korean grocery stores; and easily found on the Web (Amazon.com). Although the salt content of tamari is similar to regular soy sauce, the taste intensity of the saltiness seems reduced. The aroma and overall flavor is very complex, with a darker color and enhanced viscosity. Taste both, and see which you prefer. Tamari's complex aromas and taste are best appreciated in dipping sauces and in meat applications.[5,11]

Here are some of the uses of soy sauce in food product development and cuisine (taken from the Kikkoman Web site and based on my experience):

a.   SS adds a depth of flavor to cured meats like beef jerky (quite essential, actually).

b. In many savory dishes SS can add color, richness, and saltiness (of course) and can reduce bitterness.

c. SS is useful in such systems as baked goods when adding color and flavor and boosting the natural savory nature of wheat proteins.

d. SS adds a balance of flavor in sweet systems like cookies and even chocolate dishes. Add just a little—one or two teaspoons is plenty.

e. SS contains MSG that may activate other receptors as well, including those for heat and cold perception. Thus, adding a bit of soy sauce to a gingersnap cookie may actually wake up the ginger flavor.

Therefore, sneaking in a little soy in many food preparations will boost the flavor and the ultimate pleasure of that food. I particularly like it in reduction sauces, beef stews, chocolate chip cookies, refried beans, and almost any dish that needs a bit more umami to make it stand out. Please note that soy sauce is quite salty; resist the temptation to add extra salt until near the end of cooking. Salt taste is difficult to mask in foods once it is added, although adding a little sugar and acid may help reduce salty perception. Try adding small amounts of soy sauce to such dishes as Caesar salad, *beurre rouge* sauce, and even *crème brûlée*. Adding SS and honey to pizza crust adds additional flavor and enhances caramelization (Maillard reaction).

<u>Soy sauce makes a great base for quick cuisine formation:</u>

a. SS with green onion and brown sugar approximates *teriyaki* flavor.

b. You might like the following recipe for Hawaiian Huli Huli sauce for BBQ chicken:

   * 4–5 pounds chicken pieces
   * ½ cup soy sauce *paste* (a thicker soy-find in Chinese stores; regular will work)
   * 1 tablespoon minced fresh ginger (if powder, use 1 teaspoon)
   * 1 tablespoon minced garlic (more if you prefer)
   * 1 tablespoon lime juice (lemon will work)
   * 1 tablespoon Chinese red chili paste

- 1 tablespoon brown sugar (add more for additional flavor)

- 1 tablespoon vegetable oil

- (Pineapple juice and honey can be substituted as a flavor variation)

Mix all ingredients in a saucepan and cook over low heat until well blended. Put chicken pieces in a plastic bag; add some of the marinade and let sit in the fridge for three hours. BBQ the chicken and baste with the remaining sauce during cooking. Regular soy sauce works just as well if soy sauce paste is unavailable.

c. SS with red chili paste (use a 50/50 blend) is my wife's favorite—brush on corn on the cob or other vegetables before grilling.

d. SS works well in this ersatz brown steak sauce (bordelaise type), about one cup:

- 1 shallot, minced

- 1½ cup red wine

- 1 tablespoon soy sauce

- 2 garlic cloves, minced

- Pinch thyme

- 1 teaspoon beef stock (I like Minor's by Nestlé, but Better than Bouillon will work)

- 1 tablespoon tomato paste

- 1 teaspoon cocoa powder (Nestlé)

- 1 teaspoon black peppercorns

In a saucepan, sweat garlic and shallots in 1 tablespoon of oil. Do not burn the garlic. Then add all other ingredients and cook together, simmer for 1 hour. Reduce by half, and don't add any salt. Finish with swirl of butter. This sauce is fabulous on grilled steaks. I keep the peppercorns and shallots in. Peppercorns add a wonderful burst of flavor when they are chewed, if you don't like peppercorn simply strain them out.

This modified recipe comes closest to the classic brown sauces used in French cooking. The ingredients were selected to approximate the flavoring compounds produced during the time-honored process of making veal stock, without the veal bones and all the effort. This shortcut formula is based on food chemistry, but is no substitute for making the real thing. See page 37 of Anthony Bourdain's *Les Halles Cookbook* on how to make your own reduced veal stock or *demi-glace*. Many cookbooks contain stock recipes (see *Bouchon Cookbook* p. 318, the *Gourmet Cookbook* p. 928, or the *New York Times Cookbook* p. 586). The brown sauce recipe on page 67 of Julia Child's *Mastering the Art of French Cooking* starts with canned beef bouillon (of all things) but creates a surprisingly tasty sauce in about four hours. Well worth mastering; and if you use shallots instead of onions—so much the better!

I prefer to cook with *dark* soy sauce (richer, sweeter), which you can find in Chinese or other Asian supermarkets. (Japanese culinologists may find this type of sauce a little too strong and overbearing for more delicate dipping sauces and sushi.) One brand that I like is Kimlan; its ingredients include the following:

- Soybeans: MSG-rich, high in proteins and some fats

- Wheat: MSG-rich, high in hydrophobic amino acids, rich in gluteomorphins

- Salt: primary hedonic solute

- Sugar: primary hedonic solute (sucrose—the tastiest sugar!)

It is *very* salty, so use it with great care! One tablespoon contains 44 percent of your daily sodium intake, so hypertensives or those sensitive to salt intake (about 15–17 percent of the population) beware. In such cases reduced-sodium soy sauce (Kikkoman Less Sodium Soy Sauce) is always an excellent option.

Secret Soy Sauce

In the standard American grocery store, about the only brand available is Kikkoman, and its lower salt version in the familiar, green label. Since soy sauce has an intense, usually dark brown color and may interfere with the color of the foods, you may be able to find the lighter-colored version, which is especially useful in light-colored sauces like hollandaise. Kikkoman, by the way, is the largest producer of naturally brewed soy sauce ($2 billion in international sales) and has plants in Japan, Netherlands, Taiwan, and the United States (California and Wisconsin).

Despitethe high quality of Kikkoman's standard sauce (we buy it by the gallon), there is a secret, and more powerful flavor enhancer product that you may want to try. I have only recently discovered this soy sauce (during a recent Ranch 99 Market visit in Van Nuys, CA) while doing research for this section of my book. To sum up the reaction to *this* soy sauce, my wife said, "Wow, intense, beyond anything I have tasted." The product is made by Kikkoman of Japan. The label tells you nothing, unless you read Japanese; the back label states—"All purpose seasoning." This is Kikkoman Umakuchi Shoyu, or flavor enhanced soy sauce. Brewed only in Japan, this sauce contains soybeans, wheat, salt, high fructose corn syrup, alcohol (preservative), disodium inosinate, and guanylate (potent 5'-nucleotides). Used in a slightly smaller amount in sauces and stews (compared to the regular), it really kicks up the flavor, because of the taste synergism of MSG + 5'-nucleotides. But I caution: do *not* use it as a standalone seasoning condiment—it is much too orally overwhelming. From now on I will refer to this soy sauce as "Super Soy Sauce"—and I use this in most of my routine cooking. A very good substitute for the Kikkoman Super Soy Sause is the Taste of Asia soy sauce from Maggi Foods, distributed by Nestlé USA. This complex cooking sauce contains vinegar, which adds additional arousing and taste-enhancing properties.

In summary, soy sauce adds pleasurable taste elements to both sweet and savory systems. The judicious use of soy sauce is one of the easiest ways to improve your own cooking and increase overall food pleasure.

Numbered References

1. Bourdain, A. 2004. *Les Halles Cookbook*. New York: Bloomsbury USA.

2. MSG safety & labeling. Glutamate Association. http://www. msgfacts.com/safety/msgsafety.html

3. FDA and monosodium glutamate, (MSG). *FDA Backgrounder*, Aug., 31, 1995. http://www.cfsan.fda.gov/~lrd/msg.html.

4.   New science provides new insights into health of glutamate. *Food Insight Newsletter*, March/April, 2000. http://www.ific.org/foodin sight/2000/ma/gluamatefi200.cfm.

5.   Schultz, M. What's sauce for the sushi. *Food Product Design*, April, 2005. http://www.foodproductdesign.com/articles/462/462_0405 INI.html.

6.   Yoshikawa, M., Takahashi, M., and S. Yang. Delta opioid peptides derived from plant proteins. *Curr. Pharm. Design*, 9:1325–30, 2003.

7.   Young, V., and P. Pellet. What protein in relation to protein require- ments and availability of amino acids. *Am. J. Clin. Nutr.*, 41(5 Suppl.):1077–90, 1985.

8.   Kataoka, S. Functional effects of Japanese style fermented soy sauce (shoyu) and its components. *J. Biosci. Bioeng.*, 100:227–34, 2005.

9.   Walker, R., and J. R. Lupien. The safety evaluation of monosodium glutamate. *J. Nutr.* 130(4S Suppl.):1049S–52S, 2000.

10. Kitts, D. D., and K. Weiler. Bioactive proteins and peptides from food sources. Applications of bioprocesses used in isolation and recov- ery. *Curr. Pharm. Design*, 9:1309–23, 2003.

11. Homsey, C. Flavor enhancement: taking taste from so-so to spectacu- lar. *Food Product Design*, Oct., 2001. http://www.foodproductdesign. com/articles/463/463_1001de.html.

General information on cooking with soy sauce

- http://www.chinatownconnection.com/chinese_soy_sauce.htm

- http://www.kikkoman.com/cookbook.html

A review on soy sauce types and taste testing

- McManus, L. Searching for superior soy sauce. *Cook's Illustrated*, 84:26-27, 2007.

2. Cheese, Especially Cheddar, Parmesan, and Romano

The second most useful secret-weapon (taste-active) food is cheese, in particular, cheddar, Parmesan, and Romano. Although there are several types of cheeses that are actually higher in flavor compounds (Gorgonzola and feta cheese), not everyone can handle the fatty acid tastes and slightly stinky aromas.[1] Goat or feta cheeses owe their unique piquant flavor to the short-chain fatty acids called butyric acid, and this is the major flavoring compound used in the "vomit" flavored jelly belly in Bertie Bott's 10 flavor discovery box (from Harry Potter).[2]

Cheese is a concentrated dairy food made from milk curds (the casein protein) separated from the whey protein during acidification, or the addition of the rennet enzyme. During the aging or ripening process, the added starter cultures (bacterial or fungal) release additional enzymes that have proteolytic or lipolytic activity (break down protein and fats), giving cheese its characteristic flavors. The longer the cheese ripen, the lower the moisture and the stronger the flavor.

Cheddar's special charm is its acidity and melting characteristics, which are greatly enhanced by direct heating; Parmesan's flavor secret (hard cheese) is the high amount of free MSG that develops in the aging process, almost 1.5 percent by weight. The judicious use of Parmesan increases the taste and flavor of many cooked dishes. The secret is to use a small amount as a background flavor booster (1-2 teaspoons). And the real Parmesan, or Parmigiano-Reggiano, makes a most excellent cheese crisp. A recipe can be found on p. 37 of *The French Laundry Cookbook*.

Cheese Pleasure

a. <u>Cheese is high in energy density</u>. We have previously indicated that the brain evolved with a built-in sense of liking for concentrated energy foods, and cheese fits this description nicely. Typical cheeses are high in protein and fat (one slice of Tillamook medium cheddar cheese is 90 kcals, 5 grams protein, and 7 grams of fat). (Note that cheese is low in lactose or milk sugar; I always chuckle when people tell me they can't eat cheese because they are lactose intolerant—this is a widely held urban myth.[3] In fact, aged cheddar has *no* lactose at all!)

b. <u>Cheese is high in fat</u>. With few exceptions (the hard-grating cheeses; see below), cheese contains significant amounts of butterfat from milk. The gut, brain, and fat cells all rejoice in the presence of fat. You may recall that our taste buds have *two* sensing mechanisms for the taste of fat.

c. <u>Cheese is high in casein protein</u>. Although pure protein has little taste, casein breakdown derivatives have many taste-active peptides. Many of these umami flavorants are amino acids and di- and tri-peptides.

d. <u>Cheese is very high in flavor-active compounds</u>. Enzymes from bacteria, fungi, and with a little help from aging, create many hundreds of flavor compounds that activate both olfaction and gustation receptors. The careful use of certain cheese(s) can kick up your cooking to tasty new levels if you follow the guidelines presented here. The cheeses I use most are:

- <u>Cheddar</u>: classic flavor, good melt, emulsification properties, and great food compatibility; in other words, it goes well with many dishes. Cheddar develops the tastiest flavor compounds when baked or broiled at high heat. The cooking goal is to make sure the cheddar topping is brown and bubbly.

- <u>Gouda</u>: superior meltdown properties, stringiness, and a nutty flavor, different from cheddar.

- <u>Parmesan</u>: sharper acidic taste, high "umami" profile, superior in taste-active compounds (Romano is a very good substitute), but poor solubility because it's a hard cheese. Asiago is another good substitute if you can't find the others. Parmesan's lighter aroma profile blends well in many savory dishes and sauces.

- <u>Comté, or Emmentaler, or Gruyère</u>: for onion soup; other cheeses don't hold up to the heat and just liquefy.

What about mozzarella, which accounts for about 20 percent of all the cheese consumed in the United States (mostly pizza)? Well, this Italian-style cheese undergoes only slight milk ripening and is lightly salted. Although quite low in flavor properties, it makes a nice topping for pizza due to its structural properties (lower fat), higher water content, and great stringiness. When mozzarella is heated, however, proteins and sugars will react to form tasty Maillard reaction products—but it is not nearly as flavorful or as complex as cheddar cheese.

e.   Parmesan and Romano are very rich in natural MSG (almost 1.5 percent by weight), in both free and bound forms. When these are cut into small pieces you can taste the wonderful salt-plus-MSG pop. This hard cheese is bacterial ripened and originated near Parma in Italy. Using special, fat-degrading enzymes in the bacterial cultures, this cheese actually has a rancid-fat flavor profile. Romano is even more rancid tasting due to the longer aging (for up to two years). Real Parmesan cheese is lower in moisture and fat, which makes it difficult at times to get it into solution during cooking. This is why I tend to use Kraft Parmesan (big, green can) in general cooking, as it is easier to use and will solubilize. Adding just one tablespoon to rice dishes will really accentuate the flavor.

My favorite appetizer is French bread, cut and buttered, with a layer of Kraft Parmesan on top—nice and thick but even—broiled in the oven for about five minutes (watch it carefully). What a taste sensation! This does not work as well with the fancy Parmigiano-Reggiano due to the differences in melting points, crystal structures, and processing. Both types of cheeses have their place. Occasionally I will make popcorn for our neighborhood, and I always add one tablespoon of Kraft Parmesan to the popcorn with the Aji-Shio salt. Once (without my saying anything about how I make the popcorn) our neighbor said to me, "Why is your popcorn so much better than mine?" Now you know.

f.   Cheese is very high in casomorphins. As we have discussed, cheese is concentrated in a type of protein called *casein;* during digestion, the proteolytic enzymes act on the casein molecule to create short-chain amino acid fragments called *casomorphins.* The casomorphins may have opioid-like effects in the body, such as constipation or pain relief. Some researchers believe they lend an addictive quality to food, although the science is mixed in this regard. I certainly think they do make cheese and cheese-flavored food more pleasurable due to subtle effects upon digestion. In his book *Breaking the Food Seduction*, Dr. Barnard expresses his opinion that the four most addictive foods are sugar, cheese, chocolate, and meat.[4] I tend to agree; tastiest snack food I know is Doritos, and it *is* Nacho Cheesier, isn't it? Although it sounds as if this is a bad thing, casomorphins may have some positive biological or evolutionary values, such as increasing learning ability, reducing anxiety, and protecting the gastrointestinal tract from noxious invaders.[5,6,7] It is interesting to note that cow's milk is much higher in casein (80 percent) than human breast milk (40 percent), which suggests that cow's milk may have more psychoactive properties. This "addictive" response may have evolutionary value; as casomorphins may help with maternal bonding during breastfeeding.

References

1. Georgala, A., Moschopoulou, E., Aktypis, A., Massouras, T., Zoidou, E., Kandarakis, I., and E. Anifantakis. Evolution of lipolysis during the ripening of traditional Feta cheese. *Food Chem.*, 93:73–80, 2005.

2. Bertie Bott's 10 flavor Discovery Box. Amazon.com. http://www.amazon.com/Bertie-Botts-Flavor-Discovery-Box/dp/B0002EXSZS

3. Newer knowledge of dairy foods. National Dairy Council. http://www.nationaldairycouncil.org/NationalDairyCouncil/Nutrition/Products/cheesePage5.htm

4. Barnard, N. 2003. *Breaking the Food Seduction*. New York: St. Martin's Press.

5. German, B., and C. Dillard. Health implications of milk containing β-casein with the A^2 genetic variant. *Crit. Rev. Food. Sci. Nutr.*, 46:93–100, 2006.

6. Sakaguchi, M., Makoto, K., Wakamatsu, M., and E. Matsumura. Effects of systemic β-casomorphin-5 on learning and memory in mice. *Eur. J.Pharmacol.*, 530:81–7, 2006.

7. Trompette, A., Claustre, J. Caillon, F., Jourdain, G., Chayvialle, J. A., and P. Plaisanae. Milk bioactive peptides and ß-casomorphins induce mucus release in rat jejunum. *J. Nutr.*, 133:3499–503, 2003.

3. Garlic: Flavor Powerhouse

We discuss in chapter 9, why we like garlic. In summary, garlic has the following sensory properties:

• Garlic aroma has a long-lasting aroma complex that forms a very strong food-aroma memory in the brain—cooking garlic instant signals that dinner is being prepared.

• Garlic aroma contains a molecule (methyl furyl disulfide) that excites the "umami" taste receptor in the mouth, especially in combination with MSG—thus increasing the savory nature of food.

• Garlic flavor stimulate the mouth's trigeminal taste systems for heat, texture, tactile, and temperature perception.

Do Vampires Hate Garlic?

In the original Bram Stoker version of the Dracula story, professor, Van Helsing placed garlic flowers through the room to protect Lucy from the "un-dead" or vampires.[1] Garlic aroma does possess some mosquito-repellent activity, and this may have fostered the association. I came across a paper published in the *British Medical Journal*, which is also available on the Web.[2] Many of the comments are tongue in cheek, but it appears to be a *real* study! The authors wanted to test the hypothesis that garlic wards off vampires, but owing to the lack of such creatures, they used leeches instead. They smeared garlic on one hand and used a clean hand as a control. The leeches actually preferred the garlic hands and moved toward them. The authors concluded that since garlic attracts vampires, the use of the flavorant should be restricted in Norway!

In a subsequent experiment, these same researchers smeared garlic on their forearms and placed the leeches directly in contact with the garlic. They wiggled and failed to start a feeding response, which they normally do very quickly. The leeches died two hours later. Although the leeches crawled toward the garlic, direct contact was quite lethal. The scientists concluded this was a case of *fatal attraction*. Garlic can be a powerful prooxidant, and it also inhibits blood from clotting. Garlic volatiles are lipophilic and are rapidly absorbed by oral tissues. Perhaps the leeches absorbed a massive dose of anti-blood clotting factors and bled to death. Vampires may sense this, and like the poor leeches, they have a similar reaction.[2] In my garden, I use garlic as a bug spray and long-term repellant. Although it is poor as a rapid knock-down pesticide, bugs will begin to fall off the plants after a few hours. And it appears harmless to the good bugs like ladybird beetles, bees, praying mantis, and spiders. Check out http://www.garlicbarrier.com/catalogue. By the way, *don't* make your own; fresh garlic juice burns delicate plant tissues.

Garlic Facts[3]

- Garlic has a long history of use, as noted by several mentions in the Bible, ancient Chinese writings, and the early Greek, Roman, and Egyptian cultures.

- Garlic possibly originated in Central Asia, around Siberia.

- Garlic intake is soaring—probably due to the many health claims associated with it, including: boosts immunity, fights cancer, thins blood, has favorable effects on blood lipids (reduces cholesterol), and has antibiotic, antiseptic, and antihypertensive effects.

- California grows the most garlic; crops are concentrated in Kern, Fresno, and Monterey counties. (I have actually been in a garlic processing plant—you might as well throw away your clothes after a visit.)

- Elephant garlic is a leek and not a true garlic.

- Chinese chives also have garlic flavor without the bite. (I have this plant growing everywhere in my backyard—be careful; it acts like a weed and is nearly impossible to pull it out by the roots.)

Numbered References

1. Stoker, B. 2004. *Dracula*, Cambridge, Mass.: Candlewick Press.

2. Baerheim, A., and H. Sandvik. Effect of ale, garlic and soured cream on the appetite of leeches. *Brit. Med. J.*, 309:1689, 1994. http://www.bmj.com/cgi/content/full/309/6970/1689

3. Garlic: Flavor of the ages. *Agricultural Outlook*, June–July, 2000. http:www.ers.usda.gov/publications/AgOutlook/Jun2000/as272e.pdf

General References

For a good discussion of umami in foods

- http://www.oznet.ksu.edu/extrapidresponse/images/june2005.pdf

For a discussion on Asian flavors and sauces

- http://www.foodproductdesign.com/archive/2004/0404CC.html

Those interested in garlic chemistry should check out the following:

- http://www.herbalchem.net/GarlicAdvanced.htm

- http://www.healthy.net/asp/templates/interview.asp?PageType=Interview&ID=173

4. Butter/Cream—the French Cuisine Secret

Why we like butter is discussed in chapter 5. To summarize, the most important sensory aspects of butter are:

- Butter is a water-in-oil emulsion; the human palate naturally prefers the taste of emulsions made with salt, sugar, and fat.

- Butter is 80 percent fat, and the unique combination of long-chain and short-chain fatty acids excite fat and taste receptors in the mouth.

- The butter salt content is concentrated in the water phase, which effectively creates a hypertonic salt solution and greater hedonic appeal.

- Butter is high in dynamic contrast because it melts down quickly when warmed in the mouth.

- Butter's aroma profile is distinctive, yet resistant to sensory specific satiety.

- Butter's high caloric density is an attractive sensory and post-ingestional property.

- Butter contains flavor boosting glutamates and the 5'-nucleotides (IMP, GMP, and AMP).

Butter

Butter is made by churning sweet cream. In this process the fat globules tend to stick together into a semi-solid but emulsified form. Butter acquires additional flavor complexity through the fermentation of cream by bacterial cultures. The typical mixture contains cultures of *S. cremoris, S. lactis, Diacetyl lactis*, and *Leuconostocs*. The cream is ripened to a pH of 5.5 at 21°C and then pH 4.6 at 13°C. Most flavor development occurs between pH 4.6–5.5, and the colder the temperature during ripening, the greater the flavor development. This produces many flavor components, such as diacetyl (the signature butter-flavor compound, which is very powerful in small amounts), acetoin, and acetaldehyde.[1] In addition to the water and oil, butter has additional emulsification properties due to its whey protein content. Adding butter to finished sauces will help stabilize and maintain the sauce emulsion.[2] Cream, on the other hand (due to its casein content), has *stronger* emulsification properties, but the emulsion must be formed by the use of a wire whisk or blender. Knowledge on how to manipulate these ingredients is absolutely essential for skillful cooking at home.

Ghee, or clarified butter, a supposedly Mongolian invention (and popular in India), is butter with the milk solids and water removed. Many chefs cook with it, and when I worked at Carnation Company we used to sell quite a bit to the food service industry. It's easy to make but a bit messy during the separation process. When butter is melted, the fat rises to the surface, and you need to discard the watery and cloudy fluid on the bottom. If you plan to use lots of ghee, you can find specialized gadgets to help you easily separate the surface butter oils from the watery whey solution below. If you don't want the hassle of making ghee yourself, just remember, when cooking with butter, let the butter bubble and subside as the moisture boils off; then proceed with frying. Moisture in butter will *steam* the meat surface rather than fry it; all those good flavor compounds won't form when the food is steamed. Even if you mix butter 50/50 with other oils, wait until the foaming subsides. Ghee is an excellent frying medium, generating more flavor compounds than any other vegetable or animal oil; with the possible exception of duck fat. Using butter to fry ground spices (such as cumin) in the pan before adding other ingredients is a popular Indian food technique called "blooming." In a skillet, add a little butter and your spice blend (curry, chili), fry for a few minutes, then add the rest of the recipe. Blooming intensifies spice flavors, increases flavor complexity, and creates fat-soluble flavors trapped in the butterfat. Additional spices that improve with blooming include Chinese five spice, coriander, cumin, ancho chili pepper, turmeric, and Old Bay Seasoning.

Thomas Keller's Butter Base (*Buerre Monté*)

Chef Keller frequently uses this butter base in the preparation of meat, poultry, and seafood dishes. It is basically a simple butter sauce, but it allows for great versatility in cooking. For a good discussion of this technique see p. 135 of *The French Laundry Cookbook*, or see below. Here is the basic technique:

- 2 tablespoons dry white wine, stock, or water (liquid)

- 8 tablespoons (¼ pound or 1 stick) unsalted butter, at room temperature

  Simply bring liquid to a boil in a 1½- to 2-quart saucepan—this does not take long, so watch constantly. Reduce heat to low (this is key) and add 2 tablespoons butter. Immediately start whisking, continue to whisk until butter has blended smoothly into liquid. Add remaining butter in 2-tablespoon pieces, whisking constantly after each addition until smooth. Do not let mixture boil, which will break the emulsion. Makes about a cup.

Chef Keller uses *buerre monté* to poach lobster, baste meats in the final oven cooking, and make sauces *à la minute* (for example, *canapé* sauces). I tried marinating a steak in *buerre monté* overnight in the refrigerator, and then barbequed the steak on my Weber for dinner. The meat had a wonderful aroma and taste (enhanced Cookivore aromas) and seemed to cook more evenly. I doubt the chef would approve of such a marinade, and it did seem extravagant, but it was fun and tasty culinary experiment. Try it for yourself—just watch for butter oil flare-ups.

Cream

Milk (hugely complex with over 10,000 different chemical constituents) can be readily separated into its two main constituents, cream and skim milk. These fluid creams can vary in fat content, from as little as 10–12 percent in half-and-half to a full 40 percent butter fat in heavy whipping cream. Most all modern creams are made in a centrifuge, which spins the milk, a process that separates out the lighter milk fat. Most creams are also homogenized to stabilize the fat globules and pasteurized to extend shelf life. Some heavy creams are *ultra* pasteurized (high temperature and short time) to *really* extend the shelf life. In fact, a container of heavy whipping cream from Costco can last a long time in my fridge: over two months with repeated opening and closings. Since butterfat is 9 kcals per gram, the caloric load varies greatly, depending on whether you use half-and-half or heavy cream in your cooking. Most French recipes use heavy cream, as demonstrated by Chef Bourdain in his *pommes purée* recipe (see page 243 of *Les Halles Cookbook*).

Cream Liking

a. <u>Cream is high in butter fat</u>. We have shown that the oral cavity has a liking for fat and may sense it both from fatty acid content and a texture component. Butterfat is very unique, it has a wide variety of different fatty acid chain lengths. This gives cream and butterfat a unique mouthfeel property that is not duplicated by any other fat, although coconut fat comes close. Butter excites the taste buds better than any other fat, since it has very short fatty acids like butyric and medium-chain fats and a host of complicated fatty acid derivatives, like diglycerides, sphingolipids, phospholipids, and lipoproteins. After all, milk is complex because it is the *sole* source of nutrition for young animals and infants. The shorter chains of fatty acids (up to 10 percent in butter) tend to be more water soluble (4 carbons or less), and the higher chains are quite fat soluble (carbons at 18 chain length). And when you fry using butter, the short-chain fats tend to volatize into the characteristic "butter" aroma.

b. <u>Cream has a low aroma profile</u>. Unlike butter, which is cultured and has its own flavor, cream has a very subtle aroma profile. You can use a lot without aroma burnout. We know that certain "bland" foods seem not to turn on the natural food satiety mechanism in the brain, and I suspect cream is one of them, along with butter, French fries, and vanilla.

c. <u>Cream is loaded with taste-active compounds</u>. Like butter and *unlike* solid oils, cream contains the following interesting palatability enhancing components:

- Carbonyl compounds (flavor)

- Nucleotides (umami tastants)

- Nucleic acids (umami tastants)

- Flavor compounds (sulfur-containing compounds, alcohols, carbonyls, acids, and esters)

- Carbohydrates (lactose—important sugar that creates many flavor compounds and derivatives, especially when fermented by bacterias)

- A number of milk salts like $Na+$, $K+$, $Ca++$, and $Mg++$

- Anionic compounds such as citrate, chloride, carbonate, and sulfate

- A number of nitrogenous substances (amino acids and derivatives like taurine, carnitine, and acetyl glucosamine)

- Vitamins (some vitamins play a huge role in flavor generation, such as thiamine)

d. <u>Cream is the ultimate emulsifier</u>. The major proteins in milk are casein (80 percent) and whey (20 percent), in a complex biological fluid with many interesting and perhaps addictive properties. There are four types of casein in milk, all of which add valuable nutrition, milk stability, and antibacterial properties. (Recall that cheese is all casein and not whey.) Since humans like emulsions, cream is an excellent way to help form them. Milk fats have some emulsification properties as well, due to the more water-soluble short-chain fatty acids (about 10 percent of the total fatty acids).

References

1. Flavors that develop upon cooking. http://webexhibits.org/butter/com pounds.html

2. Butter manufacture. University of Guelph. http://www.foodsci.uoguelph.ca/ dairyedu/butter.html

Excellent Web site for butter recipes

• http://www.moomilk.com/cuisine/recipes-13.htm

5. Shallots

> Shallots should be used more often; they increase the taste and flavor of everything.
> J. Koch[1]

Rare in the home kitchen but plentiful in fine restaurants, shallots (*Allium cepa*) are a world-class ingredient in the professional kitchen. Roman scholar, Pliny the Elder, in the first century praised the role of shallots in sauce making.[1] Anthony Boudain, in *Kitchen Confidential*, says this ingredient makes "restaurant food taste different than your food."[2] I decided to study this key ingredient in French cuisine and I found some surprising sensory properties:

a. Less oral lingering bite. Ingesting shallots cause less "onion taste" in the mouth vis-à-vis the yellow onion; so the use of raw shallots (vinaigrettes) is more socially acceptable. However, the lacrimator activity is many times that of onions. I was surprised just how strong a lacrimator chopped French shallots can be (the grey shallot or *griselle*). The tearing effect is similar to onions, where sulfur volatiles (syn-propanethiol-S-oxide) arise from the crushed onion cells, dissolve in the tears of the eye, and irritate the cornea. Since the cornea has more nerves per square millimeter than any other tissue in the body, the stinging sensation is very intense.[3] Based on my experience, one shallot has more tearing activity than one large chopped onion. Garlic does not appear to produce lacrimators in abundance, but they are there nonetheless.

b.   <u>No shallot breath</u>. Shallots, although they have a strong flavor, do not create shallot breath (or sulfur compounds that actually are breathed out of the lungs). Garlic contains unique flavor compounds that are actually absorbed from the digestive tract and travel in the bloodstream to the lungs, where they volatize into the aveolar tissue of the lung (these include allyl mercaptan and methyl sulfide). I have noticed from personal observation that the bad breath offenders in the allium species are, from worst to least offensive: garlic, green onions, onions, shallots, and leeks. Shallots are a great way to add flavor to a variety of foods without smelling like a basket of onions the next day!

c.   <u>Distinctive flavor</u>. Shallots have a slightly different flavor profile from most of its allium cousins. Shallots are particularly rich in a thiosulfinates fraction called *n*-PrS, which includes *n*-PrSS(O)propenyl-(E) and its derivatives.[4] If you run out of shallots use the white portion of a green onion, as it contains many of these same flavor compounds as the shallot. My wife noted that the Chinese use green onions extensively in their cuisine; perhaps green onions are the shallot ingredient of China. Julia Child, in *Mastering the Art of French Cooking*, also suggests using green onion as an acceptable substitute. (But beware: using green onions carries the risk of bad breath, almost as lingering as garlic breath, although I can find no references on the topic beyond personal experience.)

d.   <u>Long hang-time flavor generation</u>. Chopping shallots generates dozens of volatile sulfur compounds that have a long hang-time in the olfactory mucosa and can form strong aroma-memory associations. The enzymes released during the chopping of the cell wall act on precursor compounds to create the myriad aromas and tastes. Shallots, however, do *not* have any alliin, the flavor compound unique to garlic, but share many of the other classes of flavor compounds.[4]

e. <u>Shallots and sugars</u>. Compared to onions, shallots are slightly higher in protein, contain more essential oils (flavor compounds), and are higher in sugars (glucose, fructose and sucrose). The higher sugar content not only increases the generation of aromatic Maillard reaction products (caramelize), but also increases the burning susceptibility in the pan. As with garlic, sauté shallots carefully on lower heat.

f. <u>A healthier allium species</u>. Shallots contain significant amounts of phenolics and flavonoids, which not only add great flavor but may be significantly healthier than many other types of onions. Leelarungrayub et al. (2004) noted that shallots have the highest antioxidant activity and phenolic content of the onions tested, as well as a very high level of the potent anti-inflammatory flavonol, quercetin.[5] Hence, the consumption of shallots may reduce the risk of both cardiovascular and cancer as well (the author's own words). By the way, the weakest antioxidant performers of the onions tested were Vidalia sweet onions—they are still wonderful when used fresh in sandwiches—but a less flavorful substitute when the recipe calls for sautéed onions.

As an experiment, my wife made a classic broccoli stir-fry two ways; one using garlic, and the other using garlic *and* shallots. We both agreed that the addition of shallots intensified the flavor in a dramatic way. The key is not to add too much; keep the amount at a 2:1 level of shallot to garlic, and mince it very fine. Since shallots have more flavoring power per gram than the common white onion, just one shallot will provide plenty of additional flavor.

Researcher Thomas Scott has also described each allium species based on its sensory property: the *rowdy* onion; the *aristocratic* shallot; the *herbaceous* chive, the *sharp* scallion; and the *assertive* garlic. Dr. Scott's descriptions of each allium species are quite *apropos*. *Rowdy* means to create a brawl with flavor generation (onions are potent lacrimators); *aristocratic* means something precious, expensive, and unique (shallots have a unique spectrum of flavor volatiles); *herbaceous* refers to chives onion flavor melded with chlorophyll; *sharp* means quick onslaught and bite (green onions and garlic are potent breath destroyers); and *assertive* refers to distinctive and lingering garlic aromatics.[3]

The nutritional benefits of garlic, onions, and shallots are well known and are the subject of hundreds of scientific and epidemiological reports. The plants produced the phytochemicals to ward off ingestion by animals and act as a bacteriostatic and antifungal agent. As we see so often in nature, if humans ingest these plants they acquire some of the same phytochemical protections as well (powerful antioxidants).[5]

Let's take a quick look at the relevant Biblical passages on onions and leeks, since they contain some interesting physiological principles of food perception. I quote from the New American Standard version.

> *Exodus 16:2–3*
> And the whole congregation of the sons of Israel grumbled against Moses and Aaron in the wilderness. And the sons of Israel said to them, "Would that we had died by the Lord's hand in the land of Egypt, when we sat by the pots of meat, when we ate bread to the full; for you have brought us out into this wilderness to kill this whole assembly with hunger."

Note that in Egypt and probably elsewhere in the Middle East, meat, bread, and onions were part of the established cuisine. However, some scholars suggested that this diet may not have been the actual daily fare of the Israelites and may have been a (literary?) exaggeration of their culinary condition.

> *Exodus 16:4 (Emphasis is mine.)*
> Then the Lord said to Moses, "Behold, I will rain *bread* from heaven for you: and the people shall go out and gather a day's portion every day, that I may test them, whether or not they will walk in My instruction."

Manna (Hebrew for "What is it?") became the new staple in the diet, but it was now available 24-7 and appears to have lasted throughout the forty-year transit in the desert (Exodus 16:35).

> *Exodus 16:12*
> I have heard the grumblings of the sons of Israel; speak to them, saying, "At twilight you shall eat meat, and in the morning you shall be filled with bread; and you shall know that I am the Lord your God."

In time, the Lord gave them the ultimate comfort food, meat, and bread. Studies disclose that meat hunger is actually highest in the evening, but in the morning—when humans have lower blood glucose and are mildly ketotic—the stomach prefers a meal of fat and carbohydrates (bread). In a later passage we get more information on manna composition and the preferred diet of the Israelites. Note the references to the allium family and how eating the same thing day in and day out induces *sensory specific satiety*!

> *Numbers 11:5–8 (Emphasis is mine.)*
> "We remember the <u>fish</u> which used to eat free in Egypt, the <u>cucumbers</u> and the <u>melons</u> and the <u>leeks</u> and the <u>onions</u> and the <u>garlic</u>, but now our *appetite* is gone. There is nothing at all to look at except this *manna*." Now this manna was like coriander seed, and its appearance like that of bdellium (color of pearls or myrrh). The people would go about and gather it and grind it between two millstones or beat it in the mortar, and boil it in the pot and make cakes with it; and its taste was as the taste of cakes baked with oil.

> *Numbers 11:18–20 (Emphasis is mine.)*
> "… Therefore the Lord will give you meat and you shall eat. You shall eat, not one day, nor two days, nor five days, nor ten days, nor twenty days, but a whole month, until it *comes out of your nostrils* and becomes loathsome to you; because you have rejected the Lord …"

Sometimes people cannot eat even their most beloved foods every day—or can they? The answer appears to depend on the nature of the food itself and its sensory properties. Brain imaging studies on SSS found that certain foods do *not* trigger a decrease in food pleasure, even if the food is eaten repeatedly. Vanilla flavor is an example of a food aroma that doesn't seem to decrease in hedonics with repeat exposure. Other common foods that probably fall into this same category include milk, French fries, bread, and other very bland or nondistinctive foods. A person might be able to eat plain, white bread or rice every day but not parmesan-rosemary foccacia or brown rice as the flavors are too distinctive. Manna was probably very bland (breadlike) and adaptable to spicing and cooking variations.

References

1. Koch, J. The other onion: for a more refined flavor, savor the subtle shallot. *The Seattle Times: Pacific Northwest Magazine*, Sept. 7, 2003. http://seattletimes.nwsource.com/pacificnw/2003/0907/taste.html

2. Bourdain, A. 2000. *Kitchen Confidential.* New York: Bloomsbury USA.

3. Scott, T. Ask the expert: What is the chemical process that causes my eyes to tear when I peel an onion? ScientificAmerican.com. http:// www.sciam.com/print_version.cfm?articleID=000C5FF7-5DB5-1C72-9EB7809EC588F2D7

4. Block, E., Naganathan, S., Putman, D., and S. H. Zhao. Organosulfur chemistry of garlic and onion: recent results. *Pure & Appl. Chem.*, 65:625–32, 1993.

5. Leelarungrayub, N., Rattanapanome, V., Chanarat, N., and J. M. Gebicki. Quantitative evaluation of the antioxidant properties of garlic and shallot preparations. *Nutrition*, 22:266–74, 2006.

General References

- http://www.shallot.com/gb/1e.htm

6. Sugar and Reaction Flavor Additions

- Sucrose (table sugar)

- Brown sugar

- Honey

- Maple syrup

Sucrose

Cooking frequently uses heat to generate flavor and taste-active compounds. The raw materials that generate the most flavor are usually proteins and amino acids that interact with carbohydrates, specifically *reactive* sugars of glucose, fructose, and sucrose. Knowing how to optimize this reaction and how it forms (Maillard compounds) can add immeasurably to your cooking style, especially when you want those fabulous browning colors, flavors (yeasty, malty, coffee-like, BBQ), and tastes. Technically, the reaction involves a nonenzymatic browning reaction of a reducing sugar with an amine group of an amino acid or protein. This is a complex, unstoppable reaction that starts like a chain reaction and keeps on going with time and heat.

The Maillard reaction that creates these delicious tastes and flavors can be maximized in cooking. Food scientists have found that an oven temperature of 375°F seems to create the best flavor compounds without the cogeneration of burnt off-flavors. To maximize the flavor reaction, one uses compounds that are highly reactive like sucrose (technically a nonreducing sugar but heat changes that), brown sugar, honey, and maple syrup. Sucrose is a disaccharide that is composed of a bonded molecule of glucose and fructose. Fructose, a free-form sugar in honey, apples, pears, and peaches, is very reactive (seven times more reactive in Maillard reactions), and one should use caution to avoid burning with these ingredients. The reaction is also greatly slowed by too much water or dilution. Thomas Keller understands this and cautions his readers to get the water out of the skin of fish and duck in order for this flavor reaction to occur, and to crisp the skin. And microwave cooking is a complete disaster for creating these compounds! Microwaves tend to steam food and not brown them. In my experiments, honey, butter oil (ghee), and salt generate very nice flavor and browning compounds (regular butter works as well). Ironically, in biological systems, we want to *inhibit* this reaction. In diabetes, high blood glucose levels increase protein glycation, which causes many negative physiological effects, like basement membrane damage to red blood cells and blood vessels, and cataract formation. Some scientists even suggest that ingestion of fructose accelerates these negative diabetic neuropathies, as the fructose molecule is more reactive than glucose. Interestingly, fructose is more reactive in cooking as well, and burns at a much lower temperature.

I believe that the best sweetener to use in cooking is sucrose. The reasons are:

a. Sucrose combines sweetness with a special mouthfeel not found in any other simple sugar. The combination of taste and mouthfeel is more pleasurable than just sweetness alone.

b. Sucrose is a powerful releaser of dopamine in the nucleus accumbens shell, which acts as strong "wanting" and alerting stimuli.[1] Repeated exposure to sugar actually increases the desire to consume it; unlike the satiety response to most other foods.

c.   Sucrose activates a "hot spot" in the medial shell of the pleasure center and increases μ–opioid response that creates both "liking and pleasure" and activates food ingestion in general.[2] Sucrose, therefore, increases food pleasure and the pleasures of the eating experience.

d.   Cannabinoid CB-1 receptors may also play a major hedonic or reinforcing role in complex sweet (sucrose) taste emulsions. The brain's cannabinoid receptors are particularly fond of sweet and fat *combinations*.[3]

Brown Sugar

Brown sugar is a semi-refined white sugar with a variable amount of molasses still present during processing. Molasses is the liquid product of boiling, concentrating, and clarifying sugar cane juice, a complex flavor mixture of reaction compounds with some very strong hang-time odorants. I substitute light brown sugar for table sugar when I wish to add just a little more flavor complexity. Dark brown sugar is a wonderful complement to systems that are already rich in Maillard reaction products, like BBQ sauce, cookies, and certain soy-sauce based marinades. Cooking with brown sugars increases the depth and complexity of your cooking, since the preformed flavor compounds will become precursors for continued flavor development.

Honey

My botany professor at UC Davis used to call honey "bee vomit"! Honeybees make this complex substance by ingesting flower nectars (mostly sucrose), and storing the liquid in stomach pouches (crop), where it mixes with intestinal enzymes. The crop contains the enzyme "invertase," which breaks apart (inverts) the sucrose into fructose and glucose. Thus, honey is sweeter than sugar because fructose is sweeter than sucrose. Honey composition, beyond the simple sugars, is surprisingly complex and contains bioflavonoids (antioxidants), numerous vitamins and minerals, pigments, flavors, sugar alcohols, and a variety of organic acids.

One of my favorite food personalities (food-smart and brims with enthusiasm) is radio host Chef Jamie Gwen (Chef Jamie on 790 KABC-AM). One of her recipes uses a 50/50 mixture of butter and honey glazed over a turkey or chicken to create impressive color and flavor. But be careful not to roast the chicken over 350–375°F to prevent bitter flavor note generation (from the fructose in the honey). Recall that fructose is several times more reactive to heat than sucrose. Chef Jamie's 50/50 combination can be used with *real* maple syrup as well. I never cook chicken without it! Check out Chef Jamie's Web site (www.chefjamie.com) and her interesting spice rubs and food garnishing sauces, available for sale on the Home Shopping Network. Cooking with blended rubs and sauces (as long as they are of good quality) takes the guesswork and mess-work out of food preparation.

Honey is approximately 80 percent sugars (fructose, glucose, maltose, and sucrose) and 20 percent water. Honey also is surprisingly acidic (gluconic, formic, acetic, butyric, lactic tartaric, and malic), adding extra bite (low pH) to many marinades and dishes. When honey crystallizes, it is the glucose that is the problem, since it is less soluble in solution than fructose. Honey is also rich in compounds called lactones, which are flavor-active components that impart a slight sweet and fruity flavor, similar to those found in butter. Therefore, butter and honey combinations may actually be synergistic and boost the overall pleasurable flavor we associate with cooked butter.

Another unique characteristic of honey is the presence of numerous enzymes such as sucrase, amylase, and glucose oxidase. Hence, the use of unpasteurized or raw honey in marinades and sauces may generate additional interesting flavor compounds.

To see how Chef Emeril uses honey (and many of the other power foods) check out his recipe for Spicy Honey Barbecued Chicken on the Food Network online.[4] Emeril, by the way, although classically trained in the French style, prefers to cook with a high flavor flare. He is a master at using our list of power foods (such as spices, pork, and garlic); he seasons everything he touches, whether it is flour or bread crumbs—or just the plate.

Maple Syrup (Real, Not Fake)

The product of the sap of black and sugar maple trees, maple syrup's major carbohydrate is sucrose. The maple sap starts with a sugar content of only 2–3 percent, and then, through various methods of concentration, the final sugar content nears 68 percent. It takes 40 gallons of maple sap to make 1 gallon of finished syrup. The concentration process obviously creates many flavor compounds, but *real* maple sugar syrup is a much more complex physiological mixture—not unlike human blood serum.[5] Maple sap is not just sugar water as some believe, if that were true, sap would not sustain the life of the tree. Maple sap is actually a biological liquid that contains amino and organic acids, phenolic compounds, hormones, minerals and salts, and other components that act as growth promoters for the tree.

The special aroma of maple can evoke memories of food ingested in the past. For example, after a night's fast, just the aroma of maple syrup conjures up the breakfast experience. Learned food associations occur best when body energy stores are depleted. Most people are mildly ketotic upon awakening, and the stomach and brain are primed to form very good food memories. Maple syrup volatiles are potent and have a long hang-time, thus promoting a good aroma and calorie relationship.

Check out the online recipe from Bobby Flay, the celebrated Food Network chef, a fabulous recipe for maple glazed ribs.[6] The cooking technique, in addition to the maple syrup, insures moist, tender and flavorful ribs. Ribs are roasted at high heat to form Maillard reaction flavors (350°F), followed by a maple coat, wrapped in foil and extended cooking at 250°F. This allows a long contact time with the meat and the potential for complex flavor compounds to form. Bobby finishes the dish with another glaze of maple syrup. Maillard reaction flavors form best in meat at 350-375°F; in vegetables, higher heat is required to first break down the tissues then release the sugars for caramelization. The magic roasting temperature for most root vegetables, asparagus, cauliflower, and (even) broccoli is approximately 425–475°F.

So the question may arise: "Can't I use imitation pancake syrup instead of the more expensive maple syrup?" Fake maple syrup contains high fructose corn syrup (which burns easier) and artificial flavors (lack flavor depth). Since there is no sucrose in fake maple syrup, the Maillard reaction products that are the tastiest do not form; we have discussed earlier that the mouth prefers the taste of sucrose. Finally, the ersatz syrup does not contain the amino acids, organic acids, vitamin and minerals, and bioflavonoids that create numerous flavor compounds. Your guests deserve the best—don't be a *sap*; use the real thing!

References

1. Rada, P., Avena, N. M., and B. G. Hoebel. Daily bingeing on sugar repeatedly releases dopamine in the accumbens shell. *Neuroscience*, 134:737–44, 2005.

2. Peciña, S., and K. C. Berridge. Hedonic hot spot in nucleus accumbens shell: where do µ–opioid cause increased impact of sweetness. *J. Neurosci.*, 50:11777–86, 2005.

3. Ward, S. J., and L. A. Dykstra. The role of CB1 receptors in sweet versus fat *Behav. Pharmacol.*, 16:381–8, 2005.

4. Lagasse, E. Spicy honey barbequed chicken. Food Network. http://www.foodnetwork.com/food/recipes/recipe/0,FOOD_9936_181 76,00.html?rsrc=search

5. Nutritional value of pure maple syrup. Michigan Maple Syrup Association. http://www.mi-maplesyrup.com/Information/info_maplenu trition.htm

6. Flay, B. Maple glazed ribs. Food Network. http://www.foodnetwork.com/food/recipes/recipe/0,FOOD_9936_25813,00.html

7. Worcestershire Sauce (WS)

Somewhat of a cross between soy and fish sauce, this Lea & Perrins creation has many uses in the kitchen, and without adding too much sodium. It can boost the flavors of marinades and add complexity to sauces, and it can be used as the main flavorizing agent. Developed commercially in 1837 by two chemists, John Lea and William Perrin, the formulation has been made the same way ever since. Similar to the Coke formula or the spice blend for Colonel Sanders' chicken, no one seems to know the exact formula, as it is shared among the select few.[1]

The Additions and Purposes of Ingredients

a. <u>WS contains both malt and regular vinegar</u>. This acidulant is a strong trigeminal stimulus (feeling) and salivary stimulant *par excellence,* promoting both food arousal and attention.

b. <u>WS uses flavor-rich molasses</u>, a sugar cane extract. Molasses' major sugar is sucrose, most preferred by the taste buds, and an excellent Maillard reaction promoter. Molasses also has proteins and complex, potent sulfur-derived aromatics.

c. <u>WS adds high fructose corn syrup (55 percent fructose and 45 percent glucose)</u>, which heightens flavor generation, especially with fructose-protein interactions. Fructose is a particularly reactive sugar and browns more quickly than sucrose.

d. <u>The use of anchovy paste</u> in the fermentation of WS contributes a tremendous variety flavor active compounds. This oily fish is rich in protein (natural MSG), omega-3 fatty acids, and 5'-nucleotides—amplifying both umami taste and aroma complexity. Fish sauce is, of course, a favored condiment in many Asian cuisines; Thai, Vietnamese, and Filipino cuisine use it just like soy sauce. Lea & Perrins must have figured out a way to get rid of the inherent fishy smell of anchovies (probably by keeping the acidity high, and the use of antioxidant spices). Cooked anchovies are also high in the classic cookivore flavor family known as the "pyrazines."

e. <u>Onions</u> add powerful sulfur aromas, sucrose, and orosensation.

f. <u>Garlic</u> contributes long lasting aromas, umami-boosting tastants, and activates the pleasure-producing hot and cold oral receptors.

g. <u>Tamarind extract</u> is processed from a fruit commonly used in East Indian, Middle Eastern, and Asian cuisines; it flavors many soups, curries, and sour seasoning mixes. High in fruit acids (tartaric) and sugars, but still very sour tasting, this may be the integral (secret?) ingredient in Worcestershire sauce. Other constituents include the antioxidant flavonoids and anthocyanins, pectins and starch, and terpene aroma compounds.[2] I speculate that the addition of tamarind acts as a souring and preservative agent that counteracts the fishy (anchovy) oxidation aromas.

h. <u>Cloves</u> are the dried, unopened buds of a myrtle-like tree called *Syzygium aromaticum*. From the French word for nail, cloves have interesting antiseptic and oral numbing properties. The characteristic flavor comes from an essential oil called *eugenol,* which happens to be a potent stimulator of cold receptors in the mouth. In other words, it provides an added blast of orosensation by activating cold-TRP receptors. Cloves are considered the most aromatic spice and, like cinnamon, can work well in both sweet and savory dishes. (I recently made a cinnamon bordelaise sauce, and it was outstanding.) It is a powerful antibacterial, and the addition of clove probably kept the nasty bugs from forming during the two-year extraction process (although I doubt they do this today).

i. <u>Natural flavorings</u> add more aroma and taste complexity.

j. <u>Chili pepper extract</u> combines well with the sour taste and fruity aromas of tamarind. The main ingredient in chilies is capsaicin, and we now know that this compound binds to heat-sensing receptors that have a direct role in increasing opioid response. Capsaicin also activates the CB-1 cannabinoid system directly affecting the food pleasure response. Chilies are a good source of vitamin C, which helps protect flavor and color as well.

Worcestershire sauce, an essential ingredient in Caesar salad and Bloody Mary, can really add depth and complexity to many savory dishes, with its spicy (clove) aroma, acidic character, fatty acid top notes, and plenty of fish-derived umami flavors. The secret to using WS is to use it in sauce blends, not as the major flavoring ingredient. If your final sauce or marinade tastes too similar to WS, then you may have added too much.

<u>Quick recipe: great accompaniment for steaks</u>

Take 1–2 pounds of white button mushrooms, discard the stems, and cut them into 3/8-inch slices. In a saucepan, add 2 tablespoons chopped shallots at the beginning and sauté first with 2 tablespoon butter, then add 2 tablespoons WS, 2 tablespoons soy sauce, 1 cup red wine, and the mushrooms. Simmer it over

medium-low heat and reduce it down to where the liquid is almost evaporated, which should take 30–40 minutes. Correct the seasoning at end with salt and pepper. Final product should be nice and brown, and glassy in appearance; all the liquids should be absorbed into the mushrooms. I adopted this from a recipe I saw on the Food Network, and it is a family favorite. Variations include using fresh shitake or portobello mushrooms instead of agaricus (white button). One to two pounds of fresh shitake will be quite expensive, and you may want to save this dish for that special rib eye roast during the fall holidays. Portobello will work well, but slice them a bit thinner and discard the stem and gills—unless you like a very inky preparation. Remember to keep the lid off the pot, or it won't reduce!

References

1.   Worcestershire sauce. Wikipedia. http://en.wikipedia.org/wiki/Worcestershire_sauce

2.   Tamarind. Gernot Katzer' Spice Pages. http://www.uni-graz.at/~katzer/engl/Tama_ind.html

8. Bacon ("Pork Fat Rules!"—Emeril Lagasse)

Good-quality smoked bacon is an easy way to improve the flavor and tastes of many dishes. In a recent interview, a fast-food company executive was asked what he did to make his company's food tastier. "Easy," he said, "we just add more cheese or bacon." Emeril is also famous for saying "pork fat rules." And Anthony Bourdain writes:

> "Is there any better, more noble, more magical animals than the pig? Not from a cook's perspective there isn't. Virtually every single part of a pig can be made into something delicious. Pork makes just about everything taste better, and no beast offers more variety, more possibilities, and more traditional, time-tested recipes per ounce than the humble piggy."[1]

Bourdain further suggests that salted pork, fatback, and smoked hock—cured pork—were the essential ingredient(s) in many ancient cultures and cuisines. He even believes that the history of interplay between salt and pork is the history of the world!

Bacon is typically of the most taste-active foods used in cooking. Starting with cuts of pork belly, bacon is cured with salt, spices, and flavorings, in both wet and dry processing methods. After curing and preservation, the bacon is then smoked over wood chips for up to two weeks. The result is a high salt- and sugar-cured meat with hickory-smoked flavors. Alton Brown, one of the stars of the Food Network, has a recipe to make your own bacon, which uses salt, sugar, molasses, black pepper, and apple cider in the water-curing process; all of these are flavor-active compounds.

Bacon is also hickory or hardwood smoked. Hickory smoke provides much more than a memorable aroma. The smoke contains taste-active flavor potentiators for salt taste that are quite noticeable. Hardwoods contain cellulose, hemi-celluloses, lignans, and complex proanthocyanidins, all of which produce a number of interesting aromatic compounds. Hence, bacon is high in compounds that make food taste great: salt, fat, sugar, brown reaction flavors, and innumerable taste-active components of hickory smoke:[2]

a. Wood celluloses actually are complex sugars, and when they are burnt, they produce thousands of fruity, floral, and smoky notes (depending on the wood).

b. Carbonyl compounds react with surface proteins of meat to increase color and add "bite."

c. Hemicelluloses primarily lower the pH and tighten the surface proteins of the meat.

d. Lignin, or cellular glue, produces smoky, spicy, and pungent compounds.

e. Wood smoke is a powerful antimicrobial agent.

f. Phenolic compounds in wood produce strong, vanilla-like aromas.
    A few tips on cooking bacon. I've found that slow cooking with a cold-start skillet is best—nonstick, of course. Lay the bacon in the skillet, and then turn on the heat. This method seems to prevent excessive curling of the bacon. Pricking the bacon with a fork and

oven-roasting (not broiling) at 400°F may work as well. After cooking, save the bacon fat; it adds a depth of smoky and sweet flavor that livens up many dishes. Just pass it through a sieve first, while it's still hot; it will congeal at room temperature and store very nicely in the fridge. Use a light hand in cooking with bacon fat. A few teaspoons added to a Chinese stir-fry or in roasted potatoes add the memorable cookivore flavors.

Bacon Recipes

Bacon is a strong flavorant and combines well with other strong flavors, such as Roquefort cheese. The Web has numerous bacon-inspired creations. Here are some creative ideas from the Food Network—it lists over 1,100 recipes containing bacon as a featured ingredient!

a. Low-carb Bacon Wrapped Shrimp and Scallops (Rachel Ray)

   • This is a classic bacon-wrap recipe that uses several pleasure foods: lime juice, red pepper flakes, black pepper, and green onions (scallions).

   • http://www.foodnetwork.com/food/recipes/recipe/0,FOOD_ 9936_27789,00.html?rsrc=search

b. Pizza with Caramelized Onions and Crispy Bacon (Wolfgang Puck)

   • Recipe demonstrates Puck's flavor layering expertise. Note the liberal use of pleasure foods: multiple cheeses, onions, nutmeg, Parmesan, black pepper and, fresh thyme.

   • http://www.foodnetwork.com/food/recipes/recipe/0,FOOD _9936_26714,00.html?rsrc=search

c. Corn Biscuits with Bacon (M. S. Milliken & S. Feniger)

   • A classic combination of corn, buttermilk, and cumin flavors. Uses cracked black pepper as a topping and bacon fat in the batter for extra flavor. Toast the cumin first and grind for an enhanced aroma punch.

   • http://www.foodnetwork.com/food/recipes/recipe/0,FOOD _9936_4063,00.html?rsrc=search d.　Crispy Potatoes with Bacon, Garlic, and Parsley (Food Network Kitchens).

　　• Note the cooking techniques—potatoes are parboiled first, then cooked in bacon fat, and stirred only as needed (to keep a crust). When potatoes are tender, add the seasonings of garlic, parlsey, black pepper, and cooked bacon, cook for just a few more minutes. Potatoes are crisp-tender, the flavorants are bright, and colors remain fresh looking.

　　• http://www.foodnetwork.com/food/recipes/recipe/0,FOOD _9936_26570,00.html?rsrc=search

e.　Chili Dog Bacon Cheeseburgers with Fiery Fries (Rachel Ray)

　　• Add pleasure-boosts into the hamburger patty with: diced hot dogs, chili powder, Montreal seasoning (my wife's favorite), Worcestershire sauce, hot sauce, and ketchup! In the final assembly, chili sauce is added to Kaiser rolls and the burgers are topped with cilantro, lettuce, and lime juice! Whoa.

　　• This recipe is a "trigeminal-rush." The fiery fries are made by using baked fries with a spicy coating of raw garlic and chives.

　　• http://www.foodnetwork.com/food/recipes/recipe/0,FOOD _9936_30954,00.html?rsrc=search

f.　Chunky Cheese Potato Soup and Wilted Spinach Salad (*Food Fight*)

　　• Liberal use of the pleasure foods bacon, bacon fat, cheddar cheese, onions, and heavy cream. The wilted bacon spinach salad, using a sauce of sugar, vinegar, and warm bacon fat, is one of my all-time favorites.

　　• http://www.foodnetwork.com/food/recipes/recipe/0,FOOD _9936_23906,00.html?rsrc=search

g.　*Frisée aux Lardons* (Anthony Bourdain)

　　• Classic French bistro recipe that boils the fat from the bacon before frying.

　　• Roquefort on toasted baguette compliments the strong flavors.

References

1. Bourdain, A. 2004. *Les Halles Cookbook*. New York: Bloomsbury USA.

2. Decker, K. Where there's smoke, there's flavor. *Food Product Design*, July, 2003. http://www.foodproductdesign.com/articles/0703AP.html

9. Egg Yolks—Taste-Active Emulsification (TAE)

Many of our favorite dishes contain egg yolks, sometimes in huge amounts. For example, *crème brûlée*, my favorite dessert, consists simply of egg yolks, sugar, and cream. For recipes, see http://www.gourmetsleuth.com/index.asp. Emulsions often contain egg yolks, with mayonnaise as the quintessential vinegar, salt, and fat emulsion. My favorite sauce, hollandaise (and its cousin béarnaise), is another egg-enriched emulsion, although it is a bit tricky to make both of these properly.

The chemistry of the egg yolk is worth investigating. Yolks contain about 60 kcals, 5 g of fat, 2.7 g of protein, and more than 200 mg of cholesterol. Happily, studies indicate that the cholesterol from eggs is poorly absorbed and therefore not the menace it once was thought to be. The yolk, rich in fat-soluble vitamins A, D, E, and K, is also high in phospholipids that contain lecithin, chemically known as phosphatidylcholine.[1] These stabilizing components actually coat the fat oil droplet and suspend it in solution. Egg yolks are also surprisingly high in glutamic acid, which probably contributes to the taste-active property of eggs. Egg yolk protein is also easily and quickly cooked by heat. As little as 65°C or 180°F, will cause coagulation of the protein and ruin the emulsion. Hence the trickiness of making egg-based sauces.

Incorporating egg yolks into a food creates an emulsion, and the hedonic solutes are concentrated in the water phase. Yolks are also high in fat taste and can potentiate the taste of other food combined with them. Here are some examples:

a. <u>Caroline's hamburgers</u>. My wife makes a hamburger patty that is simple but receives good reviews every time. Take ground beef and add garlic, and onion powder, some salt, a little soy sauce, and one whole egg. Mix it by hand; but don't overmix. Let rest one hour in the refrigerator, and then form the patties. You may add one extra egg *yolk* for richness. I have also experimented with adding 1 tablespoon of cream to the mix with excellent moisture-retention results.

b. <u>Steak tartar</u>. In the *Les Halles Cookbook*, Anthony Bourdain says this is Les Halles signature dish that packs people into the restaurant. He uses 2 egg yolks, along with many other flavor-active ingredients: mustard, anchovies, Worcestershire sauce, Tabasco, pepper, onions, cognac, and capers.

c. <u>Hollandaise sauce</u>. I experimented with making and breaking the emulsion of hollandaise sauce with egg yolk, and it is amazing how tasty the emulsion version is in the mouth. The ability to create emulsions is an essential technique of great cooking, and certainly worth the effort to learn. See page 129 of *How to Read a French Fry* for tips on making hollandaise sauce.[2]

d. <u>Aioli sauce</u>. This garlic-oil-based emulsion makes a great accompaniment to vegetables or fish. Fresh garlic, minced finely, adds a huge taste and flavor impact. I like to make this sauce and let it mellow for a day before using it. The major taste-active compound in garlic (allicin) is a prooxidant and can irritate oral tissues at high levels—so don't use in excess amount of fresh garlic.

Adding a few egg yolks to soups and stews can improve the flavor. But they must be *tempered* first—to whipped egg yolks add some of the hot mixture, whip, add more liquid, stir or whip again, then add the mixture back to the soup.

For an excellent food-science discussion of the culinary use of egg yolks and the making of sauces, see pages 127–133 in *How to Read a French Fry* by Russ Parsons.[2] Some of his observations include the following:

a. Start your mayo- or sauce-making with all ingredients at room temperature.

b. The ideal proportion of yolk to oil is one yolk to ¾–1 cup oil. (I use 2 for added richness.)

c. For mayo: Beat egg yolks with all dry ingredients first, and then add oil in a small stream.

d. I use a Cuisinart food processor; hand blending is just too much work and creates variable results. Mayonnaise made from the new weight-management oil, Enova, makes a very stable and tasty emulsion.

Reference

1. Jiang, Y., Noh, S. K., and S. I. Koo. Egg phosphatidylcholine decreases the lymphatic absorption of cholesterol in rats. *J. Nutr.*, 131:2358–63, 2001.

2. Parsons, R. 2001. *How to Read a French Fry*. New York: Houghton Mifflin.

10. Salt Sense, Spice Blends, and Super Salt(s)

"The ability to salt food properly is the single most important skill in cooking."
Thomas Keller[1]

Joyce Barnathan and her husband, during a vacation trip to Sante Fe, New Mexico, attended a Southwest cuisine cooking school, and wrote about their experience in *Business Week*.[2] The couple learned two important culinary points: the ability to salt a dish properly distinguished a cook from a chef; and using fresh herbs and grinding your own (in a coffee grinder) can dramatically elevate your home cooking. Although the correct salting of food would seem elementary, in my experience, many aspiring cooks under-season their dishes, as if sodium chloride is a metabolic poison. Luckily, the level of salt most of us prefer happens to be just about the same, approximately 1 percent. When cookbooks say to correct the seasoning, they are saying, in essence, "Get the salt level correct; what you like is probably what the other guests will like." Now, if you are a supertaster (those individuals with a higher proportion of taste buds and taste cells), then you may have a tendency to undersalt prepared foods, because your taste perception is stronger.

The *1 percent rule* for salt in food is the single most useful principle I can give to my readers. Since our bloodstream is near 1 percent salt, we tend to like this concentration level (or just a little bit higher; most snack food is up to 1.5 percent). Although much effort is made to reduce sodium in foods (Campbell Soup Company is investigating natural sea salt), the sodium ion is uniquely tasty, and most substitutes generally taste bitter. It is simply impossible to eliminate sodium and still have a food taste *good*. By using MSG, we can drop the salt level by 25 percent, and with the addition of 5'-nucleotides we can reduce the sodium content by another 10–15 percent. The search continues, however, for salt substitutes and salty taste potentiators. The use of sea salt is intriguing; perhaps there are other taste-active compounds or synergisms that I am unaware of. I do know that sea salts have become more commonplace in high-end restaurants of late.

There is yet another salting secret that one should know. A sauce that is placed upon a food must take into account the *lack* of salt in the food. In other words, the *final* concentration should be 1 percent. For example, a steak sauce should have a salt concentration higher than 1 percent, because the steak will further dilute the entire salt concentration to less than 1 percent. I learned this lesson when I was developing a cheese sauce (in my product-development days). I noticed that panelists tend to rate the preference of the cheese sauce (over unsalted corn chips) highest when it was actually much saltier than 1 percent. Hence, when making a sauce—whether it is a hollandaise or a brown steak sauce—make it just a little saltier to your palate; when it is diluted with the food the final strength will be just about right. Most good cooks and chefs know that they have failed in seasoning foods properly if the guests add salt to the foods presented to them.

Spice Blend

I'm a big fan of Emeril's Original Essence seasoning blend. The spices are very fresh (which is unusual in premade blends), and you can actually see pieces of the herbs, which add visual interest to any food. I really like the thyme pieces and subtle Italian herb notes. The quality of the seasonings in the jar is quite superior; you are unlikely to find this quality unless you are a food scientist and contact the spice vendors directly. Emeril's spice blends are made by BG Foods (see www.bgfoods.com), a manufacturer and distributor of high-quality, shelf-stable food products, such as Ortega taco shells, Accent (MSG), Las Palmas Mexican Sauces (my favorite), and Regina vinegars. Emeril's seasoning blends also come in other varieties (Bayou Blast, Southwest, Asian, and Italian) and are worth experimenting with. For example, are your taste buds tired of the same old fried chicken recipe? Just substitute a different flavor of Emeril's Essence for the spice blend—instant *alternative* cuisine. This sensory trick works by using flavor (taste and smell) to reduce or eliminate food boredom (sensory specific satiety).

Ready made spice blends are certainly easier than making your own, and they are a quick way to enhance food pleasure with an instant flavor principle. Just make sure you store them properly to prevent stale or oxidized aromas. If you want to make your own, here is a recipe from the chef:

Emeril's Essence (courtesy of Chef Emeril Lagasse)[3]
2½ tablespoons paprika
2 tablespoons salt (I prefer popcorn salt here)
2 tablespoons garlic powder (fine or granular)
1 tablespoon black pepper
1 tablespoon onion powder (fine)
1 tablespoon cayenne pepper (more or less to taste)
1 tablespoon dried leaf oregano (powdered)
1 tablespoon dried thyme (pieces)

Combine all ingredients thoroughly and store in an airtight jar or container. Yield is about 2/3 cup. What makes this work is to use the best ingredients you can find, and the thyme should be in small leaf pieces, if possible, for visual contrast. I find it easier to just purchase the Emeril blend, because I can't find really fresh individual ingredients in the stores.

Here is a recipe using Emeril's Original Essence for simple BBQ chicken legs. In approximately 2 quarts water, add: 3 tablespoons of minced garlic, 1 tablespoon supersalt (if available), 3 tablespoons kosher salt, 2 tablespoons Lawry's seasoned salt, and 1/2 cup vodka. Place 10-15 chicken legs in the brine solution for a minimum of three hours and a maximum of 24 hours, and best placed in the refrigerator to minimize bacterial growth. The brine should taste pretty salty, almost like ocean water. Remove chicken from the brine, sprinkle Emeril's Essence fairly thickly on the wet chicken as a coating, and let the chicken dry out a bit. Cook about 30–40 minutes at approximately 375°F or until done. Brining seasons the meat, increases fluid retention during cooking, and creates additional flavor compound during heating. For the science behind brining poultry, see the discussion in *Cook's Illustrated, The New Best Recipe.*[4]

There are many other interesting seasoning salts and herbs that can be used for cooking. For example, Chef Paul Prudhomme has a complete line of herb and spice blends that are worth exploring (See http://www.chefpaul.com/. There are many great recipes). Following is a list of some of my other favorites. Costco carries many of these. I buy the larger containers; the herbs and spices seem to have a superb freshness level not always found with the smaller sizes at the supermarket.

- McCormick's garlic, onion, peppercorns, Italian seasoning, and red pepper flakes (these are kitchen staples).

- Lawry's Seasoned Salt (LSS) and seasoned pepper are good choices for marinades and brining. Note that the LSS contains *both* salt and sugar; this is very useful for added food pleasure, since the sugar will caramelize and create more complex (Maillard) flavors. McCormick's Season-All is similar to LSS but a bit higher in certain flavor notes like celery and nutmeg. It does *not* contain sugar.

- Red Robin's (gourmet burgers) Seasoning Salt contains flavor ingredients found in no other commercial blend that I am aware. The taste enhancers in this spice blend greatly amplify the umami taste. Kudos to the food scientist who developed this powerful general purpose seasoning salt.

- Tradewinds Seasoning Salt contains a spice blend (paprika, pepper, onion, garlic, and celery) that includes MSG. Find at Smart & Final (a West Coast, grocery warehouse).

- Lawry's Perfect Blend of spices and rubs—the blends have very interesting colors, textures, and flavors. The larger granules have visual appeal.

- McCormick's Montreal Steak Seasoning is a personal favorite. It's great on pork ribs and as a seasoning for hamburger (mixed in, *not* on top). Roasted vegetables (broccoli) come alive using this blend.

- Pappy's 50 percent Less Salt Seasoning (found at Smart & Final), adds flavor without excess salt and comes in a number of flavor varieties.

- Old Bay Seasoning has excellent celery and bay aroma notes with plenty of spice depth from cloves, allspice, and mace (an unusual blend). New research indicates that these spices may activate vanilloid, CB-1, and temperature-sensitive receptors in the mouth, adding enhanced orosensation.

Some mail order companies make excellent spice blends. My favorite is the Penzeys spice catalogue. Check it out at http://www.penzeys.com/cgi-bin/penzeys/shophome.html. The advantage of mail order is that the spices tend to be fresher, and Penzeys has a huge selection of herbs and spices in single and multiple blends. With Penzeys spice blends, you can endlessly and effortlessly vary your food flavor signatures. For example, I received a boxed gift of their spices as a Christmas present, and I use them to add variety to my dishes. The spice set included: Northwood's Blend (traditional, paprika-based seasoning), Jamaican-inspired jerk seasoning for chicken and fish, Galena Street (Southern-style) rib and chicken rub, and the Trinidad Lemon-Garlic marinade.

Herbs and spices you should not use:

Certain herbs do not dry well, and their use can actually *hurt* your cooking by invoking stale and musty notes (unpleasant evoked qualities). Here is a list of herbs that you should not use in your home cooking unless there is little choice:

a. Dried basil. The annual herb with the delicate licorice flavor stores very poorly. Unless the basil is dried under special, low-temperature conditions, even then one can only discern a slight basil scent. In addition, this herb is easily destroyed by cooking, so adding it to food with applied heat is a waste of good basil. A great substitute for the licorice flavor of basil is tarragon, and herbs whose aromas are actually enhanced by heating. Just a small pot of the fresh plant in the kitchen will provide enough for fresh use; and we now have new basil species that grow more leaves and less seedpods; and one species acts like a perennial, and will grow through the winter months.

b. Dried parsley. Truly dreadful when dried. First, it doesn't smell like real parsley, and second, the texture could not be more removed from the real thing.

c. Ground black pepper (not fresh). Pepper loses much of its aromatic punch during storage. To make things worse, it can develop musty and fecal (skatole and p-cresol) off-notes over time, which you want to avoid in your cooking. You *must* use freshly ground pepper in your cooking!

Other Tips

- See *Cook's Illustrated*, July & Aug., 2003, p. 16–17 for an excellent summary of fresh versus dried. The article recommends that you avoid using the dried versions of the following herbs: basil, chives, dill, parsley, and tarragon.

- Tip: Dry roasting whole spices can dramatically increase their aromas, activate the essential oils, and boost intensity. Cumin, coriander, and fennel seeds increase in both aroma intensity and complexity with roasting (use a heavy skillet, watch carefully, and don't let them burn). Whole spice blends may be slowly toasted as well—for example, curry blends. See http://spiceadvice.com/usage/staple_spices.html.

Nutmeg, Cloves, and Nitric Oxide

Freshly ground nutmeg and cloves is used in a variety of savory French sauces and desserts, and is an essential part of the flavoring complex in egg nog. These spices, however, have interesting pharmacological properties that may have fostered their use in cooking. Nutmeg, in particular, contains powerful essential oil compounds, including pinene, camphorene, eugenol, and myristicin. Researchers found that ethanolic extracts of nutmeg and clove, given to male, Swiss mice, release nitric oxide in a manner similar to Viagra.[5] The authors suggest that the spices have both central and peripheral stimulatory effects, based on nutmeg's ability to increase peripheral vasodilation. Other scientists believe that nutmeg may act as a monoamine oxidase inhibitor and thus has a stimulatory action on central neurotransmitters. In this author's opinion, nutmeg, cloves, cinnamon, and mace may actually increase one's perception of or interest in the food being spiced via peripheral effects on taste sensation and central effects on neurotransmission. But as Anthony Bourdain cautions, use a light touch when using nutmeg in the spicing of sauces and foods, you want a subtle background note, not the flavor of eggnog![6]

Salts of Special Distinction

Salt comes in many grinds, types, and textures. At first blush, it would seem that salt is just sodium chloride, and that's the end of it. Since the proper salting of food is the number one principle of good cooking, the choice of salts in cuisine design has a major impact on food pleasure and palatability. Let's take a look at the common salts and then explore what I call the *enhanced* pleasure salts.

Table Salt

Common table salt is a ubiquitous seasoning aid, and there is nothing wrong in using this condiment to attain the preferred 1 percent solution. One common mistake is using the *iodized* version of sodium chloride. Iodine, an essential nutrient, does have an off-flavor metallic taste that can be quite overpowering, especially in delicate food systems. I much prefer to use Diamond Kosher salt (Thomas Keller's and my wife's choice) in general cooking and food (meat) brining. Iodine deficiency is rare in the United States. By the way, like Chef Keller, my wife uses the *feel* of the salt in her fingers to judge the amount to use.

Sea Salts

Fancy table salts are now offered in a variety of forms and flavors. Thomas Keller, of *The French Laundry* fame, probably started the focus on salt with his wonderful series of cooking articles in the *Los Angeles Times*. In his restaurant, he offers Jurassic or Italian Chianti salt, French *Fleur de Sel,* and salt from the Sea of Japan.[7] Do we really need these fancy salts? Karen James, a food writer, investigated the use of these specialty salts in upscale restaurants. She found that sea salts are very popular with professional chefs and come in over fifty varieties, with an elevated price tag to match. She notes that with prices twenty times higher than kosher salt, they are mainly used to finish, or "plate," the final dish. Her article mentions Chef Theo Roe, an instructor at the Culinary Institute of America in Hyde Park, NY, who seasons with kosher salt in his kitchen and *finishes* food with a flurry of *Fleur de Sel.*[7] Excellent assortment of sea salts are available in the mail order catalog called Chefs or go to chefscatalog.com. My current feeling is that the sea salts may have taste properties *beyond* salty taste; such as activation of dynamic contrast (the crystals meltdown *rapidly* upon contact with saliva). I am currently investigating their physiochemical properties.

Campbell Soup Company announced the use of a special sea salt to reduce the amount of sodium in some of their soup lines (Chicken Noodle, Cream of Mushroom, and twelve soups for kids), by up to 40 percent. Campbell would not use these salts if they didn't have some secret synergistic (and taste-active) properties. Perhaps the minerals such as magnesium, potassium, calcium, and a whole host of up to sixty trace minerals (for instance, vanadium) amplify salty taste perceptions, or boost umami flavor.

Another possible explanation for the oral popularity of larger-size salt granules is that the crunch or meltdown of the seat salt on the tongue may "surprise" the taste buds with an "unexpected" blast of hedonic solutes (suddenly) dissolving in saliva. According to Read Montague's surprise theory and food pleasure, unexpected rewards are the *most thrilling* of all.

Chef Keller recommends trying sea salt in salads or sprinkling just a little over cooked meats. As the salt dissolves in the saliva, it "explodes" on the tongue. In fact, this is why I like Montreal Steak Seasoning; it has different tastes and textures and contrasts and a larger salt crystal—a dynamic mixture that enhances food pleasure.

AJI-SHIO (Supersalt I)

You've probably never heard of this unusual salt made by Japan's largest seasoning manufacturer, Ajinomoto (Japanese for "Essence of Taste"). But it is a very special salt that can greatly improve certain dishes, and it possesses a "wow" factor for many who try it. Found in Chinese, Japanese, and Korean supermarkets, this flavor enhancer is 90 percent salt and 10 percent MSG. What is even more unique is the physical structure of the salt itself. The MSG is actually coated *around* a salt granule; this is not a fine powder. If people use this salt in place of table salt, they can use about 20–40 percent less and have *more* salt and savory flavor! Since the salt is somewhat expensive for routine cooking, save it for special dishes in which the savory success is of utmost importance, for example:

a. Popcorn—use about 25 percent less of this salt versus popcorn salt.

b. French fries—just a stunning flavor boost.

c. Finishing savory dishes—I sometimes just sprinkle a bit over cooked meats, pastas, and salads.

d. It is superb in mayonnaise and salad dressings, sauces, and gravies from scratch.

Aji-Shio is hard to find and only sold in Asian supermarkets, if you want to match the blend for general seasoning, use 9 parts of salt to 1 part of MSG (Accent). Since this mix does not replicate the special Aji-Shio salt structure don't use as table salt.

MSG has surprising little taste on its own; but in combination with sodium, in the right proportions, this amino acid heightens the hedonic dimensions of food. If you are hypertensive or on a salt-restricted diet, just a pinch of this unique Supersalt I will greatly enhance food pleasure. I *do not*, however, use this salt for brining; kosher salt is the choice here, or use Supersalt II, which I will discuss shortly.

Benefits of combining salt with MSG:[8,9]

- Amplified salt signal (increased pleasure)

- Induction of "umami," or deliciousness (increased pleasure)

- Suppression of off-flavors

- Increased salivary flow

- Increased depth and meaty flavor to many dishes

- In small amounts, increased pleasure in sweet foods such as cookie.

Supersalt II

Several months ago, I discovered another salt blend during a trip to a Korean supermarket in my hometown of Valencia, CA. Since I am a curious cook, I constantly scour the aisles looking for interesting food ingredients, even if I haven't a clue as to what they are (my wife reads Chinese, which helps). A trip through a Ranch 99 Chinese supermarket or the Japanese chain, Marukai, is an eye- and palate-opening experience. The seafood is absolutely fresh (swimming in tanks!), and the selection of "umami-predominant" snacks is amazing.

There is a Korean salt that is made from a unique combination of ingredients: 90 percent salt, 9.9 percent MSG, and 0.1 percent 5'-nucleotides. Although Supersalt I is a powerful tastant, Supersalt II is in a class by itself. This salt blend is *serious* seasoning—and must be used wisely. Sensory studies demonstrate that the combination of salt, monosodium glutamate, and nucleotides increased the "umami" taste to the greatest extent (up to 4–8 times more umami than MSG and salt alone).[10] Words alone do not fully describe the tremendous hedonic taste impact of just a few grains of Supersalt II. It will literally take your culinary breath away. Now I know that food purists and chefs will be taken aback by the suggestion of using such a simple chemical soup to improve the taste of food. And I certainly understand that *real* cooks and chefs will prefer to make their stocks from scratch for depth and complexity of flavor. But few of us have the time or culinary to make our own stocks and demi-glace. The judicious use of Supersalt II can greatly improve the taste, appeal, and lusciousness of almost any savory dish.

How to Use Supersalt II (SSII)

Although I prefer to use more complex seasoning in my cooking (such as soy sauce, parmesan, and egg yolks), there are instances in which this salt can improve the savory or "umami nature" of any savory dish. I brine *all* my meat before cooking and use SSII in the brine mix along with kosher salt. In dishes where you add salt and you want to substitute SSII, try adding 2/3 less, then check the seasoning. In some dishes where soy sauce can't be used, I will use SSII instead, since it is much more complex, but one can't add soy sauce to everything.

Try boiling pasta in water salted with SSII instead of plain salt. In potato recipes substitute SSII for regular table salt (it's excellent in oven-roasted potato dishes). Soups and sauces are greatly boosted by SSII, especially if they are simple in preparation and you don't have the necessary and fancy ingredients to boost the flavor naturally—like real Romano cheese (in fact, you may not *like* Romano cheese). Remember to use this salt at half or less the amount as regular table salt, and taste the dish carefully.

SSII is so powerful that it is best used sparingly and never as a tabletop salting agent—it's simply too overwhelming. But in small amounts and used wisely, SSII will make your cooking better, sometimes *much* better. All three ingredients are also derived from natural sources, such as molasses. Perhaps there is one interesting additional benefit to using such a salt. The 5'-nucleotides found in SSII (part of our DNA) are actually added to infant formula to boost immunity and improve intestinal health.[11] For those who are salt sensitive or concerned about their blood pressure, try using SSII instead of table salt. You may be able to cut back your sodium intake by up to 80 percent and still find the overall taste and umami flavor to be quite acceptable.

How to Find Supersalt II

This is the tough part. Only Korean stores carry this, and I can't make out the brand name, since it is written in Korean. The store I frequent has two brands. The one I am looking at says the product is made by CJ companies and imported by Rhee Bros, Inc. The Web site is www.cj.co.kr. You need to visit Asian grocery stores and look for three colored spoons on the front of the package and a small sticker on the back that says, "Salt, MSG, and Ribonucleic acid." The salt is not expensive and is worth the effort to find.

If this salt proves elusive, there is another substitute that is more readily available in Chinese and Japanese food stores—an Ajinomoto Co. product called Hi-Me or instant cooking base. It is comprised of 92 percent MSG, 4 percent disodium 5'-inosinate, and 4 percent disodium 5'-guanylate. This is very similar to SSII, but without the added sodium chloride. It is useful for soups, stocks, and sauces or in the brining of food. One needs to add salt, of course, but by itself Hi-Me has an interesting brothy, slightly meaty, mild salty taste. In brining meat, only half a teaspoon per gallon of water is needed to boost umami taste.

Food Pleasure Honorable Mentions

We have not exhausted the pantry of pleasure foods, and a few comments are in order for additional ingredients that add depth, complexity, and—ultimately— pleasure.

Hot Peppers

"I'm surviving Szechuan. I'm making it through this most incendiary of incendiary meals in the fire capital of the world. And I'm loving it. The effect of all the peppers is almost narcotic in its endorphin-producing qualities."
Anthony Bourdain[12]

See chapter 15 on why we like spices for an in-depth discussion of hot pepper ingestion and the pleasure sensation it generates. Hot Peppers add heat, of course, but a different type and intensity than black pepper (piperine). Hence, both can be used in cooking without interfering with each other, and Cajun cuisine frequently uses both. Capsaicin, the active compound, adds tremendous trigeminal stimulation to foods, but it doesn't have to be blazing hot to be pleasurable. After all, hot pepper is a *painful* stimulus that activates the capsaicin-sensitive vanilloid receptor TRPV1, which causes the brain to release opioids in response to the painful stimulus.

Even for those who don't like hot food—supertasters mostly—a small amount of red pepper can increase food pleasure by subtle activation of increased sensation. Many French sauces and even mayonnaise recipes include some powdered red pepper. We are not making Mexican food here, but adding *subtle* threshold sensation. I also like to add some white pepper, which gives the food a sharper piperine component. A few drops of Tabasco are an excellent option if fine red pepper is not available.

Roasted and smoked hot peppers add another dimension of food pleasure and are worth experimenting in your cooking. Smoked jalapenos (chipotle) are a surprisingly good addition to many dishes. The smoky element, of course, ties into the cookivore theory. For recipes see Epicurean.com. Roasting a pepper over a flame and letting it steam in a paper bag adds tremendous flavor compounds not present in the fresh peppers. Actually, roasting just about *anything* increases caramelization, breaks down the sugars and amino acids, and creates Maillard reaction products. As we have discussed, many of these flavor-enhancing compounds, by the way, *don't* form in a microwave oven!

Acidulants—Vinegars and Fruit Acids

A unifying theme in the pursuit of excellent cooking—one I often repeat—is that *dry food is sensory death!* Foods that fail to elicit saliva upon mastication will greatly reduce the food's sensory pleasure. Saucing theory, moistness in food, dynamic contrast, and proper seasoning—all contribute to enhanced salivation and food appreciation.

What is the most potent stimulator of saliva? Any food that stimulates the *sour* sense of taste will induce salivation, an unappreciated sensation in food pleasure.[13] Sour taste itself is not directly pleasurable like salt and sugar; it is actually termed "aversive" in the taste journals. But combined with the other pleasurable tastes, it is a booster of food pleasure. In physiological circles we call it food *arousal*. Thomas Keller knows this well; he wrote that vinegar is an overlooked seasoning, but used in the background it builds flavors; many of his *à la minute* and meat sauces use a little vinegar at the finish.[1]

Keller uses white wine vinegar because of its low flavor profile; it blends in well in the background. Many sauces and dressings are acidic at the core, whether it's lemon juice or balsamic vinegar. I frequently add an acid ingredient in many food recipes. For instance, I love roasted potatoes with just one tablespoon of lemon juice and/or balsamic vinegar prior to oven roasting. The acidulants retard non-enzymatic browning (food looks brighter), and add a "mouth watering" dimension to the food. The vinegar additions, in the finished sauce, should be low enough to build flavor only; the taste and smell of vinegar should not be noticeable.

Experiment with using small amounts of vinegar or other acidulants in your cooking. Add a dash to scrambled eggs, or add some vinegar to pasta in boiling water. Recall that many of the great sauces contain acidic ingredients—such as lemon juice in hollandaise sauce. Pull out the acid, and you have a very flat and bland creation. What would a *beurre blanc* sauce (a great sauce worth mastering) be without the acid component? What would be the point of Caesar salad dressing without the Worcestershire sauce and lemon juice? In the making of French fries I often use a few tablespoons of vinegar or lemon juice in the soaking water to reduce the browning of the potatoes and to help brighten the flavor.

Research indicates that certain acids have taste enhancement effects, in both animals and man. For example, citric acid increases food consumption in horse feed, and phosphoric acid enhances the flavor of cat food.[14] Citric acid may enhance the taste of sucrose, high-intensity sweeteners, and amino acids in man as well. The famous English chef, Simon Hopkinson, interviewed by Emily Green, says that lemon juice improved the taste of "everything."[15] Lemon juice, of course, is a major source of *citric acid*. The acid in vinegar (acetic acid) is the most efficient food acid that elicits salivation; in addition, it also activates trigeminal nerve endings in the mouth (sensation) and in the nasal cavity (aroma)[13] Perhaps this explains Chef Keller's fondness for vinaigrette—the combination of fat and acid.[16]

References

1. Keller, T. 1999. *The French Laundry Cookbook*. New York: Artisan.

2. Barnathan, J. Cooking school: don't get burned. BusinessWeek online. Sept. 19, 2005. http://www.businessweek.com/magazine/content/05_38/b3951130.htm

3. Lagasse, E. Emeril's essence. Food Network.com. http://www.foodnetwork.com/food/recipes/recipe/0,FOOD_9936_8489,00.html

4. Collin, J. The basics of brining. *Cook's Illustrated*. Nov./Dec., 2001. http://www.cooksillustrated.com/images/document/howto/ND01_ISbriningbasics.pdf

5. Tajuddin, S., Ahmad, S., Latif, A., Qasmi, I. A., and K. M. Y. Amin. Aphrodisiac activity of 50 percent ethanolic extracts of *Myristica fragrans* Houtt. (nutmeg) and *Syzygium aromaticum* (L) Merr. & Perry. (clove) in male mice: a comparative study. *BMC Complement Altern. Med.*, 3:6, 2003.http://www.biomedcentral.com/1472-6882/5/16

6. Bourdain, A. 2000. *Kitchen Confidential*. New York: Bloomsbury USA.

7. James, K. Want the salt? But which flavor, which color? Columbia News Service. Nov. 29, 2005 http://jscms.jrn.columbia.edu/cns/2005-11-29/jamesk-gourmetsalt

8. Umami: the fifth element (fifth element in taste, includes recipes). *Art Culinaire*. Summer, 2003.

9. Halpern, B. P. Glutamate and the flavor of foods. *J. Nutr.*, 130:910S–914S, 2000.

10. Kawai, M., Okiyama, A., and Y. Ueda. Taste enhancements between various amino acids and IMP. *Chem. Senses*, 27:739–45.

11. Newburg, D. S., and W. A. Walker. Protection of the neonate by the innate immune system of developing gut and of human milk. *Pediatr. Res.*, 61:2–8, 2007.

12. Bourdain, A. 2006. *The Nasty Bits*. New York: Bloomsbury USA.

13. Lugaz, O., Pillas, A. M., Boireau-Ducept, N., and A. Faurion. Time-intensity evaluation of acid taste in subjects with saliva high flow and low flow rate for acids of various chemical properties. *Chem. Senses*, 30:89–103, 2005.

14. Ogawa, K., and J. Caprio. Citrate ions enhance taste responses to amino acids in the Largemouth Bass. *J. Neurophysiol.*, 81:1603–7, 1999.

15. Green, E. Simply Simon. *Los Angeles Times Magazine*, Jan. 15, 2006.

16. Keller, T. 2004. *Bouchon*. New York: Artisan.

CHAPTER 21

▼

CULINARY SECRETS OF THE TOP CHEFS

"How many times, and in how many ways, can I say it? Fish tastes better on the bone! As every cook from every serious food culture from every generation knows."[1]
"The absolute foundation of professional cooking, and the most useful thing I can teach you, is the concept of *mise en place*."[1]
"What's missing in your home cooking? … What's wrong with your soup, your sauces, your stews? The answer is almost certainly 'stock'."
Anthony Bourdain[1]

Introduction

In this section we explore the talents of a few top chefs and show how their techniques and ingredient selections follow my principles of food pleasure. We start with a brief discussion on the first discourse of good food, *The Physiology of Taste*, written in 1825 by J. A. Brillat-Savarin, a French lawyer and gastronome with an uncanny understanding of food and cuisine. Next, we follow the principles of French bistro cooking by the witty cook and peripatetic gourmand Anthony Bourdain, famous for his book *Kitchen Confidential* (for adults only).[2] This book chronicles his sometimes harrowing experiences as a chef and includes a wonderful chapter on culinary techniques that the home cook can use. I wrap up with a brief discussion of the more advanced techniques of America's celebrated chef, Thomas Keller of Bouchon, French Laundry, and Per Se restaurant fame (he's won numerous awards, accolades, and honors). When I studied Mr. Keller's writings, I was astonished to find that his exacting techniques followed the top six food pleasure theories—to the letter. This suggests an unusual ability to perceive how food construction and ingredients affect the sensory pleasure response.

These two chefs have an absolute passion for what they do, and it shows in their restaurants, cookbooks, and cooking styles. Keller is the neurosurgeon of cuisine design and construction; his recipes are innovative and demanding, and they require time (for instance, his onion soup takes four hours; Bourdain's takes 1.5 hours). Recipes in the *Les Halles Cookbook* are easier for an amateur (like me), but what I enjoy most about these cookbooks is the food chatter surrounding most of the recipes. One can learn much by just reading the sections on *mise en place*, making stock, and "the importance of ..." sections. I will summarize some of their most important thoughts below.

Chefs' Comments on How to Make Food Taste Great

> Inviting a person for dinner requires that you care for his happiness.
> J. A. Brillat-Savarin (1755–1826)

Jean Anthelme Brillat-Savarin

Jean Anthelme Brillat-Savarin wrote the first treatise (or at least the most famous) on good food appreciation; *La Physiologie du Gout* or *The Physiology of Taste*, self-published in 1825. Brillat-Savarin was undoubtedly one of the greatest gastronomes the world has ever known. His work is still quoted in foodie circles, and his aphorisms are now classics. But the underlying purpose of his work was to discuss the pleasures of the palate and gastronomy in general.

Brillat-Savarin was a lawyer by training, but he examined food perception and pleasure with a scientific bent. As I went through his book, page by page, I was struck by the fact that I was, in essence, updating this classic work. Much has been learned in the ensuing 180 years, and I thought it would be instructive to revisit and update his writings with the most recent studies in food perception and physiology. I found his work inspirational—and the present effort is not only an update but serves as a small tribute. In fact, I discovered his book about two years *after* I started my explorations into food pleasure, in 1985. The entire work is available on the Internet from eBooks@Adelaide.[3]

He wrote twenty aphorisms at the start of his book; I've selected a few for an updated physiological review. The aphorisms are in my own words:

1. A nation's fate depends upon their food supply.

- Food and culture have always been closely linked, whether it's the soybean in China or the potato in Ireland. The spice and salt cravings alone accounted for spirited human interaction among nations in trade, commerce, and warfare.

2. You are what you eat.

- Humans require the most diverse diet of any species, with a daily requirement of over fifty macronutrients, vitamins, minerals, and vitamin cofactors. This requires an equally complex food sensory system for the detection, appreciation, and assimilation of these essential nutrients.

3. God created appetite, to reward us for eating.

- Dr. Robert Hyde, a professor at San Jose State University, has written about the importance of ingestion and pleasure; he refers to cuisine and food intake as the *primary pleasure*. Consuming enough salt, fat, sugar, and protein would indeed be tedious unless they excited pleasure sensations—both oral and gastrointestinal.

4. Of all the senses, the pleasure of eating remains the strongest and most comforting.

- The sense of taste is a very durable sensation, with little loss in acuity over time in healthy adults. Olfaction, however, is more fragile, with perceptible losses in discrimination starting as early as sixty years of age; and the deterioration in aroma detection and discrimination is higher in men than women.

5. The first hour of dinner is never dull.

- The pleasures of eating can be sustained if the courses and construction are interesting and varied. Escoffier used to say that the perfect meal should last about two hours. And in French cuisine, the serving of hors-d'oeuvres (or the British "elevenses," the Chinese "dim sum," the Spanish "tapas") *extends* the pleasures of the palate as long as the dishes are small, light, and varied in flavors and textures.

6. Creating a new dish is more important than finding a new star.

- Certain dishes do inspire us, whether it is the simple French fry potato or the fancier cone-shaped coronet found at the French Laundry. When *steak au poivre* was first invented in France, it became a national sensation. Paul Prud-homme's blackened fish technique, served at his K-Paul restaurant in New Orleans, was emulated by just about every culinary cognoscenti and upscale restaurant.

The next three aphorisms deal with E. T. Rolls' (neural) discovery of sensory specific satiety, where after about ten minutes of food ingestion one dulls to the sensory characteristics of that food (color, texture, taste, and aroma). He found that certain neurons in the orbitofrontal cortex stop responding to that food, thus reducing food pleasure.[4] Thomas Keller calls this effect the law of diminishing returns, a phenomenon he experienced a long time ago—the first beer on a hot day is great tasting, but the pleasure soon decreases in the second or third.[5]

7. Dining should start with the strongest flavor food and move toward the lightest.

8. Drinking during eating should be from the lightest to the most perfumed and aromatic.

9. Appreciation of good food and wine is dulled by too much wine.

The next observation fits in perfectly with humans as cookivores, where fire and food became the perfect natural partners with our inborn, meat-eating genetics.

10. All men prefer the roasting of meat, right from birth.

Brillat-Savarin took his guests' happiness very seriously. The next set of aphorisms reveals his commitment to food excellence and camaraderie. These are very similar to the comments by Keller and Bourdain, who maintain that preparing food for your friends and seeing them satisfied are the only reasons you create the best food you can. Bourdain writes that "the greatest and most memorable meals are as much about who you ate with as they are about what you ate ... just as you must respect your guests, however witless and unappreciative they might be. Ultimately, you are cooking for yourself."[1]

11. A man should not have friends unless their dinner needs are met.

12. The house coffee must be excellent and all liquors first-rate.

13. Proper entertaining requires that dispensing happiness to all in the house.

These aphorisms—or, more appropriately, observations—are actually principles on the importance of food intake in humans, its reinforcing power, and how to maximize the reward potentials in the food and wine served. The rest of his book is sprinkled with similar physiological observations of food perception, intake, digestion, and the proper techniques of cuisine appreciation. So let's examine some additional Brillat-Savarin's culinary observations comparing them to modern food and physiological research. (In his book, he often calls himself the *professor* and the reader the *student*!)

1. Brillat-Savarin lists at least six senses—sight, hearing, smell, taste, touch, and physical desire. I believe the number is closer to twenty, as humans possess increasingly complex sensations that seem to be separate and distinct, such as the positional sense (you innately know where your body parts are in space). And some scientists believe that each sense of taste (salty, sweet, sour, bitter, vanilloid, umami, water, and fatty taste) may be its own *separate* sensory dimension.

2.   Brillat-Savarin notes that each sensation has an artistic and hedonic component, which I believe as well. Taste and smell are primary reinforcers and are intricately wired into the pleasure centers—in fact, they are the drivers of ingestion and proper food selection. And as we have discussed, visual interest in movies and video games is guided by endorphins even at the highest levels of processing.

3.   Taste, notes Brillat-Savarin, is roused to action by appetite and hunger. His observation has now advanced to even single-cell recordings in the brain as performed by E. T. Rolls, who discovers that feeding induces a satiety to the sensory properties of that food, whether it's texture, color, aroma, or taste; certain neurons in the orbitofrontal cortex just stop responding. In addition, Brillat-Savarin correctly points out that taste is a pleasure, and it encourages food consumption; it is the gatekeeper of the mouth that protects us from harmful substances. His description of taste in a man whose tongue was cut out—well, you will need to read it for yourself—demonstrates that we have taste receptors over the entire oral cavity, but most of them are sensitive to *bitter* and *sour* substances.

4.   Brillat-Savarin brilliantly deduces that some of us have more taste sensation in the mouth than others; we now describe this phenomenon as those who are "supertasters." The term was coined by Dr. Linda Bartoshuk to describe individuals with elevated taste response. Supertasters may have many more taste buds than nontasters (25 percent of the population), and medium tasters (50 percent).[6]

5.   Brillat-Savarin says water has no taste. However, we know from the work of Dr. Edmund Rolls that water does indeed have a *sensation* all its own—in the orbitofrontal cortex—and that water taste is naturally rewarding, because it may activate the hedonic tastes of salt and sugar.[7]

6.   Brillat-Savarin correctly points out that the act of swallowing is the crescendo for flavor and taste reward. Swallowing activates the final perception of food via retronasal aroma perception (back of the throat).

7. Brillat-Savarin comments on the sad truth that the strength of suffer-
    ing in man is stronger than pleasure. This is an astute but unfortunate
    fact of physiology. The perception of pain is vital to sustain (protect)
    life itself, but the perception of pleasure is the driver of higher-order
    functions and complex behaviors. As Biederman and Vessel (2006)
    explain, humans are "infovores"; the brain craves *sensory* information
    and uses pleasure as the common currency to influence advanced
    behaviors.[8] Individuals who do not feel pain, due to a brain lesion or
    similar incident, usually don't live very long, because cuts, abrasions,
    and bumps lead to infection and death.

8. Brillat-Savarin says that when we eat we have the sensation of feeling
    good. We now know that foods contain nutrients that interact with
    many receptors, nerves, and hormones—all of which affect higher
    brain centers in a complex and rewarding manner. For example, stud-
    ies in both humans and animals demonstrate that food ingestion pro-
    duces a calmness, and feelings of conviviality. And the act of just
    filling the stomach with nutrients is pleasurable as well.[9,10,11]

Anthony Bourdain's Cooking Tips

In his highly amusing book on the culinary underground, *Kitchen Confidential*
(KC), Anthony Bourdain has a wonderful chapter on how to cook like the pros. I
think it is worthwhile to compare his insights with the food pleasure principles
we have been studying. His chapter is one of the best short courses on good cooking I've seen. In the discussion below I will enumerate each principle and then
explain the physiology behind it. In addition, we will discuss a few additional
cooking principles found in his *Les Halles Cookbook* (LHC)—an equally humor-
ous but surprisingly instructional tome for the home cook.[1]

1. A Decent Chef's Knife (KC)

Bourdain prefers the knives manufactured by the famed Japanese cutlery company, Global. The blades were designed by Komin Yamada and use ice-tempered
molybdenum and vanadium stainless steel. In my own kitchen, I have dozens of
knives and consider myself somewhat of a chopping knife hobbyist. My favorites
are the simple Chinese chef knives made in Taiwan: flexible blades; stainless steel;
short, blunt handles; and fine, vertically serrated cutting edges. For many uses, a
standard chef's knife (6 of 8 inch) is sufficient. I also like the new hybrid cutleries

that are called Japanese-style santoku knives. Pick the one with a hollow-ground edge with oval circle cuts near the cutting surface—these help prevent food from sticking to the knife blade. I bought mine at Chefscatalog.com. You should always use a steel sharpening blade *each* time you slice; the proper technique is to run the steel away from the top of the blade. Just three or four runs will straighten out the blade tip, which usually forms a "U" shape during cutting. The difference is dramatic. Try to cut a tomato with a U-shaped blade; it will just not go through the skin properly. However, just a few short runs of the steel, and it cuts like a knife through butter.

2. Garnishing Tools (KC)

Many chefs use squeeze bottles to add a decorative touch to plated foods. This not only applies a tasty sauce to a dish, but also creates for added visual interest or contrast, which is arousing. Humans, as visual animals, find food more interesting with added colors and visual contrasts (drizzles, sprinkles, and spots). Emeril is a compulsive plate-splasher—sometimes with two or three added sauces, food garnishes, or BAM! Original Essence. Many chefs will splash the plate with colorful sea salts, or use a powder shaker filled with sweet or savory ingredients for dusting the plate. Try this at home at your next party. You will definitely receive compliments from your friends (as well as a few snickers). When I tried this technique, one neighbor told me that I spend too much time watching the "Iron Chef." If you don't wish to make your own squeeze bottle sauces, Chef Jamie Gwen sells four types of garnishing sauces on her Web site.[12]

Mr. Bourdain also recommends heavy-bottomed stock pots and pans and a good, nonstick pan that you clean by simply wiping it with a damp cloth. In fact, Anthony says he never washes it! (My food scientist wife is skeptical of this practice.) The major reason to spend the cash on a heavy-bottomed pan is to avoid burning or scorching food. Burnt food creates long-lasting aromas and bitter tasting compounds; even a small amount of improperly cooked food can taint the entire batch. You don't want to form a long-lasting negative association between you and the burnt food you just served your guests—toss it and start over!

Food toys are fun, and I have my share, but they won't create food like the pros if you cannot grasp the fundamentals of good cooking. Boudain agrees, if one has no sense of good food construction, and you basically can't cook, then no kitchen gadget will help.

3. *Mise En Place* (LHC)

This is French for "put in place." This principle simply states that, you should do all your prep work ahead of time and put ingredients within reach. That includes, gathering pots and pans and towels, keeping softened butter at the ready, preheating the oven, and coordinating and thinking through all parts of the recipe—even premeasuring—as you see so often on Emeril's live show. One important caveat I should add is this: making dishes for the first time for guests is usually asking for trouble. Practice ahead of time, or give yourself some wiggle room in the schedule if things go awry. Caveat two: prepare the dishes and cover them to retain the heat, or simply reheat them in the oven. As the dish cools, so does the pleasure; and most fish dishes cool *very* quickly (fish flesh is less dense than that of meat). Bourdain recommends that you cook as much of the meal ahead of time, and just reheat and garnish. Save the last minute cooking for dishes that won't keep very well—for example, French fries.

4. Shallots (KC)

Rare in the home pantry but plentiful in fine restaurants, shallots are a world-class ingredient in the professional kitchen. Boudain says this ingredient makes restaurant food taste different than the food you cook at home. And restaurants strive to make food you *can't* readily duplicate at home. If you can easily make perfect fries, why would you go to McDonald's?

This member of the onion family has a few special properties:

- It has less oral bite than an onion, so raw use is more acceptable.

- It has slight garlic-like volatiles.

- Its flavor profile is distinctive in its own right, but similar to green onions.

- The chopping of shallots (*Allium cepa*) generates hundreds of volatile sulfur compounds that have a long hang time in the olfactory mucosa and can form strong aroma memory associations.

- Shallots, although they have a stronger flavor profile than onions, do not create garlic or onion breath (sulfur compounds that are actually breathed out of the lungs).

5. Garlic, Cooked and Roasted (KC)

On a visit to New Orleans, I tasted my first roasted garlic mayonnaise and was a convert right then (Galatois restaurant). Learn how to roast garlic, and you will instantly elevate your home cooking. Just about everyone likes the flavor of roasted garlic. As an added bonus, the roasting process kills the enzyme that makes allicin, reducing or eliminating garlic breath.

Bourdain loves using garlic as well, but he does not use a garlic press. He notes that whatever comes out of the press, it doesn't resemble garlic. Why? I really don't know, but my wife agrees. She said, "No self-respecting Chinese cook would *ever* use a garlic press." Perhaps the instantaneous puréeing action interferes with flavor development or does not allow the proper ratio of garlic aromas to form, or the absence of small garlic bits lowers visual and textural contrasts. Another sensory possibility is the activation of surprise theory; biting down on a small piece of cooked garlic releases a sudden "rush" of umami flavorants. My wife takes a large, flat knife and smashes each clove, gingerly teasing off the outer, paper-like layer. Then she either chops it fine (for flavoring) or delicately slivers it (more elegant look) for use in stir-fry dishes.

Roasting garlic completely changes the sensory character; the bite and sharp aroma mellow into a smoky and silky creaminess, here is a recipe:

<u>Roasted Garlic Bulbs</u>

> 2 garlic bulbs, papery outer skins discarded
> 4 sprigs thyme
> 2 tablespoons extra-virgin olive oil

- Preheat oven to 400°F.

- Cut a small slice (about ¼-inch) from the top of each bulb, exposing the tops of most of the cloves; discard.

- Place bulbs in a baking dish (I add a little water to the bottom to retard burning) and top with thyme (optional). Drizzle with oil. Cover with foil.

- Roast bulbs until soft and golden, about 1 hour.

- Don't over-roast the garlic, if it burns, it becomes bitter and will ruin any food it's mixed with.

The softened garlic will now squeeze out of each bulb. Use it in just about anything edible. What a great flavor when added to mashed potatoes or in vinaigrette. Add it to a cream sauce and get "oohs" and "ahs" from the family. Bourdain mixes *raw* with roasted garlic for a flavor enhanced and more interesting Caesar dressing. Recall that raw garlic activates cold and hot oral receptors.

Roasted-Garlic Aioli Mayonnaise
(Makes about 1 cup)

    1 roasted garlic bulb (garlic squeezed from cloves)
    1–2 teaspoons fine popcorn salt (depending on your taste)
    2 large egg yolks (yolks add emulsification and richness)
    1 tablespoon Dijon mustard (emulsifies and adds hedonic aromas and tastants)
    1 teaspoon fine sugar (Bakers)
    1 cup olive oil (Enova or Resetta works well here)
    1–2 tablespoons fresh lemon juice (add citric acid, a palatability enhancer)
    ½ teaspoon white ground pepper (activates sodium taste, adds bite)
    ½ teaspoon cayenne (or a few drops of Tabasco adds capsaicin)

- Combine garlic cloves, salt, egg yolks, lemon juice, white pepper, sugar, and mustard in a food processor until combined, about thirty seconds.

- With processor running, pour in the first tablespoon of oil— blend it well for twenty-five seconds.

- Add the rest of the oil in a slow and steady stream; process until mixture is slightly thickened, about one minute.

Note: The yolks in this dish are not cooked, so to eliminate salmonella contamination one should heat the yolks (very carefully) over low heat until they are slightly thickened and heated through, then proceed.

I must reemphasize that garlic, with a high content of fructose, burns readily and forms bitter tasting compounds. Use lower heat when cooking garlic, or combine it with other ingredients. If it burns, toss it out and start over. When sautéing garlic, if it starts to brown, you are burning it.

You can control the pungency by the chopping technique: finely chopped garlic makes the most flavor compounds; slivers of garlic are intermediate in heat and flavor; and a clove crushed with the side of a knife blade is the lowest. And what about dehydrated garlic? It is lower in flavor but has enough bite left to be very useful in rubs, marinades, and spice blends. Not all dehydrated garlic products taste and smell the same because of differences in processing. You may want to shop around to find a brand you like; I am heavily dependent on McCormick's Garlic Powder with Parsley (for marinades, brines, and quick pasta sauces), available in bulk (24 oz.) at Costco. Of all the spice blends I use, the garlic aroma in Emeril's Original Essence contains a very potent and surprisingly "fresh" smelling; this is probably why I use so much of it. Please see the section on secret-weapon pleasure foods for more information—on using spice blends.

6. Butter (KC)

Please see my section on butter as a secret-weapon pleasure food.

Bourdain uses a lot of butter in his restaurant. He notes that it is the *first* and *last* thing in the pan. Bourdain sautés dishes with a mixture of butter and oil (50/50) for a nice, brown, caramelized color and flavor (I like unsalted butter with olive oil or Nisshin Resetta Oil). The whey solids in butter contribute a unique, hazelnut-like aroma. In sautéing meat dishes, remember to wait for the mixture to stop bubbling, as the water in the butter can add an unacceptable stewed or steamed flavor; water evaporates at 212°F and greatly inhibits the formation of Maillard flavor compounds.

Some butter sauces are easy to make. Just heat the butter till it browns a bit (to develop aroma), add a little salt and lemon juice, and then pour it over fish or other lighter dishes. Bourdain also finishes most sauces with butter, which means to swirl a little in at the end of the sauce-making—for added texture, flavor, and taste hedonics (recall that butter is an emulsion). Here is an example of classic hotel butter, tasty on steaks and cooked vegetables:

Maître d'Hotel Butter
1 stick softened butter
1 tablespoon shallot, finely chopped
1 tablespoon lemon juice
1 tablespoon chopped Italian parsley
½ teaspoon cayenne pepper, to taste
½ teaspoon white pepper
½ teaspoon popcorn salt (or MSG-coated salt)

Blend it all up in a food processor (or by hand with a fork), put into a container, and chill it down again. With cooked meats like steak, place a pat of the butter on top and let it melt. To be a bit more artistic, place the butter mixture into a wax paper sheet and shape into a log, then slice off into "medallion" pieces.

7. Chopped Parsley and Garnished Food (KC)

Parsley that is finely sliced makes an interesting visual addition (splash) to the food plate or mixed into many foods and sauces like mashed potatoes. Bourdain cautions against chopping—slice it instead with a chef's knife, for a more elegant presentation. This is a finishing touch that is easy to perform, and increases over-all food appeal. I found, through experimentation, that the action of chopping releases enzymes that will dull the color of parsley; slicing helps keep the color a bit longer. The ideal would be to tear it into tiny pieces with your hands (the leaf fractures along the cell line and will prevent the enzymes from leaking), but it would not look uniform. This technique, however, works well when tearing lettuce bits for salads (less enzymatic browning reactions).

Parsley Liking

1. <u>Parsley is green</u>. This simple color addition adds interest and contrast to food. Remember that humans are visual animals, and color additions are welcome to reduce food boredom (or sensory specific satiety).

2. <u>Parsley has a unique flavor profile</u>. Parsley's fresh "green" flavor, does not conflict with the existing food aroma complex. Parsley is a distinguished member of the *Umbelliferae* family, a genus that includes such important culinary herbs as celery, cilantro, caraway, dill, fennel, anise, and cumin. Thus, parsley adds aroma interest and visual contrast to most savory-based foods.

3. <u>Parsley contains interesting flavorants</u>. These are primarily essential oils and terpenes such as myristicin, apiole, and beta-pinene. In folklore, parsley has been used as an appetite stimulant, to lower blood pressure, and to increase libido in women (probably via an increase in DHEA formation and estrogen production, according to James Duke, PhD).[14] Myristicin is considered a MAO inhibitor and is a hallucinogen at high doses. MAO inhibitors tend to increase the amount of dopamine and serotonin in the body—similar to the action of anti-

depressants. With all its health and happiness benefits, I suggest always eating the garnish on the plate!

4. Parsley is a garnish. Just adding parsley to a plate reminds people of a restaurant experience. Remember that as people eat, the brain memorizes the environment in which they have dined. This ancient brain striatal program is useful for finding food again when hungry. So the next time you cook at home for friends and family, garnish like the fancy restaurant you took mom or dad to on a Hallmark holiday. Bourdain agrees—even a talentless hack can decorate food.

5. Parsley reduces "stale" flavor. Freshly chopped parsley "refreshes" cooked food by reducing off-flavors and adding "bright" aromatics.

8. Fresh versus Dried Herbs and Spices (KC)

(For a detailed discussion on why we like spices see chapter 15.)

Bourdain's cooking only utilizes fresh herbs. This is good advice, but it must be tempered a bit by further culinary clarification.

Fresh herbs and spices *always* have a more complex and distinctive aroma profile and may contain two to three times the volatiles of the dried versions. But dried spices and herbs have their place in cooking, especially if the quality is high. Modern methods of spice and herb drying and concentration now create surprisingly good copies of their fresh counterparts. In addition, the low moisture content makes for terrific rubs and marinades and allows infinite combinations. And these spice blends are much more soluble than their fresh counterparts. Emeril's Essence is an example of a spice blend that combines high sensory quality with just the right amount of salt. In fact, his Original Essence blend would be a bust if he used freshly chopped herbs (raw herbs can be surprisingly bitter when eaten fresh). Dry rubs and "BAM!" blends are as much about taste as the aroma. There is a place for both in your cooking.

9. Stocks and Demi-Glace (KC)

Bourdain says: "Stock is the backbone of good cooking. You need it—and you don't have it." I could not agree more! In fact, Escoffier, the dean of French cuisine and author of one of the most famous and influential cookbooks, *The*

Escoffier Cook Book, proclaimed that stock is the basis of French cooking; if the stock is of high quality, the rest of the cooking is easy.

Of all the techniques in the kitchen that are the hardest to master, the saucing of food is by far the most daunting for the average cook. In fact, it is quite harrowing sometimes for even the most accomplished chef. Chef Keller once said he "feared" making a hollandaise sauce. Just open a typical upscale cookbook on sauce-making and start with the preparation of the stock, then look at the mother sauces and all the variations. We soon just glaze over when contemplating the complexity, effort, and the mess; that's why we don't bother. Doing so would be a shame, as the ability to make a tasty sauce to complement food is absolutely critical for sensory pleasure and appreciation. One of the greatest compliments I've received in my simple cooking was over a red wine sauce that took me a good part of the day to prepare. On another occasion my son actually called from Canada for directions on how to make a mushroom-onion sauce for steak. So don't give up!

For the adventurous, the best single book on the topic may be *Sauces: Classical and Contemporary Sauce Making* by James Peterson.[15] This food-science-like textbook describes hundreds of sauces and contains amazing information on saucing ingredients from French to Mexican cuisine. Plus, it contains dozens of tips and techniques that are hard to find elsewhere. The best sections to study are Ingredients, Stocks and Glaces, Brown Sauces, Egg-Yolk Sauces, Mayonnaise, and Butter Sauces. For a less daunting treatise, see Mark Bittman's amazing *How to Cook Everything* for his chapter on sauces, salsas, and spice mixtures, starting on p. 759. The section on mayonnaise is especially well done.[16]

Stock Preparation

In French cuisine, almost all preparation of a finished sauce starts with a good beef stock; and Bourdain starts with roasted bones and vegetables, and puts them in a big pot with water. Cook without boiling and reduce the liquid by 25 percent or more; strain and freeze the stock. Many books detail the stock-making process, and if you have the time and the inclination it would be a good learning experience to try it. I suspect that only the most adventuresome will try making stock. This would be a shame. I've made stock and demi-glace many times, and the house does smell *very* nice, as Bourdain suggested it would.

If you wish to avoid the hassle of the stock-making process, you still will need superior beef or chicken bouillon stock already made for use. Bouillon cubes are a salt-infused abomination; don't use them. Not only are they mostly salt, the flavor tastes oxidized and reeks with a cheap food quality. Good alternatives are the reduced stock preparations found in small containers at your local supermarket. The best I can find in the stores are: Better Than Bouillon brand of beef and chicken bases, the Chef's Review Beef Base (Smart & Final) and Knorr Concentrated Beef Flavor Broth (very flavor active). Good choices for ready-made broths include the Lower Sodium Beef Broth from Swanson's or the Organic Low Sodium Beef Broth from Pacific Natural Foods. Start with these as your stock base, and follow Julia Child's recipe on page 67 of *Mastering the Art of French Cooking* to create a refreshed and flavor concentrated two step brown stock, using added onions, carrots, celery, wine, parsley sprigs, bay leaf, thyme, and tomato paste. Cook thirty to sixty minutes. Strain and proceed to the next step, which is the creation of a brown *sauce*—start by frying (in clarified butter) bacon carrots, onions, and celery—add flour to make the roux. Add tomato paste, parsley, bay, and thyme (again). This will create a good brown sauce. Finish by simmering for two hours, and strain. Be mindful to get rid of the fat that floats to the top (in other words, degrease). Note how the flavorants are added *twice* in the preparation of the brown sauce (chefs call this technique food *layering*).

Nestlé Foodservices' unit, known as Minor's, makes some of the best concentrated meat and vegetable food bases for commercial (mainly restaurant or food service) use. I had the honor of working with Dr. Minor at Michigan State, where I assisted him in teaching his course on food appreciation. He was a brilliant man and the creator of the fabulous L.J. Minor's food bases back in 1951. He told me once that only by using good ingredients and classic French techniques could one make *great* food bases. If you work in an upscale restaurant or even in a fast-food joint, I highly recommend the use of Nestlé's Minor's food bases. You can find them on Amazon.com. The simple addition of Dr. Minor's demi-glace to your sauces and stews will increase the flavor of the dish to new heights—or depths!

Companies with prepared food bases

- Eatem Foods Co.'s Eatem Food Bases

- Custom Culinary Gold Label Food Bases

- Minor Corp. (Nestlé division) Food Bases

- Demi-Glace Gold (http://www.gatewaygourmet.com/demi.htm)

- Williams-Sonoma Demi-Glace (see the company's Web site for ordering details)

Demi-glace: Bourdain creates demi-glace by greatly reducing a combination of beef stock, red wine, shallots, peppercorns, bay leaf, and fresh thyme.[2] This is now the base or booster for many types of sauces. Just add a little butter, and you have an excellent steak sauce. And for those who would rather buy it than make it, Williams-Sonoma carries an excellent demi-glace; and is available to the general public. Since it is a true demi-glace (a super-concentrated reduction of stock and seasoning), sauce-making is *really* simplified. It is available in beef, veal, chicken, and wild game versions. For less than thirty bucks, you can make dishes that (almost) taste like the pros.

Sauce Liking

Fanatical stock and sauce preparation may seem a bit over the top in the pursuit of food pleasure, but as top chefs have emphasized, saucing food is one of the great achievements of French cooking and of good cooking in general.

So what is the physiological function of a sauce? In the simplest sense, it adds to the enjoyment of eating. Sauces made from stocks are rich in taste-active components that complement the dining experience. Let's summarize why we use sauce:

Sauce-making entails the creation of a food complement (sauce) that is highly concentrated in solutes, tingles as many taste buds as possible (taste and orosensation) without being unbalanced, induces saliva, eases the act of mastication, maintains food familiarity (reduces neophobia to food), and evokes memories of past great meals (evoked qualities). A perfect demi-glace contains the solutes in a suspension of (quick meltdown) gelatin. All the impurities (which impede taste activation) and non-emulsified fat should be removed, by the use of a chinois or strainer.

Some functions of sauce include the following:

1. <u>Sauce adds moisture to food</u>. As mentioned above, Edmund Rolls and his group at Oxford reveal that there is a water taste.[7] Moisture

(water) in the oral cavity can activate a large percentage of the taste receptors in the mouth. And those taste receptors are hardwired into the pleasure center; this is nature's way to encourage water ingestion—by activating the pleasure centers of taste. The brain likes to taste foods in solutions! Dry food really is sensory death.

2. <u>Sauce encourages salivation to food</u>. Like Pavlov's dog, the taste and smell of good food ignites and arouses the food-eating experience. Sauce components include salts, acid, MSG, and vanilloid receptor agonists (bay leaf, thyme, and pepper) that allow you to eat a chewy cut of meat without choking.

3. <u>Sauce adds salt, fat, MSG, and sugars to foods</u>—these ingredients are rich in hedonic taste solutes that may not be present in the base food (*filet mignon* is actually quite flavorless). Each one of these tastes is hedonically active (fires up the pleasure center). In the creation of a sauce, acids, glutamates, and the 5'-nucleotides are formed and are released during the initial roasting (especially if you cheat and add tomato paste). The bones add gelatin (and glucosamine breakdown products), and the marrow inside the bones contains the magical ingredients—rich in fatty acids and blood cell precursors brimming with DNA and RNA breakdown products—the 5'-nucleotides. As little as 0.1 percent of free nucleotides are synergistic with MSG, greatly boost overall umami flavor and salt perception.

4. <u>Sauce contains aromatics</u>, which evoke cookivore memories of roasted meat and BBQ food. Roasting and frying create potent pyrazine flavors (that we can detect as low as 0.006 ppb), reminiscent of ancient repasts. Boiling meat will not create these desirable pyrazine compounds; one must fry or roast meat at high temperatures (at least 350°F).

5. <u>Sauce can add complementary flavors and colors</u>, adding visual and texture interest and/or increased food arousal.

6. <u>Sauce stimulates and improves the digestive process</u> because of the added sugars, acids, and amino acid breakdown products in the sauce itself. Sauce stimulates the so-called "cephalic" phase of food diges-

tion, in which food anticipation and oral taste increase pancreatic enzyme output and stimulate gall bladder contraction (bile).

7. <u>Sauce also helps evoke "memories" of past eating experiences</u>, "evoked qualities," wherein the sensory properties of our favorite foods bring forth memories of past consumption. Food writer James Peterson, author of the classic book on sauce-making, understands this phenomenon when he suggests that much of the pleasure of dining is based on the flavor memory of the comfort foods eaten in the past.[15]

Every meal we consume lays down sensory food memories that include (encode) how hungry we were, how much effort it took to acquire the meal, and who was with us. The brain wants to find the place where we dined (calories) when we become hungry once again. Many food psychologists believe this is the basis for the phenomenon known as food "craving."

Now let's take a look at a typical recipe for beef stock and some of the physiology behind it:

<u>Beef Stock</u>

6 pounds (approx.) cracked beef shanks or beef soup bones or veal bones
1 marrowbone, cracked (optional, easily obtained in Asian markets)
2 yellow onions, chopped
2 carrots, chopped
1 celery stalk, chopped (some use the leaves, others think it makes bitter stock)
1 leek, chopped (optional)
2 cups water
2 tomatoes, halved, or 1 can tomato paste (I prefer the paste; much more flavor)
6 garlic cloves or 2 tablespoons garlic powder
5 fresh parsley sprigs
2–4 bay leaves (I use more to prevent oxidation off-flavors)
3 fresh thyme sprigs (5–6 inch) or 1 tablespoon powder
8 peppercorns
2 whole cloves
1 bunch fresh parsley
6–10 chopped button mushrooms or 6 rehydrated shitake pieces (better flavor)
Flour (optional)

Typical preparation: Bones are washed and cracked, placed into an oiled baking dish, smeared with tomato taste, coated with flour, mixed, and roasted for an hour at 350°F. Vegetables are chopped and roasted as well until nicely browned. Into a large pot, add bones, vegetables, and the rest of the flavorings and fill the pot with plenty of water to cover everything (around twelve cups). Bring to a full simmer (never boil) for six to twelve hours, reduce, and skim off the scum, and strain like mad.

Roasted bones and meat shanks
Animal meat and bones are sources of taste-active compounds called the 5'-nucleotides (from red blood cells in the marrow). RBCs are a rich source of taste-active components as well. The addition of meat provides twenty amino acids, which have many complex but savory tastes. Meat protein is also 20 percent glutamic acid, which quickly turns into MSG with the addition of salt, acid, and gentle heat. Bones also contain the gelatin protein that adds "shine" to sauce and viscosity.

Vegetables
Aromatic vegetables and herbs (carrots, celery, leek, parsley, bay, and thyme) add essential oils with herbal aromas that give complexity and depth (food layering). They also act as potent antioxidants, which retard off-flavor during stock making. This is important with foods that contain lipids and fatty acids that easily oxidize. Off-flavors from rancid fats are hard to eliminate once they are formed. Thyme is an especially powerful antioxidant and is particular excellent at preventing off-flavors in meat and poultry (used in the classic *bouquet garni*: thyme, bay leaf, parsley, and leek).

The addition of tomatoes adds a generous helping of glutamic acid, soluble acidulants (especially citric acid), and sugars as well. Tomatoes are also rich in lycopene, a carotenoid with a cookivore aroma, and an antioxidant that the body tissues avidly store (skin and prostate). Remember that a sauce should stimulate saliva, and acids do it better than any other tastant.

Allium additions
Garlic, as noted previously, is a powerful, long-lasting aroma and a potentiator of the umami taste. I use fresh and dried garlic in just about every dish, mostly as a subtle background note. Onions and leeks also provide many taste-active components (sulfur-based alkyl sulfides) and large amounts of the antioxidant quercetin. The sugar content of alliums is surprisingly high, the sucrose caramelizes and

develops rich flavors during slow cooking and frying. Garlic is very sticky to the touch, since it contains high amount of fructooligosaccharides (short-chain sugars). All members of the allium family develop aromas that are very distinctive and long lasting. Just frying an onion will evoke brain memory that shouts: FOOD!

<u>Bottom line</u>: Saucing creates a highly concentrated and hedonically active solution that stimulates saliva and digestion, and enhances the whole eating experience. The tastes or solutes become very concentrated (technically known as osmolality) and generate rapid, strong, and reliable local and cephalic responses from the taste buds to the brain.

10. Onion Soup (LHC)

French Onion Soup is my favorite dish in a French restaurant; I know the chef will make it the "right" way, with butter, lots of onions, real stock, *bouquet garni*, and imported Gruyère cheese. Most non-French restaurants make a poor imitation that reeks of canned, tinny stock, and flavorless cheese. Two key recipe steps are the proper caramelization of the onions and the broiling of the cheese on top—they create intense flavor compounds and the major pleasure producers of this classic dish. Bourdain writes, "You want crispy, near burnt stuff … molten brown hues … with a few black spots where it is blistered and burned."[1] Use the real French cheeses, Gruyère, or Comté; the common cheddar cheese will not work. It will either melt away or burn excessively. (Every time I make this dish for guests, someone asks for the recipe; my trick is to use freshly baked garlic-bread croutons, and add one tablespoon of soy sauce to Bourdain's recipe.)

11. Tartiflette (LHC)

Bourdain's fancier sautéed and baked potato gratin illustrates the magic of secret pleasure food additions. He concurs that bacon, cheese, and starch make for a pleasurable combination. In the preparation of the dish, diced cooked potatoes are sautéed with onions and bacon, then layered with Reblochon cheese and baked. Layering adds more dynamic contrast. The key here is to get the mixture golden brown and bubbling—if the mixture looks pale at the end of cooking, just give it a quick broil. Cheese contains flavor-active compounds and casomorphins; bacon is smoked pork belly and loaded with taste-active curing compounds, lots of salt, and the irresistible hickory smoke. Potato starch is digested very quickly and is highly glycemic—more so than even table sugar. Easily digested carbohydrates raise blood glucose levels very quickly, reduce hunger pangs just as quickly—this is a rewarding experience in itself.

12. Rillettes (LHC)

Anthony Bourdain says that rillettes is about as traditional as French cuisine gets. "It gets right to the heart of what's good: pork, pork fat, salt, and pepper." Basically, take pork belly and shoulder and slow cook them for six hours with *bouquet garni,* then add salt and pepper. Add the mixture to a mixing bowl and shred, add some pork fat, and chill for three days. Serve with toast points or sliced baguette rounds.

Pork Liking

I have discussed why we like bacon in the section on secret pleasure foods, but I thought we would focus on the pork protein and fat structure for any insights into an animal that makes some chefs like Bourdain wax poetic. He is not alone; I found a number of porkaphiles on the Web, discussing their favorite food, and some even selling "Pork Fat Rules" T-shirts—inspired by Emeril, no doubt. Peter Kaminsky, who calls himself a *ham*thropologist and author of *Pig Perfect*, waxes eloquently when he compares Spanish Iberico ham to a fine wine, or a magnificent and complex symphony.[17] Bacon and pork flavor appear to be a universal liking (religious constrictions aside); pork is the most consumed meat on the planet (followed by beef and chicken).[18] Is there a physiological explanation for the universality of pork liking?

My research found that pork muscle has less of the fibrous connective tissue (collagen) present in bovine (beef) muscle tissues, resulting in a more tender and flavorful meat, especially under moist-heat conditions (like braising). Today's pork is much leaner than it was thirty years ago (USDA 2001 report), almost as lean as chicken breast meat.[19] Many professional chefs, however, consider this a flavor drawback, as pork fat is very unique, adds great richness, and has a uniquely melting mouthfeel. In addition to the lower collagen content, pork meat is also higher in glutamic acid than beef muscle. Glutamic acid is, of course, the taste of MSG—just add a little salt to pork during roasting or a slow braise, and *plenty* of "umami" is created. In the dry-curing of ham, a combination of proteolysis and lipolysis occurs, creating free amino acids and peptides—all loaded with taste and flavor.[20] Studies indicate that pork tenderness is a function of collagen content, degree of proteolysis, and muscle fiber length.

Consider the following recipe (from my wife's grandmother), which was handed down for centuries in Taiwanese cuisine. I consider this a most excellent pork dish, resulting in pork meat of magnificent flavor and a melting consistency, and the best *au jus* I have ever tasted.

Pork Stewing Cubes Recipe

Take 2–3 pounds of a fatty and cheap cut of pork meat (like the shoulder) and cut into 1½" cubes; place them into a large stew pot with a tight-fitting lid. The Le Creuset Dutch oven is perfect for this, with its superior heat-dispersion and moisture-recirculation properties. To the pork cubes add: 1/2 cup vodka, 25 peeled garlic cloves (smashed but not chopped), 1/3 cup soy sauce, 1/3 cup black vinegar (found in Asian supermarkets), and 1/3 cup brown or plain rock sugar. Bring mixture to boil at medium heat, then turn heat down quickly and simmer (low heat) for one to two hours with the lid on. Add *no* water; this, I was told, is the secret to this dish. The tight-fitting lid *must* recycle the moisture into to the pork-shoulder cubes. After cooking, the cubes can be served over white rice or noodles, or just by themselves. My wife uses the broth to flavor Japanese-style noodles.

13. Beef

Bourdain explains that the French cut beef differently than Americans, trimming off most of the fat, rarely keeping the bone in (no T-bones please), and keenly evaluating every cut to maximize the sensory contrasts of flavor and texture, fat, and lean. He notes that expensive, tender, and fork-friendly steaks (for example, *filet mignon*) are *not* the most flavorful cut, and they are often served with a sauce. He also notes that the French have no tradition of dry-aging beef. As for cooking meat, he says that over cooking any meat dish is a sin. Well done meat tends to be dry and the fibers toughen, neither condition is sensorially attractive. I have a hard time convincing my wife that cooking meat medium rare is a good thing; one speck of blood in a chicken leg or a *slightly* rare beef porterhouse never fails to invoke terror and thoughts of food poisoning. And heaven help me if the pork is undercooked (fairly difficult to get this right actually)—off to the microwave it goes, even though trichinosis is unheard of these days! As a solution, I now brine all meat; I can cook it more thoroughly and still enjoy juicy and tender meat!

My favorite cut of beef (as is Bourdain's) is the rib eye, bone in, about six inches thick; it is the perfect blend of fat, beef taste, and tenderness. I like to slow roast it on the BBQ with small amounts of hickory (the temperature never going over about

250°F) and a pan of beer nestled nearby to reduce moisture loss. I treat this cut of meat with all the respect it deserves; including serving it with a wine-shallot reduction sauce modified from Chef Keller's recipe (I use half a bottle of wine). The fat on the rib eye is the best part; it excites the fatty acid receptors (and feel) in the mouth and absorbs the lipophilic hickory aromatics.

Bourdain concludes the chapter on beef with a challenge: "I urge you to buy the cheapest, toughest—but best quality—beef you can get. Then challenge yourself to make something delightful out of it."[1]

14. Roast chicken

Both Keller and Bourdain believe that the ability to make perfect roast chicken is the hallmark of a good chef and home cook. Bourdain maintains that the popularity of Chicken McNuggets is the direct result of poor chicken-cooking techniques: most people throw some salt and pepper on an untrussed chicken then cook the living daylights out of it. Bourdain's method involves washing (and drying for a crisp skin) the chicken; trussing the chicken; applying a very even external and internal coating of salt and pepper; and finally stuffing the cavity with lemon, onion, rosemary, and thyme. One lump of herbed butter is also placed under the skin on the breastbone. He also rubs softened butter over the salt-and-peppered chicken and bastes with the fats that collect during the 375°F roasting. In slight contrast, Keller's roast chicken (in the cookbook *Bouchon*) begins with a complex and flavorful brine (which I highly recommend), then the chicken is trussed (tied up), thoroughly salted and peppered, placed in an oven-proof pan, and roasted at 475°F. When the roasting is complete, remove the chicken and let it sit and baste with fresh thyme leaves. He uses a higher temperature because he has found that the faster the legs cook, the moister the breast meat will be.

15. Béarnaise and Hollandaise Sauce

I have argued, in chapter one, that humans love food emulsions, and one of the tastiest is the classic béarnaise sauce with shallots, red wine vinegar, tarragon, black peppers, and egg yolks. Bourdain's recipe works just fine, but cautions that béarnaise sauce senses fear and will curdle easily. One key ingredient is to use *clarified* butter, as the whey solids can ruin the emulsion effect. For an easier version see the Food Channel recipe by Emeril Lagasse.[21] Julia Child has a foolproof blender method for making hollandaise that she says "cannot fail"; see page 81 in her book *Mastering the Art of French Cooking*. No matter which recipe you use, knowing how to make a hollandaise or béarnaise sauce is worth learning; it will be *much* better than the powdered mixes in the stores. And if you are successful at these sauces, the rest of the dish will be a cakewalk. Final note: these sauces don't hold or reheat very sell: prepare them right before serving.

Thomas Keller, the Neurosurgeon of Cooking

"I frequently return to classical preparations and look for a way to reinterpret
them, using the standard elements but surprising you with them."
Thomas Keller[22]

We have enumerated many cooking theories in this book, in an attempt to explain food pleasure and fine-cuisine construction. I have studied many food masters, but nothing compares to the exacting techniques of the self-taught but classically apprenticed French chef, Thomas Keller. When I first studied *The French Laundry Cookbook*, my wife, an excellent Chinese cook and food scientist, quipped, "Gosh, many of the recipes are very intricate and intimidating for the home cook. Will anyone be *cooking* from this?" And this would be a shame, for all the major principles of good food construction are in the pages of both (the *French Laundry* and *Bouchon*) cookbooks.[22,23] Keller's astute observations and understanding of food perception are almost peerless in their physiologic accuracy. In this concluding section, we will parallel his cooking comments with our psychobiological explanations. The ultimate goal is to understand what it takes to make food taste great from another great chef's perspective. (Interestingly, he calls himself a *cook*.)

Food Pleasure Theories and Keller Technique

Thomas Keller's overall culinary philosophy is to take classic French recipes, that have been refined over the years, and make them the very best they can be. After studying both books, I think his cooking style can be summarized in six points:

1. Master of Flavor Intensity (Color and Aroma). Keller maximized sensory stimulation via his techniques of flavor concentration and aroma intensification. For example, his canapé soups are called *amuse-gueule*, or "to make the mouth happy"—an explosion of aroma intensity and color that excites the senses. The carrot soup recipe is designed so that one spoonful of the soup contains the flavor of several carrots. In the Puree of English Pea Soup with White Truffle Oil and Parmesan Crisps, Keller strives to retain the intense green color of the pea, chlo-

rophyll. And in the strawberry shortcake recipe, lemon juice is used to brighten the strawberry flavor. His tomato sorbet recipe is an example of an intensified dish—it has a much stronger flavor than the original via a gentle 50 percent reduction step.

2. Master of "Dynamic Contrast" (DC). This theory states that people prefer those foods with sensory contrast and those that rapidly melt down in the mouth. Keller takes this concept to the highest level in his cooking; his style of mashed potatoes is an example of what extreme measures he will go. The mashed potato recipe uses Yukon gold potatoes (which emulsify better than other varieties), pressed through a tamis, creating, in effect, a solid emulsion that melts down rapidly in the mouth. Keller excels at making foods with high DC— especially the melt-in-your-mouth aspects of DC. For example, his lobster consommé is jellied, and melts quickly in the mouth; and the blini recipe dissolves on the tongue for a fast flavor burst. Keller describes a traditional French dish of pureed cod and potatoes; the cakes are sautéed to develop a perfect crust on the outside and a sumptuous inner creaminess.

3. Master of "Surprise Theory." Neuroscientist Read Montague argues that foods that surprise us in the mouth (unexpected food pleasure) are preferred or more pleasurable.[24] Keller uses culinary techniques that tap into this largely unknown physiological response to food. We have already discussed in point 1, that flavors and colors that are "intensified" activate "surprise" as well—a familiar flavor, but with explosive character. Many of Keller's dessert preparations use hot and cold *surprise* (you don't expect them) to delight the palate—velouté of bittersweet chocolate with cinnamon-stick ice cream, and slow-baked meringues with crème anglaise.

4. Master of "Emulsion Theory." We have talked about how humans have a built-in preference for salt-fat and sweet-fat emulsions. Keller understands this and takes great care to create stable and flavorful emulsions in his sauces, vinaigrettes, and even solid food preparations. We've also seen that concentration of the hedonic solutes in the aqueous phase magnifies the excitation of the taste cell. This is why the average home cook *must* be able to create these pleasurable emulsified sauces.

In the preparation of the staff meal (for the other chefs), Keller uses many principles of tasty food construction and emulsification theory. The house vinaigrette recipe is one such example. He combines: raw garlic (excites umami and cold and heat receptors), shallots (additional orosensation), Dijon mustard (another orosensory and emulsification aid rich with vinegar and acid), balsamic vinegar (potent aroma and taste-active solutes), salt, and an egg yolk (eggs have taste-active phospholipids and provide emulsification). Throw in a little black pepper to activate the vanilloid and possibly the cannabinoid receptors as well. Now, is this better than the bottle dressing in the fridge—*naturellment il est?*

5. Master of Reducing "Sensory Specific Satiety." Keller knows that food's sensory properties slowly dull the appetite, and he uses interesting culinary techniques to reduce satiety and increase overall food pleasure. To keep food arousal high, he prepares dishes that have either more intense flavors than the original or uses differing food preparation techniques with the *same* food. He might, for example, serve liver and onions with four different *style of* onion preparation—confit, roasted, "glazed red, and glazed white." The whole point, Chef Keller states, "… is to isolate and enhance flavors, not confuse them."

During my annual Thanksgiving dinner party, hosted for a few neighbors and friends, I tried the cooking variation technique. I cooked five classic dishes (turkey, potatoes, gravy, green beans, and stuffing) *three* different ways; for example, one turkey was brined and deep fried, another hickory smoked, and another garlic-infused and oven roasted. The meal was well received, and our guests sampled all the various preparations; but I was exhausted from the effort—I can't imagine doing this for a living.

Keller points out that most chefs satisfy the palate with just a few big courses, but the sensory attributes quickly deaden after just a few bites. We now know this phenomenon as sensory specific satiety (SSS), wherein we quickly decrease our hedonic response to the sensory properties of food (taste, aroma, texture) during ingestion. When food is on a plate, hardly anyone eats each portion in its entirety before moving onto the next (unless they have serious issues). We vary what we eat on the plate (in other words, one bite of this, and one bite of that) to keep SSS from decreasing our overall pleasure response.

6. <u>Master of Food Color</u>. Humans are visual animals, and Keller *understands this*. He uses techniques to keep colors bright and intense, even to the point of making his own fruit and vegetable powders. I've never seen this before in cooking; usually these powders are available only to industrial food scientists. Keller favors a technique called, big pot blanching; wherein a great deal of water and salt (at an ocean water concentration of about 4.5 percent) and fast cooking keeps the colors and the flavors of vegetables bright and dramatic. Numerous neuroimaging studies demonstrate a close linkage with color and flavor in the brain perception areas. If the color is dull, the food is dull—it's a linkage that is hard to reverse. Give this cooking method a try—it is a very classic French vegetable technique.

The following selected (and not exhaustive) culinary tactics by Chef Keller will improve your cooking at home:

1. <u>High quality and unique food ingredients.</u> Keller constantly seeks out the best meats and produce, which are high in both taste and flavor— food ingredients that we rarely use, but are readily obtained by searching the web. For example, he talks about his specialty melons, the *Chanterais* type, only available in produce markets or specialty organic stores. The melons are small, heavily perfumed, and quite sweet; they're a favorite of the French. He also uses hundred-year-old Balsamic vinegar, fruitwood-smoked salmon, wild chanterelles, and farmhouse cheddar. The addition of one flavorful ingredient can elevate the pleasure of the entire dish.

2. <u>Strain and skim your sauces.</u> Keller never lets a single sauce, puree, or liquid move from one place to another without being strained or skimmed. Particulates in food (especially solid fats) interfere with the binding of hedonic solutes with the taste buds and can build unwanted viscosity.

3. <u>Salt, pepper, and vinegar are critical cuisine elements.</u> What's the number one mistake in home cooking? It is improperly salting food.

Keller states that the "ability to salt food properly is the single most important skill in cooking," and it's the first cooking principle he teaches new chefs at his flagship restaurant, the French Laundry. Salt is a primary hedonic solute; the pleasure response was wired into our brains long ago. Keller uses Diamond Crystal Salt (the brand that my wife prefers) because you can *feel* the amount you are adding—and it has no iodine taste. Keller also likes the taste of sea salt—an instant oral flavor burst (or surprise). Chef Keller likes to salt his meat prior to cooking thus allowing the salt to penetrate into the muscle tissue. *Cook's Illustrated* showed that this is a very effective salting technique and a great alternative to brining.[25] In my experiments, coating steaks with seasoned salt and letting them rest in the fridge for twenty-four to twenty-eight hours, allows the salty taste *and* aromas to penetrate into the meat, and moisture loss during cooking is greatly reduced. In addition, this technique adds flavor layering; the surface proteins interact with the flavoring agents and create the cooked and smoky tastes and aromas, and the spice mix that penetrated into the meat retains the fresh character of the original spice blend—the perfect (cookivore) flavor-generation (and surprise) technique.

A few drops of vinegar finish many sauces in the French Laundry restaurant. This adds oral and nasal nonspecific trigeminal stimulation. (Don't use the flavored vinegars; you want the *feel* not the *flavor*). Sensory studies also reveal that acidic elements may boost sweetness and umami perception (MSG) as well.

4. <u>Bouquet Garni and specifically, thyme and bay leaf, add flavor and orosensation</u>. A combination of leeks, parsley, thyme, and bay leaves, *bouquet garni*, is the classic French flavoring blend that adds plenty of flavor to stews and marinades, and just about any recipe. Keller uses the combination of thyme and bay leaves quite often in his recipes. After additional flavor research, I think I know why. Bay leaf is a very unusual aromatic; some of the flavor compounds demonstrate tight binding to the vanilloid receptor, in a manner similar to piperine or capsaicin. This is very odd, since we don't taste the burn in the same way as capsaicin. Bay leaves also contain menthol, which activates cold-sensitive TRP receptors, adding more depth and sensation. Thyme has a number of volatile aroma compounds, but the content

of one particular compound, 1,8-cineole, exhibits unique pain-killing effects—perhaps it acts as a producer of endorphins similar to the effect of capsaicin, or perhaps it reduces the production of inflammatory cytokines, which make us feel better.[26,27] Thus, the classic pairing of thyme with bay leaves may have additional interesting physiological actions that complement their complex aromas.

Final Thoughts

Keller has many other keen insights on cooking, and they may be found in his bistro cookbook, *Bouchon*. Many of Chef Keller's recipes in this cookbook are upscale or *haute* versions of everyday American classics and are easier for the home cook to prepare. Try the recipes for roast chicken, onion soup, vinaigrette, quiche Lorraine, grilled ham and cheese sandwich, skirt steak and fries, beef bourguignon, and macaroni gratin. I invite the reader to try Keller's elegant version of tomato soup, potato chips, and grilled cheese sandwich (*The French Laundry Cookbook*)—as an example of how to "pleasurize" everyday favorites. The culinary student, or just the food curious, will find both Keller cookbooks illuminating—and well worth the gastronomic exploration.

References

1. Bourdain, A. 2004. *Les Halles Cookbook*. New York: Bloomsbury USA.

2. Bourdain, A. 2000. *Kitchen Confidential*. New York: Bloomsbury USA.

3. Brillat-Savarin, J. A. 2006. *The Physiology of Taste or Transcendental Gastronomy*. eBooks@Adelaide, University of Adelaide, South Australia. http://etext.library.adelaide.edu.au/b/brillat/savarin/b85p/index.html

4. Rolls, E. T. Brain mechanisms underlying flavour and appetite. *Philos. Trans. R. Soc. Lond. B. Biol. Sci.*, 361:1123–36, 2006.

5. Weich, D. Thomas Keller interview. Powells.com. http://www.powells.com/authors/keller.html

6. Bartoshuk, L. Comparing sensory experiences across individuals: recent psychophysical advances illuminate genetic variation in taste perception. *Chem. Senses*, 25:447–60, 2000.

7. de Araujo, I. E., Kringelback, M. L., Rolls, E. T., and F. McGlone. Human cortical response to water in the mouth and the effect on thirst. *J. Neurophysiol.*, 90:1865–76, 2003.

8. Biederman, I., and E. A. Vessel. Perceptual pleasure and the brain. *Am. Sci.*, 94:247–53, 2006.

9. Cota, D., Tschop, M. H., Horvath, T. L., and A. S. Levine. Cannabinoids, opioids and eating behavior: the molecular face of hedonism? *Brain Res. Brain Res. Rev.*, 51:85–107, 2006.

10. Murphy, G., and S. R. Bloom. Gut hormones and the regulation of energy homeostasis. *Nature*, 444:854–59, 2006.

11. Dallman, M., Pecoraro, N. C., and H. Brotchie. Chronic stress and comfort foods: self-medication and abdominal obesity. *Brain Behav. Immun.*, 19:275–80, 2005.

12. Chef Jamie Gwen Garnishing Sauces. http://www.chefjamie.com/store/

13. Rolls, E. T. The representation of umami taste in the taste cortex. *J. Nutr.*, 960S–5S, 2000.

14. Duke, J. 1997. *The Green Pharmacy.* New York: St. Martin's Paperbacks.

15. Peterson, J. 1991. *Sauces: Classical and Contemporary Sauce Making.* New York: Van Nostrand Reinhold.

16. Bittman, M. 1998. *How to Cook Everything.* New York: Macmillan.

17. Kaminsky, P. 2005. *Pig Perfect: Encounters with Remarkable Swine and Some Great Ways to Cook Them.* New York: Hyperion.

18. Davis, C. G., and B. H. Lin. Factors affecting U.S. pork consumption. Outlook report No. (LDPM13001), May, 2005. http://www.ers.usda.gov/Publications/LDP/may05/ldpm13001/

19. Fritschner, S. Today's pork is lean and quick cooking. Courier-journal.com. Jan. 10, 2007. http://www.

courier-journal.com/apps/pbcs.dll/article?AID=/20070110/
COLUMNISTS16/701100489/1010/FEATURES

20. Toldrá, F., and M. Flores. The role of muscle proteases and lipases in flavour development during the processing of dry-cured ham. *Crit. Rev. Food Sci. Nutr.*, 38:331–52, 1998.

21. Lagasse, E. Béarnaise sauce. http://www.foodnetwork. com/food/recipes/recipe/0,FOOD_9936_6401,00.html

22. Keller, T. 1999. *The French Laundry Cookbook*. New York: Artisan.

23. Keller, T. 2004. *Bouchon*. New York: Artisan.

24. Berns, G. S., McClure, S. M., Pagnoni, G., and P. R. Montague. Predictability modulates human brain response to reward. *J. Neurosci.*, 21:2793–98, 2001.

25. Roast salted turkey. *Cook's Illustrated*.com. http://www.cooksillus trated.com/login.asp?did=3689&LoginForm=recipe

26. Aydin, S., Demir, T., Ozturk, Y., and K. H. Baser. Analgesic activity of Nepeta italica L. *Phytother. Res.*, 13:20–3, 1999.

27. Lima-Accioly, P. M., Lavor-Proto, P. R., Cavalcante, F. S., Magal-haes, P. J., Lahlou, S., Morais, S. M., and J. H. Leal-Cardoso. Essential oil of croton nepetaefolius and its main constituent, 1,8-cineole, block excitability of rat sciatic nerve in vitro. *Clin. Exp. Pharmacol. Physiol.*, 33:1158–63, 2006.

About the French Laundry Restaurant

Built in 1890, in Napa, California, as the French Steam Laundry, this two-story, stone building is in a rustic setting surrounded by flowers and culinary herbs. With a two-month or longer waiting list, this upscale restaurant draws diners from around the globe. The French Laundry received the top votes as best restaurant in the world by the prestigious, London-based *Restaurant* magazine. Moreover, the Michelin guide gave it 3 stars—whoa! Keller's other restaurant, Per Se, also has 3 stars, which is just unheard of in the culinary world. French Laundry provides a distinctive three- to five-hour dining experience with only two prix-fixe menu options, a chef tasting menu, and a vegetable tasting menu. Both menus are priced at $240, menus change daily, still offer nine courses of California country French cuisine made with fresh, seasonal ingredients. Although this is California, leave your shorts at home—dinner jackets only.

Information

http://www.frenchlaundry.com/tfl/frenchlaundry.htm

About Les Halles Restaurant

Les Halles is a lively and informal Parisian Brasserie serving the fresh and simple dishes of France's everyday cuisine. The menu at Les Halles is classic bistro fare, and well suited to the meat and potatoes crowd—steak and frites is a menu favorite. Les Halles Brasseries is also the home base of Chef-at-Large Anthony Bourdain, author of the best-selling *Kitchen Confidential* (Bloomsbury, 2000), host of TV Food Network's *A Cook's Tour*, and coauthor with Philippe Lajaunie of the *Les Halles Cookbook* (Bloomsbury, 2004). The restaurant atmosphere certainly fits Chef Bourdain's personality—rowdy, loud, and fun—and bring a big appetite. Les Halles dining success has necessitated in the expansion to five locations; however, the original flagship restaurant is located downtown in the financial district of New York.

Information

http://www.leshalles.net/

CHAPTER 22

▼

EIGHT MOST COMMON COOKING MISTAKES

Where I buy this, it doesn't come seasoned.
Chef Emeril Lagasse, Emeril Live (TV show)

In this brief chapter I will summarize the most common (and easily corrected) cooking mistakes made by the aspiring home chef and perhaps even by some accomplished cooks.

1. Poor Salting Ability

"The ability to salt food properly is the single most important skill in cooking."
Thomas Keller[1]

Zuni Café's special flavor is based on prior salting.
J. Rogers[2]

Beauty does not season soup.
Old Polish Proverb

The single biggest mistake that I see in cooking is the inability to salt food properly, whether this occurs out of fear of salt and high blood pressure or perhaps the cook is leaving the salting up to the consumer. Food pleasure can be highly dependent on achieving the magic level of 1.0–2.0 percent sodium chloride. The junk and snack foods that I've studied are uniformly consistent on this level of salt addition (average 1.6 percent).

So how do you achieve this desirable 1.0–2.0 percent salt level? Luckily, and by no small accident, humans tend to all like the same level of sodium chloride; salt the food to your taste, and it will be fine for your guests. Don't be shy. Chef Keller sometimes calls for "aggressive" seasoning—some foods need more salt than others (for instance, potatoes). Many vegetables are very low in sodium and can use an extra hit; meats are much higher in sodium and need less. Properly cooked meals should need no added sodium by the consumer—unless, of course, one adds a sprinkle of sea salts to finish the plate or on foods that require sodium addition (French fries). In fact, some of my chef friends are offended if the customer salts his/her own food! In Chinese restaurants soy sauce and other seasonings are added to the food during preparation, so there is little need to add more. Drowning fine Chinese food with soy sauce is just as insulting to the chef.

So why do humans like so much salt in their foods? It's a combination of factors: the body has a limited ability to store salt in body tissues so there is always a need for sodium. Humans, being hairless, have sweat glands that can secrete surprisingly large amount of sodium; and nervous tissue is critically dependent on sodium for proper functioning. Hence, salt preference and craving is always in excess of our needs.

The Pleasures of Brining

About five years ago, I started brining food and realized a new dimension in flavor and moistness. In fact, you can now overcook the meat and still have an acceptable sensory result. Heat creates flavor but draws moisture out of the muscle fibrils to create an unpleasant dryness. Brining solves the dryness problem and allows more Maillard flavor compounds to be formed. For recipes, see the Food Network Web site, *Cook's Illustrated*, or Russ Parson's *How to Read a French Fry*, one of my favorite food-science cookbooks. The most common method of brining involves adding salt (and sometimes sugar) to water, and then immersing the meat for as little as one hour or up to ten days. In my brines, I always add antioxidant herbs that reduce off-flavor formation, like oregano, rosemary, thyme, and garlic. They protect the unsaturated fatty acids from going rancid due to oxygen exposure.

The second technique is the one used by top chefs like Thomas Keller and Judy Rodgers of the Zuny Café. They simply salt the meat, wrap in plastic, throw it back in the fridge, and let the salt penetrate the meat for a minimum of one day.[2] This method, according to Rogers, helps hold moisture in the meat for better and more uniform browning, resulting in a more flavorful product. Salting, of course, adds sodium—a primary and powerful hedonic tastant.

2. Poor Seasoning Ability

Seasoning not only involves salt but the application of "flavor principle" herbs and spices as well. Seasoning also creates flavor complexity, reduces off-flavor formation, increases orosensation, and creates a memory for that dish. And when the diner or consumer is hungry again, the exact "flavor principles" of the dish must be recreated for the same pleasure response (evoked qualities) to occur. For example, if you make roast chicken using a spice blend of oregano and rosemary, and the food is eaten and enjoyed by your family, the next time you cook it (and want to hear, "Boy, does that smell good" again), you need to recreate that exact spice blend.

The easiest way to flavor food is to use the spice blends in the stores—many excellent blends are now found at the local grocer. Just remember to store them in a cool, dry place—and certainly not above the oven or next to the stove burners. As I have discussed, I am a great fan of Emeril's Original seasoning mix, but there are many brands to choose from, so experiment. Paul Prudhomme has a line of seasonings for almost every taste and palate. McCormick's Grill Mates offer bold flavors and larger particle sizes that add visual and oral appeal. And for brining, I buy Lawry's seasoning mix by the five-pound tub from Smart & Final.

Using Herbs and Spices Summary[3]

- Fresh herbs are preferred in many applications, such as baking, and roasting, and they are absolutely essential in making stocks, sauces, and soups.

- Use three parts of fresh to one part dried.

- Dried herbs stale quickly; store them in a cool, dry place, out of the light, and not above the stove.

- Fresh herbs retain the flavor-active essential oils—dried contain less than 10–20 percent of these oils.

- Avoid using these in dried form: parsley, basil, chives, ginger, tarragon, and dill.

- The best dried herbs are: bay leaf, oregano, marjoram, thyme, sage, nutmeg, and cinnamon.

- Fresh herbs can be bitter; resist adding more than what the recipe specifies.

- Grow these herbs and vegetables in pots: thyme, rosemary, basil, chives, green onions, cutting celery, and oregano. Be forewarned, the perennial herbaceous plants (thyme, oregano, and marjoram), if planted in the open garden, will naturalize and become a weed.

Learn the techniques of blooming and toasting spice/herb blends. Blooming is cooking spice in a little butter or oil first and then adding the rest of the recipe. Toasting refers to heating spice seeds or nuts (such as coriander or cumin seed) first in a heavy pan prior to grinding. Both techniques increase aroma complexity, add cookivore flavors, and enhance solubility.[4]

3. Poor Saucing Ability

> "In England there are sixty different religions, but only one sauce."
> Voltaire (1755–1826)

I've mentioned several times that dry food is "sensory death." The simple goal is to create food that generates saliva and aids in mastication and flavor release. Given the option of a sauce with a meal, most people will prefer a sauce and will actively use it during eating. French cuisine is *based* on sauces, vinaigrettes, and emulsions; Chinese food (stir-fry) is *enrobed* in a sauce. But what about dry foods like salty snacks? Why can we consume them without choking? Potato chips may be low in moisture, but their thin structure (which melts down quickly) and higher fat and salt content create surprisingly large amounts of saliva upon chewing.

Many good cookbooks include recipes for sauces when making a dish. I am always surprised how many home cooks don't bother with their preparation. I find that the most fun part of cooking is making a tasty sauce for any given dish. We have a neighbor who likes to come over just for the steak sauce I created by using a brown sauce base, reduced with red wine and shallots. Cooks make food; chefs create sauces. Elevate your own cooking by learning how to make them. Whether it is a simple butter-lemon sauce or a fancy *béchamel* or *buerre rouge*—you can master this. *Cook's Illustrated* is a great resource on sauce-making, or check out the many specialized books on saucing, such as:

- *Sauce* by Williams-Sonoma Collection

- *The Book of Sauces* by Gordon Grinsdale

- *Sauces: Classical and Contemporary Sauce Making* by James Peterson

- *The Complete Book of Sauces* by Sallie Y. Williams

- *The Sauce Bible: Guide to the Saucier's Craft* by David Paul

- *Barbecue! Bible: Sauces, Rubs, and Marinades, Bastes, Butters, and Glazes* by Steven Raichlen

- *Get Saucy: Make Dinner a New Way Every Day with Simple Sauces , Marinades, Dressings, Glazes, Pestos, Pasta Sauces, Salsas, and More* by Grace Parisi

- *Michel Roux Sauces* by Michel Roux

- *The Encyclopedia of Sauces for Your Food* by Charles A. Bellissino

In creating a dish, the sauce could contribute to more than half of all the eating pleasure; it contains the taste-active solutes, increases salivation, promotes positive hedonic feedback, and aids in mastication. For a most excellent discussion on the creation and value of saucing (and haute cuisine in general), see the discussion in *The Perfectionist* (p. 223) by Rudolph Chelminski. He discloses that the grandmother of all sauces is the simple deglazing: pour water or wine or vinegar in a pan cooked with meat to dissolve the tasty brown bits (fond); after pouring out the excess fat, of course. Pan juices are then concentrated over high heat so that the sauce is reduced by at least half. The problem is the watery nature of the result—a runny sauce. The Chinese solve this problem with cornstarch or arrowroot; the French solution or "liaison," however, is butter, cream, egg yolks, or mustard.

(For a hilarious view on saucing see page 73 of Anthony Bourdain's latest book, *The Nasty Bits*, in which he relates a conversation with a hot new chef named Donovan Cooke. Although I can't repeat what he said, he does boil down saucing to its *essence*.)

4. Canned Versus Fresh

I grew up on canned food and quickly grew weary of its tinny flavor, muted colors, and not-found-in-nature textures. To eliminate bacterial contamination, the canned foods undergo a "retort" process, where the sealed container is subject to many minutes of high heat, and the food is usually in a water bath with added calcium chloride. The combination of heat and calcium creates off-flavors and unusual textures. Canned green beans are especially scary; the "classic" dish of green beans with canned mushroom soup and canned onion rings probably contributes 100 percent of the daily requirement of *tin*. Certain foods, however, seem to hold up better to this product than others. However, by using a sensory trick I learned from Julia Child, canned food can be made to taste bright and fresh again (within reason). Julia, in her recipe for brown sauce (*Mastering the Art of French Cooking*) says that the flavor of canned beef can be disguised by using finely minced onions, carrots, celery, parsley sprigs, bay leaf, thyme, and tomato paste. Chef Child is also very fond of the special combination of bay leaf and thyme—the Keller duo spice mix. Julia's vegetable and spice combination not only covers up the unpleasant canned tastes but creates a much more savory flavor character. Hence, the judicious use of these flavor ingredients may eliminate the nasty aromatics associated with canned or dried foods, and prepackaged rice or stuffing mixes.

I tested the theory that processed foods can be improved with the addition of fresh ingredients. Much to my surprise, I found little success with certain foods (canned gravies) and good success with others (canned corn and tomatoes). Canned whole pinto beans become glorious if you first sauté onions and garlic with a little butter and oregano, then add the beans, and slow simmer for about an hour. Canned refried beans (already flavored), however, are hopeless and cannot be resuscitated by any magic I possess. Why? I speculate that since retort heating is in a closed container, and essentially without access to oxygen, non-food, and unfamiliar flavor compounds are created from the added spices and herbs. This explains why the aseptic process, whereby the food is quickly sterilized by short term, high heat conditions, and filled into presterilized containers—has much less off-flavor generation.

The key point in breathing sensory life back into foods is to use fresh ingredients for the herbs and vegetables, nothing dried or processed (except bay leaf, pepper, cinnamon). Fresh thyme, oregano, rosemary, summer savory, and marjoram have essential oils that will completely (well, almost) eliminate the canned (retort) aromas. If fresh spices are not available, there is one last sensory trick. A few tablespoons of butter, ½ teaspoon of Old Bay Seasoning and, 1 tablespoon chopped onion make an excellent refreshing mixture. Just saute this mixture first, then add the food and simmer for a few minutes.

5. Poor Emulsion-Creation Abilities

One of the great discoveries of food pleasure is that humans love an emulsion. In my research, I discovered that emulsions highly concentrate the hedonic solutes (ingredients that taste good) and deliver a pleasure blast to the taste buds. Good cooks and chefs know this principle, and it is well worth pursuing to perfection (Keller is a master emulsifier). I believe the most pleasurable sauces are those emulsified by egg yolks—mayonnaise, hollandaise, and béarnaise. And egg yolks contain taste-active components of their own. Keller takes this to the next culinary level by creating solid foods that are emulsions, such as mashed potatoes.

The simplest emulsified sauce is the vinaigrette, a little acid and fat thrown together with an emulsifier. Keller writes in his *Bouchon* cookbook of "the sensuous nature of the fat" and the "flavor brightening" of the acid as the perfect combination. He calls it the "amazing tool" for the cook—the "perfect sauce." We now know that acid increases salivation and food arousal. And acidity is a strong trigeminal stimulant, both oral and nasal. We have seen how Keller adds a little vinegar to many of his sauces to "increase arousal" or to be more physiologically correct "attention to stimuli." Keller states that the perfect combination of vinaigrette is three parts fat and one part acid—but make sure the ingredients are fresh, or your emulsion will be mediocre.

> "I would eat my own father with such a sauce."
> Grimond de la Reyniere (1758–1837)

Top chefs are *obsessed* with sauce-making, and the average cook would do well to learn at least some of the more rudimentary techniques of deglazing, reductions, and simple compound butter creation.

6. Food Temperature Handling

> Better a man should wait for a dish than a dish should wait for a man.
> Old Chinese saying

Eighty percent of all food is served either hot or cold; until recently, the hedonic mystery of food temperature remained hidden. Hot or cold food stimulates dynamic contrast in the mouth when the food temperatures return to body (oral) temperature. As Dr. Bob Hyde has explained, it is the *changing* nature of temperature in the mouth that the brain finds rewarding. Hot or cold food also activates taste bud sensation without a person actually tasting anything. Since many taste sensations are inherently pleasant—sweet, salty, and umami—pleasure is activated automatically. French chefs know this and serve food piping hot. In fact, they even heat the plates. Mexican food is often served on burning hot plates. How often have you heard the waiter caution, "Watch out, hot plates!" Contrast the hot food with a cold margarita, and this is fine dining indeed.

Most home cooks are busy and can't always keep the food hot, but here is one simple tip that works well for even the most hurried moms. Casserole dishes can be placed in a heated 250°F oven for safekeeping and then pulled out as needed. If the food is in a dish with no lid (like hamburgers fresh off the grill), just take some aluminum foil and cover the food; it's a simple but effective way to keep food warm. As the temperature of the food drops, so does the pleasure, with every little degree. Why cook gourmet burgers and then serve them lukewarm? Would you serve ice cream melted? Of course not—it's supposed to change temperature and melt in your mouth! The oral cavity had the greatest ability of any body tissue to handle high temperatures. Scalding coffee that is a pleasure to the palate creates first degree burns if spilled. Humans, as cookivores, like hot food.

My wife thinks I am a little *fanatique* on this topic, but I put all dishes in a warmed oven for safekeeping if they can't be served right away. After all, you didn't come to my house to eat hospital or airline food. (Yes, I know, some airlines serve excellent fare. For an entertaining discussion see Airlinemeals.net.) In the food pleasure equation, we eat for both calories and sensation, and a major part of the sensation is the temperature of the food.

7. Poor Development of Taste-Active Compounds

Cooking involves heat and the generation of flavor-active compounds that excite the palate (orosensation) and activate taste receptors (hedonic solutes). Good cooks and skilled chefs know that culinary techniques and special ingredients can do both. In the chapter on secret-weapon pleasure foods, we are introduced to ingredients that will improve the flavor of most everything *you* will prepare. And the simple secret for creating flavorful compounds in your cooking is as simple as 375°F. Magic happens to foods cooked at this temperature and above. Maillard reactions (sugar and protein interactions) create all those nice brown and roasted flavors. Sugars caramelize, and salty potentiators emerge from the food depths to create hedonic sensations.

For example, in Bourdain's excellent recipe for onion soup, the onions are slowly cooked for twenty minutes, and he then adds flavor-rich ingredients like balsamic vinegar, dark chicken stock, port, and bacon. Thomas Keller, however, takes this roasting principle to the limit and cooks his onions for *four* hours! I recently slow-roasted a version of Keller's *soffritto*, a highly flavored onion-tomato-garlic sauce used as a foundation for many Italian and Spanish dishes (*Bouchon* cookbook). During the cooking process the caramelization of the onions (sucrose, sulfur compounds, and pyruvic acids) and the breakdown products of tomatoes (lycopenes, fruit acids, and MSG) produce some of the tastiest and most aromatic compounds I have ever experienced. Just agitating the cooking pan during cleaning released aromas and flavor that sent me back to the backyard BBQ and my *poulet rôti*. The *Bouchon* cookbook is worth the purchase just to learn the makings of the flavor–rich or "building-block" preparations: garlic, tomato and onion confit, *soffritto*, piperade, basil puree, house vinaigrette, basic roux, Mornay sauce, and *maître d'hôtel* butter.

8. Dried Versus Fresh Spices

"The *fines herbes* … a mixture of fresh Italian parsley, tarragon, chervil and chives … enhance salad, chicken, fish, sauces, and shellfish …"
Thomas Keller[1]

We have discussed in this book the importance of spices in good cooking. Fresh and dried herbs and spices have their place, but most chefs prefer to use fresh whenever possible in wet-cooking applications. Dry rubs and marinades, of course, utilize the dried versions, and if they are of high quality, the results can be very good indeed. Luckily, some spices (seeds, hard fruits) dry well. These include garlic, onions, black pepper, nutmeg, bay leaf, Chinese five-spice (my favorite), cinnamon, and mace. But leafy herbs do not dry well: chervil, tarragon, parsley, and basil. Use them fresh, or do not use them at all. Why add stale and musty aroma notes to your cooking?

Fresh herbs worth growing are tarragon, rosemary, thyme, basil, sage, and oregano. Fresh rosemary just oozes with flavor resins. Add one sprig of rosemary or thyme in a pot of Rice-A-Roni (a favorite), and watch it remove and rejuvenate the dried flavors and increase food pleasure. *All* boxed preparations fall prey to dried and stale flavor blends, especially when the spice mix calls for leafy ingredients (parsley is the worst offender). Another trick to remove the bad flavors is to add fresh or canned tomatoes to the rice or pasta during cooking; this assumes, of course, that you like the rice with an added Spanish flair. The tomato acids neutralize offensive aromas and the natural MSG in tomatoes boosts umami sensations.

Please try the classic spice combination that Thomas Keller and Julia Child use so often—bay leaf and thyme. As I have discussed, 2006 research suggests that these spices contain flavor actives with strong binding activity to vanilloid and possibly CB-1 receptors. This adds increased orosensation (similar to adding cayenne), perhaps even increased food pleasure (marijuana receptor binding), and greater mouthfeel (tactile).

References

1. Keller, T. 1999. *The French Laundry Cookbook*. New York: Artisan.

2. Parsons, R. Salt of the Earth, *Los Angeles Times*, July 5, 2006.

3. Herbs: fresh versus dried. *Cook's Illustrated*, July/Aug., 2003. http://www.cooksillustrated.com/images/document/howto/JA03_Herbs.pdf

4. Dresser, K. Spices 101. *Cook's Illustrated*, Nov./Dec., 2006. http://www.cooksillustrated.com/images/document/howto/ND06_Spices101.pdf

5. Keller, T. 2004. *Bouchon*. New York: Artisan.

CHAPTER 23

▼

TASTY HOME COOKING
AND HEALTHY FAST FOOD:
A SUMMARY

"Attention to health is life's greatest hindrance."
Plato (427–347 B.C.)

Improve Your Home Cooking

Can the principles of food pleasure be used to create tasty fare at home—foods that your neighbors savor and your kids will eat? Well, the answer is a resounding yes; the key is using healthier versions of common foods (lean meat, whole grain bread, high fiber ingredients), adding super pleasure ingredients to your recipes whenever possible, and applying the theories of dynamic contrast, evoked qualities, taste hedonics, salivation response, and emulsion theory. Fast foods' very existence depends on the difficult nature of making these tasty foods at home— they don't want the nature of food pleasure to be found! They certainly don't want you to duplicate their highly pleasurable tastes and flavors at home.

Throughout this book, we chronicle how each of our favorite foods are made to be the best they can be by chefs and food scientists. Now it's your turn. In the next few sections, I will list the "must-have" condiment critical for cooking success, and chronicle culinary techniques that transform food into something tasty. My hope is that, the knowledge of food pleasure will improve your own cooking, reduce the dependence on fast food, and bring the family around the dinner table again. Cooking is great fun; if not scary at times—soufflés fall, emulsions break, and pot roast burns—but imagine the feeling when your best friend says you make fries better than McDonald's, and with no trans fat. Pass the ketchup, without high fructose corn syrup, of course (Heinz Organic Ketchup is 100 percent sucrose).

Critical Cooking Condiments for the Pantry

We've discussed super pleasure foods and how to use them in your cooking. The following is a complete listing of indispensable cooking ingredients that add taste, flavor, and orosensation. None of these are exotic ingredients, all are as close as the nearest supermarket—no well-stocked pantry should be without them.

- <u>Ketchup</u>. Essential for many types of sauces; indispensable for French fries. I like Heinz regular ketchup for fries and Heinz Organic ketchup for cooking (sucrose based). Muir Glen and Whole Foods 365 Organic Ketchup are also fine sucrose-based choices. Sucrose and lycopene (tomatoes) create wonderful cookivore flavors.

- <u>Mustard</u>. Useful in sauces, vinaigrettes, and emulsions. Maille and Grey Poupon are top choices. Dijon mustard is an underutilized orosensory condiment.

- <u>Hot sauces</u>. Many choices here; critical for adding heat and increasing food pleasure. Tabasco's great for adding heat without flavor interference; Chinese chili paste with garlic is critical for Asian cuisine, and Sriracha Hot Chili Sauce is a spicy version of red chili paste with added sucrose, garlic, and vinegar. Cholula, Tapatia, Crystal, and Frank's Red Hot are all distinctive in flavor and tasty, excellent as condiments or as elements of a sauce mixture.

- <u>Soy sauce</u>. Top choices include Lee Kum Kee, Kikkoman, Pearl River Bridge, and Kimlan. If you can find it, I use Lee Kum Kee Premium Dark Soy Sauce, Kimlan Chili Soy Paste (hot), Wan Ja Shan Soy Sauce Hot, and Kikkoman Umakuchi Shoyu (Flavor Enhanced Soy Sauce). Maggi Cooking Soy Sauce is a good replacement for Kikkoman Umakuchi.

- <u>Mayonnaise</u>. Excellent as a neutral emulsion for many types of sauces. Easy to add flavorants to the water phase. Best Foods or

Hellmann's are good choices here. Miracle Whip is fine for sand-wiches but is too distinctive for sauce making. Learn to make your own using the weight management cooking oil: Enova.

- <u>Beef and/or chicken broth</u>. Essential for sauce-making and pleasure food creation. I use cases of Swanson's Chicken Broth. It flavors *everything*, and is rich in many hedonic tastants: salt, natural MSG, sugar, 5'- nucleotides, and yeast extractives. Organic and low salt versions are available. You can add it to mash potatoes, make a quick reduction sauce or gravy, simmer vegetables, and even use it as a marinade. The use of the big three (soy sauce, garlic, and chicken broth) will *always* boost flavor and are easy to incorporate into recipes.

- <u>Cream of mushroom soup</u>. A surprisingly useful addition to dishes; it contains natural mushroom nucleotides, MSG, cream, yeast extracts, and garlic—and in an emulsified creamy texture. Camp-bell's mushroom soup acts as a general flavor enhancer, and a lower sodium version is available.

- <u>Balsamic vinegar</u>. A fermented and aged product of the Trebbiano grape; this hedonic booster is loaded with sugar, vinegar, complex aromas, and nucleotides from yeast autolysis. Wood aging leeches out the vanillin, which activates the vanilloid receptor for added oral sensation. Price does not reflect quality; consult with March & April, 2007 edition of *Cook's Illustrated* for choosing both cooking and drizzling balsamic. Balsamic *glazes* are sweeter and richer than balsamic vinegar. This reduction sauce can be brushed on food prior to grilling or added to many types of meat sauces—and a gar-nishing sauce for desserts.

- <u>Worcestershire sauce</u>. A distinctive low sodium flavor booster with fish and clove flavors that adds wonderful "layering" flavors if used sparingly.

- <u>Tomato sauce and paste</u>. Excellent way to add flavor to sauces and just about any pasta dish. Tomato sauce is usually flavored; Conta-dina Tomato Paste is not—just 100 percent (Roma) tomatoes. The paste has much more flavor and is concentrated in lycopene, sug-ars, acids (citric and malic), and natural MSG. Add to soups, sauces, and stews to enhance flavor and color. Hunt's flavors their tomato paste and is another good choice.

- <u>Dried mushrooms</u>. Shitake, morels, oyster, porcini, etc., add tremendous flavor and are taste active (loaded with nucleotides). Mushrooms are greatly underutilized by the home chef. Chinese cooks use a dozen varieties. Soak in *very* hot water, for twenty minutes, and use the soaking liquid as well. Campbell's Classic green bean casserole improves in flavor with the simple addition of reconstituted shitake mushrooms.

- <u>Honey</u>. Fructose rich, low in pH, and flavor-intensive, honey improves just about any dish and will brown foods at a lower temperature. Banana bread with 100 percent honey as the sweetener is sensational.[1]

- <u>Maple syrup</u>. With a distinctive aroma, rich in acids and sucrose, maple syrup creates complex cookivore flavors. Please use genuine maple syrup, not the pancake stuff.

- <u>Parmesan cheese</u>. Buy both the green can and Parmigiano-Reggiano (PR). Romano and Asiago are good substitutes. Use the mild parmesan (green can) in popcorn and foods that need a highly soluble cheese. It is rich in natural MSG. The assertive PR is used in food recipes where the sharp taste, distinctive MSG flavor, and melting texture are of critical sensory importance.

- <u>Garlic, onions, and shallots</u>. The Allium family and humans were meant for each other. Raw, cooked, and roasted garlic add flavor to all savory dishes, and excite many type of oral receptors. Try using shallots or green onions in your recipes for their unusual flavor compounds. The shallots unique sensory property of intense flavor without onion breath (vinaigrette) is a treasured orosensory pleasure ingredient.

- <u>Brown or dark sugar</u>. Sucrose with added "brown" flavors accelerates and enhances almost all Maillard-type cooking methods, such as roasting. Try brining with a little brown sugar, and noticed the enhanced taste and aroma generation.

- <u>Bacon bits</u>. Premade bacon bits are of high quality these days. Just a sprinkle on salads, potato dishes, or pasta to liven the flavor and add visual contrast. Hormel's Real Bacon Bits (lower salt) is a fine choice.

- Lemon juice. Lemon acidity comes from the "secret" flavor potentiator—citric acid. Lemon juice, as Chef Simon Hopkinson says, improves the taste of everything. It tenderizes meat by hydrolyzing collagen fibers, prevents the oxidation of cut fruit, and reduces the fishy off-flavors by reacting with the smelly "amines" into nonvolatile and nonaromatic ammonium salts.[2]

- Cream and butter. As emulsifiers, sauce bases, and flavor enhancers, there are just no substitutes. Ersatz butters may be a bit healthier, but should not be used in routine cooking—the emulsions are too high in water and are easily broken, and the artificial flavors and colors do not combine well with other food ingredients.

- Sun-dried tomatoes. These dried paste or Roma tomatoes have an intense tomato flavor, color, and acidity that liven up cream sauces, pastas, and salads. For best results, slice thinly or chop in small pieces. Available in many supermarkets and Costco.

- Black sesame oil. This smoky, spicy, and roasted cookivore oil is a powerful food aromatic. Used in many Chinese, Japanese, Middle Eastern, and Korean cuisines. Mix 50/50 with soy sauce and brush on vegetables before grilling. Ground sesame seed, or *tahini*, is a flavor enhancer high in natural MSG, fatty acids, and other taste-active compounds. Perhaps the oldest seasoning discovered by man.

- Teriyaki sauce. The word "teri" and "yaki" mean "luster" and "grill" in Japanese. To soy sauce, add some brown sugar, ginger, garlic, and green onions (white part), and you have teriyaki sauce. Another version combines soy sauce with sugar and mirin (sweet sake wine)—used in fish dishes because the mirin's acidity reduces fishy off-aromas.

- Evaporated milk (evap). Yes, I know, it's hard to believe that this sterile milk product, developed by Elbridge Amos Stuart in 1899, can add flavor to foods. But the evaporated milk process develops flavor compounds from the lactose-protein interactions, and the added dipotassium phosphate and carrageenan form a very stable emulsion with a creamy, almost *silky*, mouthfeel. Scalloped potatoes using evap instead of heavy cream, not only are far lighter in calories, but almost melt in your mouth. Evap undergoes a specialized homogenization process that stabilizes the fat globules into a much smaller size than regular cream, creating a creamier texture.

- <u>Lawry's Seasoned Salt</u>. The perfect salt, sugar, and spice blend for brining meat or adding flavor to foods.

- <u>Black, white, red, green, and white pepper</u>. Black pepper adds complex aromas (terpene, musty and fermented), whether added before and after cooking, along with heat (vanilloid activation); white pepper is used where heat is required without the black specs. Finely ground white pepper is a *stronger* trigeminal stimulant than black and easily activates the vanilloid receptor. Green peppercorn provides fresh and bright aromas, and red gives slight sweetness, fruity aroma, bright color, but very little heat. Gourmet food shops often combine all four.

- <u>Emeril's Original Essence</u>. This is the workhorse spice blend in my cabinet.

- <u>McCormick Montreal Steak Seasoning</u>. This is useful in flavoring meats, adding visual contrast, and flavor to roasted vegetables. Nice blend of trigeminal stimulating piperine and capsaicin.

- <u>McCormick Garlic Powder with Parsley</u>. Excellent substitute for fresh; for example, just a 1/2 teaspoon to your cheese sauce enhances both aroma and taste.

- <u>Old Bay Seasoning</u>. A unique combination of celery, mustard, red pepper, black pepper, bay leaves, cloves, allspice, ginger, mace, cardamom, cinnamon, and paprika. Use in stock preparations or in the process of refreshing canned foods—at low levels has an amazing ability to reduce off-flavors and add mouthfeel.

- <u>Table-top grinding blends</u>. With the advent of new "grinder" seasoning blends, salt, and pepper shakers are almost passé. The spice blends add more sensation so that more pleasure is derived per bite. My current *favorite* is McCormick's Steakhouse Grinder, which contains: Black, pink, and green peppercorns (vanilloid activation); red pepper (vanilloid and CB-1 activation); sea salt (hedonic tastant); garlic (umami booster); onion (flavor booster); parsley (fresh "green" aroma); and paprika (color).

Flavorful Cooking Techniques

The classic French cooking techniques listed below greatly amplify flavor creation (Maillard reactions) and enhance taste pleasure. Many cookbooks describe these techniques, and the Web has many excellent food sites for guidances.[3,4,5] The success of *The Sonoma Diet Cookbook* demonstrates that flavorful cooking is a simple combination of tasty ingredients and classic flavor generation techniques, and you don't need a culinary degree to learn them.[3] And remember, tasty food is also more nutritious food; fragrant aromas and complex tastes increase digestive enzymes and food assimilation.[6]

- Brining meat. Chicken, turkey, and even pork benefit from a salt, sugar, and spice soak. My standard mix uses kosher salt, brown sugar, Lawry's Seasoned Salt, McCormick's Garlic Powder, and Italian Seasoning.

- Glazing vegetables. Place vegetables (barely cover) in a flavorful stock, add a little butter, a teaspoon of sugar, and let the water slowly evaporate to form the glaze.

- Salt, salt, salt. Salt everything at every step. Follow Emeril's advice and season the flour, season the water you cook vegetables and pasta in, even salt meat (steaks) ahead of cooking; the sodium will disperse into the meat overnight in the refrigerator. You'll be surprised by the greater depth of flavor and juiciness. If one must restrict salt, try the newer salt substitutes or make a mixture of 10 parts salt to 1 part MSG (Accent), and use to taste, surprisingly tasty even at a 50% reduction of sodium.

- Sweat (bloom) the spices. Add a little butter to a pan, add the spice mix powder, heat, and stir for a few minutes. Blooming spices and herbs "rejuvenate" the flavor compounds and create more lipophilic flavors that resist evaporation during the cooking process. Bloomed curry powder is especially fragrant.

- Toast the spice then grind. Toasting dramatically increase the flavor of nuts and grains. Experiment toasting slivered almonds, walnuts, pine nuts, cumin, coriander, sesame seeds, fenugreek, fennel, poppy seed, and mustard. Basmati rice, toasted in a little butter and spice, takes on a nutty and fragrant personality that survives the cooking process. Besides superior flavor, Basmati rice has a lower glycemic index than many other rice varieties; promoting a healthier blood glucose response.[13]

- Braise. Browning the meat, followed by a slow roast with aromatic vegetables and wine transforms tough meat cuts into melt-in-the-mouth tenderness, and just incredible flavor. Braising requires a specialized pot, however, a crock pot works beautifully. Braised short ribs are a sensory revelation; try the version by Charlie Trotter (short ribs with garlic mashed potatoes) found in the *WJS*.[14]

- Roast. High heat, properly applied, brings out the best in many vegetables and meats. Roasted root vegetables, asparagus, and broccoli are transformed—sweetness is enhanced and cookivore flavors emerge. The browning reactions, induced by sautéed meat, create flavor compound called the "fond." Dissolve this flavoring agent with wine or stock and create a quick sauce.

- Refresh. Many canned and frozen foods carry off-flavors that reduce food pleasure. After much experimentation, I find that butter, lemon juice, and Old Bay Seasoning—all sweated first, will reduce the nonfood flavors and aromas.

- Caramelizing. Refers to both sugar reactions products developed during high heat and sugar-protein-amino acid interactions (the flavorful Maillard and Strecker degredations in food). Caramelized flavors are best created using high heat and sucrose-based condiments.

- Food layering. A flavor building technique used by professional chefs, whereby food pleasure is enhanced by creating a constant *changing* of flavor perception during each bite of food.[4,7] Layering is achieved by using the same food, but cooked in two different manners, or adding two or three types of the same food (cheese) during cooking. The basic idea is to create complexity; humans as cookivores appreciate high flavor ingredients combined with high flavor cooking techniques. Classic stock preparation uses layering: roasting the bones, sweating the vegetables (aromatic ones), adding orosensory spices (pepper, thyme, and bay leave,) and wine, all at slow simmer. In a curry dish, for example, one could sweat the spice mix in butter to start the dish, and then add fresh curry powder at the end of the dish for additional aroma complexity and layering.

- Food saucing. Mastery of simple, and even scary complex sauces, improve the taste, flavor, and pleasure of food.[4] The following is the short list of essential sauces that everyone should master: 1. basic pan-fried reduction sauce (fond based); 2. pureed vegetable sauces (tomato-basil and pesto); 3. beurre blanc and rouge; 4. hollandaise and béarnaise; 5. mayonnaise (using Enova oil); 6. basic brown sauce; 7. vinaigrette; 8. compound butters; 9. fresh salsa; 10. Béchamel and cheese sauce (roux); and 11. simple browned butter and lemon sauce.

Reinventing Fast Food

With all of the advancements in food pleasure research and modern food science, is it really possible to satisfy the gut, brain, and taste bud with healthy food? We know there is a market. About half of all fast-food diners at least think about healthy food, and it's a market just waiting to be tapped.[8]

The idea of developing pleasurable fast food that is good for you (definition below) is challenging and *intriguing*, and would be a test of every theory and every principle enumerated in this book on food pleasure. In addition, it's a good thing for mankind; why just use these principles to make junk food tastier? Some general guidelines for a successful fast and healthy operation might be:

- The foods must be as tasty as their real-life counterparts; we will not be selling veggie burgers but healthier versions of *real* food. Burger King, ironically the only chain with a veggie burger, sells only three per day versus three hundred Whoppers.[9] Humans are meat-eating cookivores and the menu will reflect this propensity.

- The foods must not be more than 50 percent more expensive; people will pay more for perceived health benefits, but not *too* much more.

- The foods must be healthier versions of the top twenty, most ordered items in a fast-food restaurant.

- The menu should reflect simplicity and freshness à la In-N-Out Burger.

- The restaurant should reflect the efficiencies of McDonald's.

- The menu should be diverse enough to attract the important 30 percent of folks who bring in 70 percent of the revenue (the carnivorous "bubbas").

- The menu must attract both kids and their parents.

Since humans eat for both calories and sensation, a dramatic drop in fat or carbohydrate calories is likely to be detected by the gut and the brain, seriously reducing food pleasure. However, modest, but nutritionally beneficial changes are possible without any reduction of food palatability. A healthier menu might include the following nutritional profile:

- All cooking oils will be trans fat free and low in saturated fat. Denmark proved that reduction of trans fats is possible when they passed an Executive Order on March, 2003 to limit all fats to just two grams of trans per hundred grams of oil. Interestingly, McDonald's had no problems complying in this country![10,11] Wendy's, KFC and Frito Lay have all switched over to trans fat free cooking oils based on sunflower, soy and corn. Wall Street Journal, however, now hints that McDonald's has selected a trans fat-free oil for its French fries.[12]

- Fat calories can be reduced in most foods by at least 30 percent by using the "tastier" oils with desirable fatty acid profiles. Certain vegetable oils contribute more satiety per calorie via post-ingestional effects.

- Sodium content can easily be reduced by 25 percent using flavor boosters and specialty salts.

- Fiber-enhanced products (buns, drinks) are easy created with the advanced water-soluble prebiotic fibers. Soluble fiber increases the growth of good bacteria in the gut, increases satiety (feeling of fullness), and some even enhance calcium absorption.

- Carbonated soft drinks may be replaced by a variety of tasty fruit juices, teas and sparkling water. Other beverage options include weight management drinks like Enviga, the intriguing calorie burning green tea developed by Coca-Cola and Nestlé.

- Lower-fat (but flavor optimized) ice cream shakes with enhanced orosensation.

- Condiments (mayonnaise) can easily be made with the new-generation triglycerides that resist fat storage (Enova and Healthy Resetta). Ketchup could be made with turbinado cane sugar and high-lycopene tomatoes; Smart Balance would replace butter.

- A new generation of healthy salt substitutes are now available, rather than table salt.

- Carbohydrate containing food can be re-engineered to have a lower glycemic index—reducing insulin fluctuations and promoting fullness.[13]

(Theoretical) Food Offerings:

In America, the top food items listed as favorites (for men, women, teenagers, and children) are:[8]

- French fries

- Hamburgers

- Pizza

- Chicken sandwich

- Breakfast sandwich

- Salads (main and side)

- Chicken nuggets

- Chinese food

- Mexican food

Although most fast-food companies serve food based on a theme (Mexican, Chinese, hamburgers, and sandwiches), this menu would focus on the consumers' favorites. The simplified menu would hedonically optimize ten to twelve favorite dining entrées and appetizers. The core of the menu would be hamburgers and fries, followed by some simple but tasty versions of pizza, chicken sandwiches, nuggets, and salads.

Companies interested in exploring healthy fast food development can contact me directly. I'd be happy to discuss how we can use the principles of the food pleasure equation to improve the taste of nutritious foods that consumers will accept. In addition, food pleasure training seminars are now available for your product development and marketing staff. The physiological information on food perception, the chemical senses, and the neurochemistry of food intake is simply not available anywhere else.

References

1. Southern Living. 2000. *30 Years of Our Best Recipes*. Birmingham: Oxmoore House.

2. Lemon. Wikipedia. http://en.wikipedia.org/wiki/Lemon

3. Guttersen, C. 2006. *The Sonoma Diet Cookbook*. Des Moines: Meredith Books.

4. Corriher, S. 1997. *Cookwise*. New York: William Morrow and Company.

5. Zelman, K. Flavor-boosting tricks add spark to healthy cooking. WebMD. http://onhealth.webmd.com/script/main/art.asp?article key=78161

6. Hall, T. Discovering something new in food: pleasure. *The New York Times*. Dec. 30, 1992. http://query.nytimes.com/gst/fullpage.html? sec=health&res=9E0CE1DD133FF933A05751C1A964958260

7. Burton, M. Magnifying flavor through layering. *Food Product Design*, August, 2006. http://www.foodproductdesign.com/articles/681culi nary.html

8. Sloan, E. Trends on the horizon. 5th Annual West Coast Flavor Industry Forum Presentation. Mar., 21, 2005. http://naffs. mytradeassociation.org/prn_sloan.pdf.

9. Horovitz, B. Restaurant sales climb with bad-for-you food. USA Today. May 12, 2005. http://www.usatoday.com/money/industries/food/2005-05-12-bad-food-cover_x.htm

10. Denmark's trans fat law. Executive order No. 160, Mar. 11, 2003. http://www.tfx.org.uk/page116.html

11. Harvard School of Public Health. Hidden trans fat exposed. http://www.hsph.harvard.edu/nutritionsource/transfats.html

12. Adamy, J. For McDonald's, It's a wrap. *Wall Street Journal*, Jan. 30, 2007.

13. Home of the glycemic index. The University of Sydney. http://www.glycemicindex.com/

14. Gridiron Chefs: Game-day chow. *Wall Street Journal*, Feb. 3–4, 2007.

COOKING RESOURCES

What is the quickest way to learn to cook like the pros? Assuming you don't have the time, inclination, or money to enroll in a Culinary Institute someplace, I highly recommend the resources below.

Single Best Cooking Magazine

Without a doubt, it's the *Cook's Illustrated* magazine, published bimonthly by Boston Common Press Limited Partnership. I eagerly await each issue and determine my dietary regimen by trying each recipe. The magazine teaches the science behind each recipe, and the writers incorporate many of the principles of good food construction that you have learned in this book. I usually try to memorize each recipe along with the cooking techniques. Many of the recipes have a wonderful story of failures (which makes me feel better) in the quest for perfection. Some of the recipes are so good that they are worth the extra effort in their preparation. For example, my wife made the simple chocolate cake recipe for the neighbors (the recipe is not simplistic, however), and while we were out for a walk one day, a neighbor, driving by, stopped and shouted, "Your chocolate cake and the icing is the best I've ever tasted anywhere!" Now, that just doesn't happen every day. (*Cook's Illustrated*, March & April, 2006, p. 21.) Once you have mastered the basics, you can try recipes from my other favorites: *Bon Appétit* or *Food & Wine*.

Best "Learn-How-to-Cook" Books with Added Food Science

There are a number of excellent resources available in this category. Here are the ones I use most:

1. *The Culinary Craft* by Judy Gorman. I reach for this tome when I need to touch up my culinary skills or my when soufflé falls flat.

2. *CookWise: the Hows & Whys of Successful Cooking*, by Shirley O. Corriher. This teaches the science behind each recipe as you cook; it's just a wonderful resource. One way to learn is to try one recipe each day and cook your way through the book!

3. *The New Best Recipe*, from the editors of *Cook's Illustrated*. If you can't find the back issues of the magazine (I have most of them), then pick up (literally) this five-pound book on cooking science and recipe perfection. This is a *must-have* foodie cookbook. One warning: these recipes are a bit more complicated than most, but they are but well worth the cooking effort. (For example, the average recipe is two to three times longer in words than, say, the *New York Times Cookbook*.)

4. *The Cook's Bible*. This is another favorite of mine that specializes in American-style cooking. The "bible" is much less intimidating (it only weighs 1½ pounds) than the *New Best Recipe*, and it is a great book to learn essential cooking techniques (using knives, building a salad, perfecting cooked rice, etc.) while you are making something tasty.

5. *The Perfect Recipe* by Pam Anderson. Ms. Anderson is a gifted food writer and excellent food scientist, and this book chronicles the path to food excellence. It has lots of good stories of failures as well.

6. *How to Read a French Fry*, by Russ Parsons. Mr. Parsons is a *Los Angeles Times* staff writer with a gift for grub and kitchen science. It is an easy read with lots of good recipes. I highly recommend it—it's one of my favorites. His articles in the food section of the *Los Angeles Times* are first-rate.

Best Food Chemistry Book for the Home Cook

1. *I'm Just Here for the Food*, by Alton Brown. Hyperkinetic cook (he doesn't like to be called a chef), food scientist, and actor, this talented author has written a very unusual and colorful book on basic food science for home or professional chefs. It contains information one just doesn't see anywhere else. The book demonstrates an intense curiosity and a fundamental grasp of food science and chemistry—it's simply the most impressive recent work in this area that I have seen. The chapter on sauce-making is worth the price of the book. If I were teaching

cooking, I'd start with this book, coupled with *CookWise*. He is also author of the baking book *I'm Just Here for More Food* and a book on kitchen appliances called *Gear for Your Kitchen*.

2. *On Food and Cooking: the Science and Lore of the Kitchen*. This is the classic food-science text for the masses. When it first came out in 1984, I was stunned by the information and the superiority of the writing. It deserves to be in every-one's cooking library; it was also updated in 2004. I also enjoyed his lesser-known work, *The Curious Cook*, in which he explores all sorts of interesting kitchen mis-chief.

3. *Kitchen Science* by Howard Hillman. Mr. Hillman is a prolific and well-known author of over twenty books in the areas of food and wine appreciation. This one is built around questions of "Why does ..." It's an easy book to read and has plenty of information for the home cook or food professional. An updated ver-sion was published in 2003.

4. *What Einstein Told His Cook*, by Robert L. Wolke. Written by a chemist (you can tell) and James Beard winner, this interesting and quirky book covers mate-rial the others do not. The book is based on questions from his famous column called "Food 101" in the *Washington Post*. Mr. Wolke is a wonderful writer, and this book is filled with more humor and wit than most.

Best Cookbooks for Home Use

With 47,000 cookbook titles on Amazon.com, you have plenty of variety to choose from. My short list contains the most useful books for everyday use: cook-books whose recipes are vetted and are just about guaranteed to work. Here is a list of my favorites:

1. *How to Cook Everything*, by Mark Bittman. Mr. Bittman is a prolific author and columnist. I pick this volume up first for recipe ideas. His section on varia-tions of the recipe provides many ideas for reducing food burnout (sensory spe-cific satiety).

2. *The New York Times Cookbook*, by Craig Claiborne. These recipes are easy to follow and just about foolproof. It contains many ethnic selections and old favor-ites and is an excellent first cookbook for the budding, young gourmet.

3. *Joy of Cooking: 75th Edition–2006*. by Irma Rombauer et al. If you were stranded on an island with just one book, this would be it. The original first sparked my interest in food and nutrition when I started reading the "about" sec-tions in eighth grade.

4. *The American Century Cookbook*, by Jean Anderson. Written by my favorite food writer, this book contains an enormous amount of history on the dishes

your parents made that you loved to hate. It is an incredible work, and the recipes are tasty because this food writer knows how to improve each recipe. (How many cookbooks have the original *tamale pie* recipe?)

5. *30 Years of Our Best Recipes*, by Southern Living. This is a surprisingly good cookbook on the classics, and the recipes appear to be flavor-optimized with interesting twists and variations. My wife and I cook from this book quite often.

6. *Classics from a French Kitchen*, by Elaine Amé-Leroy Carley. This is classic French bistro cooking with lots of information on gastronomic lore, kitchen science, and cuisine in general. Amazon still carries it.

7. *The Gourmet Cookbook*, by Ruth Reichl. This is a stunning work with over 1,000 recipes; this cook book is *Joy of Cooking* on steroids. Recipes are more involved (the book is not for a beginner) and can be very eclectic, but everything you need is inside the covers, including plenty of kitchen chemistry and cooking tips. One nit: the recipe titles are in yellow, and I find them hard to read. The book lists plenty of sauces and is loaded with dessert ideas.

8. *365: No Repeats*, by Rachel Ray. Written by a prolific cookbook author with prominent TV presence and effervescence, this book contains the wildest collection of recipes of any recent cookbook I've seen. If you are at a loss to come up with something new, this is your book—as these recipes touch upon a dozen different cuisines. I still can't believe my wife's centuries-old recipe for lion's head is in this book! (A kind of meatball wrapped in Napa cabbage.)

About the Author

Steven Witherly, PhD is a twenty-six-year veteran in the food and nutraceutical field; and whether it's formulating an herbal prostate formulation that really works or designing a healthy food that tastes better, Steve can lend his expertise to your product so that it truly *performs*.

Education:

PhD Human Nutrition, Michigan State University (Rachel Schemmel, Major Professor), Minor: Psychophysiology.

M.S. Food Science, University of California at Davis, Emphasis: Sensory Evaluation of Food (Rose Marie Pangborn, Major Professor.)

B.S. Dietetics, University of California at Davis, Minor: Vegetable Crops and Pomology.

Positions: (in chronological order)

• Currently: President, Technical Products Inc. (TPI), consulting firm for the food and nutraceuticals industry. Complete product and nutraceutical development from conception to finished product. Examples of products include tablet and softgel formulation work, powdered drink mixes, boost formulations, energy drinks, and a unique stable effervescent system. In addition, inquire about or new one-hour or half-day Training Seminars on Food Pleasure and Perception. In the food industry, TPI will analyze your foods or menu for Food Pleasure Optimization (Hedonic solutes, Dynamic Contrast, Salivation Potentiation, Evoked Qualities, and Taste/Aroma Orosensation) and suggest changes for greater acceptance and palatability.

Previous Positions:

- V.P., Product Development, Herbalife International

- Director, Product Development, Leiner Corporation

- Director, Product Development, Nutrilite Corporation, division of Amway

- Manager, Scientific Affairs, Nestlé Corporation

- Food Scientist, Carnation Company

Web site:

- Technicalproductsinc.net

E-mail:
Your comments on the book and suggestions for improvement are welcome. Organizations may purchase bulk copies of the book at reduced rates (twenty-five or more books).

- switherly@technicalproductsinc.net

- techproducts@ca.rr.com

Telephone: 661-296-2214
Fax: 661-296-3370

Index

978-0-595-41429-1
0-595-41429-X